Airplane Racing

AIRPLANE RACING
A History, 1909–2008

Don Berliner

McFarland & Company, Inc., Publishers
Jefferson, North Carolina, and London

LIBRARY OF CONGRESS CATALOGUING-IN-PUBLICATION DATA

Berliner, Don.
  Airplane racing : a history, 1909–2008 / Don Berliner.
      p.   cm.
  Includes bibliographical references and index.

  ISBN 978-0-7864-4300-0
  softcover : 50# alkaline paper ∞

  1. Airplane racing — History. 2. Aeronautics — History.
  I. Title.
  GV759.B48   2010
  797.5'2 — dc22   2010008494

British Library cataloguing data are available

©2010 Don Berliner. All rights reserved

No part of this book may be reproduced or transmitted in any form or by any means, electronic or mechanical, including photocopying or recording, or by any information storage and retrieval system, without permission in writing from the publisher.

Cover image: Neal Nurmi Wingman Photo

Manufactured in the United States of America

McFarland & Company, Inc., Publishers
  Box 611, Jefferson, North Carolina 28640
  www.mcfarlandpub.com

Table of Contents

Preface   1

Introduction   3

Section One: Before World War I

1. The First Race at Reims   9
2. Overly Ambitious European Cross-Country Races   16
3. Weekly Handicap Races in England   27
4. The 1909–1913 Gordon Bennett Cup and Speed Records   33
5. The 1913–1914 Schneider Cup for Seaplanes   42

Section Two: Between the Wars

6. The Last Gordon Bennett Race, 1920   47
7. Streamlining and Power Light Up the 1919–1923 Schneider Cup Series   51
8. The 1920–1925 Pulitzer Trophy Races Stimulate American Military Racer Development   57
9. The 1922–1929 Kings Cup Races: Jolly Competition in a Garden Party Setting   63
10. The 1927 Dole Race Disaster: On to Hawaii and into the Pacific   67
11. The 1925–1928 Military-Oriented U.S. National Air Races   72
12. The 1929 U.S. National Air Races and the Thompson Trophy Race   76
13. The 1925–1931 Schneider Cup Races: Rampant Nationalism   87
14. The 1930–1934 National Air Races: GeeBees and Wedell Williams   93
15. The 1934 MacRobertson Race: The World's Greatest Air Race?   108
16. The 1933–1936 Coupe Deutsch de la Muerthe and the Sleek Caudrons   114

17. British Racing of the 1930s	124
18. The 1935–1939 U.S. National Air Races: Dwindling Participation	127

Section Three: Post–World War II

19. The 1946–1949 Cleveland National Air Races	133
20. The 1950–1960 Period: Midget Racing Keeps the Sport Alive	147

Section Four: The Reno Air Races Era

21. 1964: The National Air Races Return in the Desert	153
22. The 1960s	160
23. The 1970s	176
24. The 1980s	191
25. The 1990s	204
26. The 2000s	216
27. Formula One Invades Europe	229
28. Short-Lived and Minor Classes	233
Summary and Outlook	239
Chapter Notes	243
Bibliography	247
Index	249

Preface

Air racing is speed competition for piloted, fixed-wing aircraft around closed circuits or long cross-country courses. Aviation's primary spectator sport is pylon racing, in which several pilots take off together and race simultaneously for several laps around courses marked at the corners by brightly colored towers, called pylons. The sport began less than six years after the first recognized flight of an airplane, when the basic system in use today was in its infancy and thus varied in but minor ways.

For much of its history, air racing has combined experimentation into the techniques and equipment meant to enable aircraft to fly faster, more reliably and safely, with the more-or-less equal purposes of promoting commercial and civil aviation, and of course entertaining the spectators. Today, with government and commercial aeronautical research and development so highly advanced, the amusement aspect of air racing has assumed primary status.

In air racing's early days, most of the activity was in Europe, primarily Great Britain and France. Based on the extensive use of military airplanes in World War I, that aspect predominated through the 1920s. Not until 1929, when a custom-built racing airplane first defeated the best the U.S. Army and Navy could field, did civilians enter the sport with a wide variety of original designs, which quickly replaced the look-alike military airplanes.

After World War II, the availability of combat-proven, war-surplus, high-performance airplanes at little cost pushed the colorful custom-built racers into the background. But the sameness of factory-built fighter planes bored the spectators who had become accustomed to variety, and this led to a highly-regulated class of "midget" racers. Not only has this class continued to offer close competition at a reasonable cost, but it enabled this variation of the sport to spread to Great Britain and then to France.

It was this development that triggered my interest, as competition had suddenly moved from the laboratory and factory back to a simple, highly visible two-mile rectangle, around which sped 500-lb. airplanes that had been built in garage and basement workshops. This was in 1947. By 1952 I had served as a pylon judge responsible for determining if a pilot has cut a corner in his eagerness to win. By 1954 I was a volunteer with the Professional Race Pilots

Association, and soon had my first article published in a national magazine. In the ensuing decades, I have traveled almost 150,000 miles reporting on (and sometimes officiating at) races from California to France.

It would be both impossible and counter-productive for a single volume to include every detail of every air race in the past 100 years, and so limitations had to be enforced. Emphasis herein is on races involving airplanes designed and built primarily for racing, and those manufactured airplanes that have been significantly modified for racing. Just because an airplane has been raced doesn't qualify it as a racing airplane, any more than participating in an impromptu traffic-light drag race qualifies your aging Oldsmobile sedan as a drag racer. Moreover, only races where speed is the sole concern are covered, leaving out races where such matters as fuel economy and precise navigation are major factors.

Introduction

> *The Rheims meeting marks an epoch in the history of mechanical aerial locomotion. It is the first occasion on which a wide variety of machines has been brought together, and on which one has been pitted against the other day after day, so that one day the monoplane is to the fore and the next day the biplane takes the lead; while the fact that many of the competitors have been practicing on flyers for a few weeks only, reveals that the management of them can be acquired as quickly as one learns to drive a motor car.*— Flight, August 28, 1909

Air racing was born in August 1909, on a rain-soaked field in the French champagne country, spreading quickly to English garden parties, then to the shiny new municipal airport in Cleveland, and finally to a barren mile-high plateau near the gambling casinos of Reno, Nevada. Along the way it visited Miami and the Mojave Desert and the south coast of England, with side-trips all the way from Honolulu to Kansas City to Melbourne, Australia.

Its trip started out in a spindly 50 hp Curtiss pusher biplane, soon switched to a unexpectedly streamlined little Deperdussin mid-wing, followed by a sleek Curtiss floatplane with its screaming V-12 engine. From there it progressed to a TravelAir Mystery Racer built in six weeks, then the classic, barrel-shaped GeeBee Super Sportster and finally a compact silver Turner Meteor.

After World War II, custom-built racers made way for modified ex-fighter-planes like P-51 Mustangs and F2G Super Corsairs and soon, at the opposite end of the performance scale, 500-lb. custom-built midget racers. More recently, they have been joined by jaunty little sport biplanes, World War II–surplus advanced trainers, and then, four-seat, kit-built speedsters that had been precision-molded from high-tech composite materials.

Their pilots—heroes even to the other heroes—were initially engine-builder Glenn Curtiss and English Channel–crosser Louis Bleriot, then a lot of flamboyant Frenchmen and staid Englishmen. In America, it was future war hero Jimmy Doolittle and the swaggering, mustachioed Col. Roscoe Turner. They were replaced by professional test pilots and veteran military pilots like "Tex" Johnston and Cook Cleland. The most recent era can boast of test pilot Darryl Greenamyer and airport operator Bill Falck, corporate pilot Ray Cote and farmer Bill Destefani, as advancing technology re-shaped the airplanes and the sport.

Through it all, the wonderful thing about not just racers but all airplanes has remained the same: airplanes can fly, even better than birds. Despite take-off weights sometimes of several thousand or even hundreds of thousands of pounds, they can rise gracefully above the earth and sail along for many hours at a time. It took centuries of dreaming and creating, shaping and crashing to achieve this. It remains something of a mystery to most people who glance out the window at the long wing of a jumbo airliner as it cruises effortlessly over mountains and oceans, and try to recall something they had learned in school about invisible molecules of air.

Second in importance only to the airplane's near-magical ability to lift itself off a runway is its amazing potential for speed. While a car is limited to 65 or 75 mph on the open highway, and a few can reach 200+ mph on a race track, the most enormous airliner can cruise effortlessly at 600 mph while carrying hundreds of casually dressed passengers. The now-retired Concorde supersonic transports streaked across the Atlantic Ocean at up to 1,300 mph in great comfort and with no sense of the speed. It was to demonstrate that speed, and to glory in it, that men invented airplane racing one hundred years ago.

The history of airplane racing is very much that of all aviation, with glamorous pilots and sleek airplanes in the spotlight, backed up by steady, but less glamorous tinkerers and engineers producing improvements in engines and fuels and structures and streamlining, all of them leading to greater efficiency and usefulness. At first, closed-course and cross-country racing was driven by the simple need to inspire and motivate men to accelerate their search for ways to make airplanes fly faster and more dependably. Air racing eventually developed into a sport. And like all other forms of human competitions, its functions were then mainly to challenge the participants mentally and physically, and to entertain the rest of us.

Long before there were vehicles, men raced against each other on foot. Then they climbed on the backs of camels and horses and were able to race faster. Primitive boats were raced, first on the unreliable power of the wind in their sails, then by gangs of strong men with oars, and most recently on the power of huge engines meant for airplanes. Upon the invention of the wheel, men raced anything that moved by rolling, starting with chariots. As the industrial age dawned, they raced machines. First, they rode and steered bicycles, then motorcycles and automobiles. And as soon as more than a few airplanes could be gathered together, it became obvious that they simply had to be raced, as well.

In the early days, the airplane's speed was not particularly remarkable, for the first heavier-than-air flying machine — the Wright brothers' 1903 Flyer — was notable not for its speed but rather for its ability to defy gravity. With a top speed of no more than 20 mph, it was actually one of the slowest airplanes that has ever flown. Cars and trains of the day, no matter how crude by modern standards, provided much more rapid transportation.

It took but a few years to realize that the airplane had almost unlimited potential for speed, while its surface-bound counterparts were restricted by the laws of physics, the laws of society and sometimes even by common sense. If you double the horsepower of a passenger car, it is still limited by the same speed laws and by the rapidly increasing danger of colliding catastrophically with other cars driven less competently than yours.

But double the power of the engine in an airplane, and it will become not merely faster but more useful, delivering its load of people, freight or, sadly, bombs, to their destination more effectively. This wide-open opportunity for almost unlimited speed soon forced the introduction of practical restrictions on the design and power of racing airplanes. A literally *unlimited* class, permitting the most powerful engines and smallest airframes available, must remain a fantasy, as the speeds achieved would require courses so long as to limit the spectators' view to but a small portion of each lap. And the danger of racing such wild contraptions near the ground would almost certainly lead to discouraging government regulation, if not prohibition.

In the beginning, however, there were absolutely no limits on the airplane a pilot choose to race. It could be of any design and built from any materials. Its airframe could be of any size and shape, and use any available engine with any type of fuel. In those days, it was enough of an achievement just to get an airplane into the air and back on the ground without doing serious harm to it and to its pilot. If, during the run-up to the first air race at Reims, France, in 1909, someone had been clever enough to invent the turbojet engine, he just might have been able to build an airplane around it and easily whip the less creative pilots who were restricted to sitting behind (or sometimes alongside of (or in front of) the sputtering piston power plants of the day.

As airplanes developed into a wide range of sizes and shapes, air race organizers had to face the reality that continuing to race everything in one, all-inclusive "unlimited class" was both unrealistic and counter-productive. To improve the closeness of competition, and thus the appeal to spectators, airplanes were soon divided into classes by the piston displacement of their engines, e.g., a 200 cubic inch class, a 350 cubic inch class.

With the available power in each class being roughly similar for each airplane, emphasis was shifted to the design of the airplane, and thus the improvement of the breed. The chances of a racing class becoming dominated by one or two competitors was reduced, and in some cases the costs of building and competing were limited and therefore the number of competitors was increased.

After the Second World War, when airplane racing was no longer on the front line of technical development and found itself, instead, a spectator sport, it still faced speed limitations. To keep the participants within view of those all-important paying customers, specific courses had to be created. Like the oval racetracks and twisting road courses for cars and motorcycles, their aeronautical counterpart became the pylon-marked oval course. To keep g-loads in tight turns within reason, the courses had to take into account the speeds to be achieved, and so those for the faster airplanes had to be designed with more turns of less severity.

Airplane racing has long been "The World's Fastest Motor Sport," due not entirely to the considerable horsepower available, but also to the airplane's greater receptiveness to streamlining. Racing cars and motorcycles are forced to scrape their large, sticky tires across the pavement, thus producing considerable and inescapable resistance to their forward progress at the same time that they are providing forward thrust. The airplane's wheels, on the other hand, can be conveniently retracted completely inside, where they cannot interfere with the smooth flow of air around the vehicle. Whereas automobile and, to a lesser degree, motorcycle racing have benefited greatly in recent years from aeronautical technology, these land vehicles must still expose more of their vital parts to the wind in order for them to perform their important functions.

The need to keep pylon race courses visible to the crowd has placed a severe (but not necessarily undesirable) limitation on speeds. The highest speed yet achieved during a sanctioned race for any recognized class of propeller-driven airplanes is slightly over 500 mph, set on a course more than eight miles in circumference and with its back stretch some three miles away from the grandstands.

In the early days of airplane racing, the competitors took off individually, frequently rounding the course alone, or with no more than one or two other airplanes aloft at the same time. The serious lack of reliable engines played a major role in this system, as it would have been cruel and completely unrealistic to have required several crews to have their temperamental engines running at the same, preannounced starting time. The spectators suffered, not knowing who was winning until the last competitor had landed and all the speeds had been compared by huddled officials and posted on a large board. But in those days, simply seeing airplanes flying as fast as they could was excitement enough.

As technology improved and the needs of the spectators were given greater consideration, airplanes were started at specified intervals, so that all would be racing at the same time, though it usually wasn't clear which was the fastest until the race had ended and the times could be adjusted for their staggered starts. This was almost as confusing for the spectators as the old system, and was replaced as soon as possible by the "race horse" start, in which all the airplanes are lined up, side-by-side, and are started together when the official starter waves his flag.

As it became ever more difficult to find airports with sufficient space to line up more of the larger racing planes and start them safely, an "air start" was employed for some classes. In the air start, the airplanes form a line abreast of the pace plane, and all streak toward the race course together, steadily increasing their speed. When all is ready, they are let loose by a radioed signal from an official in the pace plane. This is almost as exciting as a "race horse" start, and is certainly safer.

The sport has rarely experienced stability. During the 1930s, the dominant Cleveland National Air Races attracted so many fans and so much press attention that they spawned dozens of local and regional races. Today, however, only the reliable National Championship Air Races at Reno, Nevada, are keeping American air racing alive, while there are alternately encouraging and discouraging stirrings in Europe.

The sport has undergone enormous changes in its first 100 years, as has the world in that same period. It is currently faced with the distracting onslaught of video games, home computers, and NASCAR, but probably will survive, though in what form, one can only guess.

Section One: Before World War I

Chapter 1
The First Race at Reims

It was the opportunity of a lifetime. Hardly anyone in Europe or America had yet to see a single airplane on the ground, let alone in flight. The first aerial voyage on the Continent had been achieved less than three years before, by a Brazilian, Alberto Santos-Dumont. And while words describing a string of daring achievements in this new realm were effectively being communicated by newspapers and magazines, the same could hardly be said for live visual images capable of expressing the amazing impact of humans actually soaring above the ground higher, faster, longer and farther than ever before.

There had been attempts to organize air races as early as 1907, but all failed due, initially, to the lack of airplanes, and then to the inability of airplane engines to run on schedule. Further development of technology would be required before any real progress toward the first competition could be expected. It would take two full years.

Forty miles to the northeast of Paris and near the great cathedral city of Reims in the lush champagne country lay the Plains of Betheny, onto which, in August 1909, poured tens of thousands of Frenchmen, from shopkeepers and common laborers to high government officials and members of the nobility. They were there for the same, quite simple reason: to watch more than three dozen pilots vie for honors in the world's first organized aerial contests.

They were greeted by ornate grandstands, two rows of hurriedly built hangars rented to airplane manufacturers (airplane manufacturing was, in itself, a brand new concept), an aerial race course delineated by tall towers or pylons at its four corners, and a sea of wet, sticky mud. It was about to become the temporary center of the known universe, as a few terribly brave men did battle with wind and rain and gravity in poorly designed airplanes that were underpowered by highly undependable engines, as they sought titles and trophies and the admiration of the great masses and their few peers.

Most had been struggling along in near-obscurity, dreaming and designing, building and testing, crashing and repairing, and modifying; and then, after briefly nursing their wounded bodies and pride, recouping their financial losses and charging right back into it. Gradually, progress was being made. Shapes were being refined. Wings were becoming less like those of birds and more like those of airplanes. Structures were being strengthened. Engines were being coaxed to run for more than few minutes before overheating or violently expelling major parts. Pilots were learning how to use flight controls that many of them had previously not realized were even necessary. Still in the future, however, were such sophisticated concepts as fuel efficiency and streamlining.

The immediate goal was still merely to take off, fly briefly and then land in one piece and near enough to the take-off area to make the next attempt convenient. The Grand Week of the Champagne — August 22–29, 1909 — would produce the first signs of direction for this new form of locomotion, with an organized attack on official records for speed, altitude, distance and duration. It would be a spur to the rapid improvement of everything related to heavier-than-air flight.

A series of formal competitions served to focus the attention of the crowd and especially of the pilots and their crews. No longer could the pilots do entirely as they pleased, arising late, casually preparing the airplane, and then waiting for perfect weather conditions before venturing aloft in hopes of doing whatever appealed to them at the moment. At Reims there were specific periods of time during which a pilot must make his attempt to win a particular trophy. Rules were starting to appear in what had been the wildly uncontrolled vagueness of the air. At least for a few days, the solitary aeronaut who could do as he wished would be replaced by a crowd of pilots who accepted guidance so as to create some semblance of order. After all, it takes at least two to make a race.

Nevertheless, by modern standards, the event was conducted in a pretty relaxed atmosphere, with no announcements such as "all the pilots wishing to compete for the silver challenge trophy must be at the starting line at five minutes past two." Considerable blocks of time were set aside for any pilot who wanted to try for a prize. He could take off at any time within that block. An unsuccessful take-off attempt would merely cause him to get in line for his next attempt, for disqualifications were as yet unheard of.

A year earlier, there would not have been enough flyable airplanes in all of France to make such an event possible. That was before Wilbur Wright had shocked European aviation with his apparently effortless flights, which left their greatest achievements in the dust. In repeated demonstrations near LeMans, France, between September and December 1908, he flew five times as far, and for five times as long, as the best of his rivals. Even more important for the long term, he revealed a mastery of control that astounded all who watched. Operating with little public notice, he and his brother bicycle builder had achieved what scores of ostensibly more qualified men were still dreaming about.

Now, having been shown that fully controlled flight of a heavier-than-air craft was a reality, the French wasted no time in taking the lead, which the Wright brothers had so richly earned and were in the process of allowing to vanish.

1. The First Race at Reims

While the design and construction of the competing airplanes would undergo rapid and drastic changes, the basic concepts of the race course with its corner pylons and the identification of airplanes with large racing numbers painted on their sides would survive the first 100 years of air racing in substantially their original form. The Reims course was 10 km. (6.2 miles) in circumference, with the two long straightaways 3.75 km. (2.3 miles) long, and the short straights 1.25 km. (0.8 miles) long. It was located on what is now the southeastern part of the Reims-Champagne Aeroport. Each airplane would be started individually; the modern "race horse" start had yet to be considered, since it was clear to all that majestic, high-strung horses were considerably easier to organize than early aero engines.

To a modern observer, the airplanes would have looked unfinished, as if they had been pulled off the middle of the assembly line rather than at the far end. The wing ribs and their connecting spars—now considered internal structure—were out in the open, for everyone to see and for the wind to tumble wastefully about. The fuselages with their strength-producing longerons, verticals and cross-bracing were, in most cases, fully exposed to the elements. The value of enclosing all this within fabric or thin sheet metal was yet to be learned. But at the speed most of these airplanes flew, such streamlining would have been of only limited value.

Aside from a couple of British pilots and a single American, the line-up at Reims consisted of Frenchmen, some of whom were among the leading lights of aviation, while others were, and would remain, little known. As significant as who was there, was who *wasn't*. Both of the Wright brothers stayed at home, busy with plans for production of their airplanes and the training of pilots. British aviation pioneers Samuel Cody, A.V. Roe and Blackburn were nowhere to be seen, nor were the first European to fly, Jacob Ellehammer, nor the popular Brazilian, Santos Dumont, who was seriously ill and phasing out his aviation activities.

The best known among those present was Louis Bleriot, who had become world famous a few weeks earlier with his flight from the French side of the English Channel to the British. The 21-mile trip, all 36 minutes of it over open water, ended Britain's centuries of physical isolation from Europe. It was the first flight from one country to another, and the first over a major body of water. The painfully shy Bleriot reluctantly became the toast of Europe, which was rapidly becoming enamored of everything even vaguely aeronautical, including popular songs and flamboyant ladies' hats.

For the various contests at Reims, Bleriot had come well prepared, with three versions of his Channel-crossing monoplane: a Type XIII with a 40 hp, 3-cylinder, air-cooled Anzani engine; a Type XII with a 50 hp, 8-cylinder, water-cooled E.N.V., and a Type XI with a 25 hp, air-cooled Anzani engine. All three used wheels for their landing gear; while only the Type XI used birdlike wing warping for roll control, the others using the soon-to-become-universal hinged ailerons.[1]

Henry Farman, an Englishman living in France, had been a well known bicycle and auto racer, and soon after learning to fly had captured both the World Speed and Non-Stop Distance Records. For Reims, he had two of his own biplanes, developed from an earlier design by the Voisin brothers. Both used ailerons, with landing gear composed of both runners and wheels. Each had a 50 hp, water-cooled, 4-cylinder Vivinius engine.[2]

Hubert Latham was a wealthy playboy who had made the first serious attempt to fly the English Channel, twice landing with a splash just a few miles out from the French Coast. He had two large, graceful Antoinette monoplanes at Reims. Both were powered by 50 hp, water-cooled, Antoinette V-8 engines, while one used ailerons and the other used wing-warping, symbolizing the major clash of philosophies on how best to exert roll control.[3]

Leon Delagrange was a student at the Ecole des Beaux-Arts (School of Fine Arts) in Paris at the same time as Farman and Gabriel Voisin. He had then given up a promising career as a sculptor to take up aeronautics. At Reims, he had two airplanes, one a Voisin biplane with a 50 hp Antoinette V-8 and "automatic" roll control. The other was a Bleriot Type XI monoplane with a 25 hp, 3-cylinder, air-cooled Anzani.[4]

The sole American pilot at Reims was Glenn Curtiss, who had started a

Hubert Latham's #16 Antoinette monoplane in front of his hangar at Reims (Anders Bruun collection).

1. The First Race at Reims

Alfred Leblanc's #24 Bleriot in flight at Reims (Anders Bruun collection).

small bicycle repair shop in 1900, built his first motorcycle in 1901, and set his first motorcycle speed record (64 mph) in 1903, shortly before the Wrights first flew an airplane. By 1904 he had built an engine that was used in a dirigible. In 1907, Curtiss was crowned the "Fastest Man on Earth" when he drove a motorcycle powered by one of his V-8 engines to 136 mph on the hard-packed sands of Ormond Beach, Florida. The record was still standing when he arrived at Reims.[5]

The first day started out in dreadful weather, with high winds and lots of rain, none of which discouraged a huge crowd bent on seeing things that had never before been seen by modern humans, let alone their primitive ancestors who had populated this land eons before. As for the would-be air racers, several braved the elements, making attempts on the course to qualify as members of the French Team that would compete for the Gordon Bennett Trophy later in the week. This constituted qualifying time trials, a system that is still in use.[6]

Paul Tissandier, the son and brother of famous balloonists, was the first to make an attempt, taking off in his Wright Flyer shortly before noon and staying up for barely a minute, but qualifying not only as a possible member of his country's team, but as arguably the world's first racing pilot. Bleriot followed, covering almost half a lap. Eugene Lefebvre, in a license-built Wright biplane, was the next to make more than a feeble try, succeeding in completing almost two full laps of the 10-km. course. As the beginning to the first air race, this had been less than a roaring success. But, as neither an airplane nor a pilot had yet been smashed, it got the sport off to a fine start. Those who had come simply to see men fly, went home happy.

A late-afternoon heavy rain storm appeared to have ended the day's activity, but then a suddenly clearing sky stirred the increasingly frustrated pilots to action. Soon the Plains of Betheny was host to a scene unprecedented in world history: seven airplanes in flight at the same time, circling the race course, vying for the Prix de la Vitesse (Speed Prize). This challenge was for three laps of the course, and offered a purse of 20,000 francs ($4,000).

The best time for a single 10-km. lap was turned in by Lefebvre, at 8:58.8 for 41.53 mph. Tissandier turned a lap at 9:26.2 for 39.52 mph, and the Comte de Lambert, also flying a Wright biplane, at 9:33.4 (39.02 mph), all of which were unofficially and briefly world speed records. Additional attempts by these men and any others would be permitted on Tuesday, the 24th, and Sunday, the 29th.

Competition for the Prix de la Vitesse and the one-lap Prix de Tour de Piste (Circuit of the Course) extended to the final day of the meet. Eight pilots competed in the Vitesse, with Farman flying two airplanes. America's Glen Curtiss turned in the lowest time of 25:39 for the 30 km. (18⅔ miles), for a speed of 43.6 mph. Hubert Latham was in second place, a minute slower, for 42.1 mph. Curtiss won 10,000 francs.

In the Tour de Piste, 13 pilots took their turns on the course, with Louis Bleriot winning by 7:47.8 to Curtiss' 7:49.4. At 47.83 mph, he came in barely

Alec Ogilvie's Wright Roadster being restrained while its engine is run up at Reims (Anders Bruun collection).

ahead of Curtiss, at 47.63 mph. Bleriot won 7,000 francs, and Curtiss added to his total with 3,000 francs.

The feature racing event of the Grand Week of the Champagne was the James Gordon Bennett Race, for two rounds, each for one lap of the course, with the total counting. Bleriot won the first round by 7:53.2 to Curtiss' 7:57.4. In Round Two, Curtiss equaled Bleriot's first round time, but Bleriot had the misfortune of running into a brief rain squall, which slowed him by 10 seconds for his lap. Glenn Curtiss thus won the trophy on total time and set a record for 20 miles of 15:50.4. He had won the first important air race in the world with a speed of 47.52 mph.

The unquestioned King of Speed for the first-ever air race was the engine-builder from Hammondsport, New York. With two firsts and one second place in the three racing events, he won 38,000 francs ($7,600), a trophy which was soon to become priceless and earn him worldwide recognition. Eighty-one years later this achievement would lead to his becoming only the second racing pilot to be elected to the American Motorsports Hall of Fame.

The sport of air racing had been born, as witnessed by a horde of Frenchmen, including journalists who would spread the word farther. News photographs would show one airplane passing another as they sped down the home stretch, bringing first the entire country and then the rest of the world into much closer contact with the latest wonder of powered flight. No longer would pilots and their airplanes be limited to staggering from place to place with few witnesses. Now they could exercise their truly novel talents for all to see.

Chapter 2

Overly Ambitious European Cross-Country Races

The First Cross-Country Race

Before there was any great interest in closed-course, around-the-pylons air racing, prizes were already being offered for cross-country competitions, flying from one specified point to another. At first, these were just cross-country flights (far from a simple achievement in those ancient days), but they developed into races at the first opportunity.

The first major prize was offered in Great Britain as early as 1905, for the first pilot to fly to a selected point and return to where he started. One hundred guineas (1 guinea = 1 pound + 1 shilling, or about $5.25 at the time) was offered by Sir David Salomons, automotive pioneer and founder of the Royal Automobile Club. The rush to win the £105 ($525) prize was understandably slow in developing, as this was almost three years before the first recognized flight of an airplane in Britain.

London-to-Manchester Race

On November 17, 1906, the *Daily Mail*, then and now one of England's major national newspapers, stepped to the fore and offered a prize of £10,000 (then equal to $50,000) for a not-necessarily-non-stop flight of about 160 miles from London to Manchester, both cities being sites of the paper's major offices. While the first flight in the country still remained in the future, the size of the prize created considerable interest, with airplane designers, builders and pilots finally having a specific target at which to aim.[1]

The first officially recognized flight by a British-built airplane was accomplished on October 16, 1908. Pilot Samuel Cody, then an American who eventually became a British subject, was the Royal Engineers instructor in kite flying at the Army Balloon Factory at Farnborough, now the site of an important biennial aerospace industry exhibition. Cody was also the designer and builder of British Army Aeroplane No.1, a spindly, Wright-style biplane with a 50 hp

2. Overly Ambitious European Cross-Country Races

Antoinette V-8 engine. His 1,390-foot (¼-mile) straight flight at Farnborough went into the record books as the historic first flight in Britain.

Six months later, the pieces which had been fluttering about in all directions came together. The first to try for the *Daily Mail* prize was Claude Grahame-White, who had become the first man to receive a British pilot's license, the year before. He soon established an airfield and flying club in 1910 at Hendon, north of London, which was taken over by the military. It later became the home of the Royal Air Force Museum, which now includes one of Grahame-White's original hangers.

He took off for Manchester from Park Royal, a few miles northwest of the center of London, in his Farman biplane in the early morning of April 23, 1910. Grahame-White got as far as Rugby, halfway to his goal, stopped for an hour, then went on to Lichfield, where engine trouble forced him to make an unplanned landing. He suffered damage in the landing and from subsequent high winds, which spelled the end of his first attempt.

Louis Paulhan, of France, had taught himself to fly in a Voisin biplane he'd received as first prize in a model airplane contest. He joined the competition a little after 5 P.M. on the afternoon of April 27, leaving from Hendon in a slightly newer model Farman than Grahame-White's. A second attempt was begun by the latter barely an hour later from Wormwood Scrubs, a few miles west of Park Royal and the site of an infamous prison. The two men raced all-out, Paulhan landing for the day near Lichfield, and Grahame-White at Roade, 57 miles further away from their goal at Manchester.

Grahame-White saw but one chance to beat his more experienced rival, and so took off the next morning at 2:30, long before sunrise. In doing do, he demonstrated either supreme courage or a lack of judgment bordering on the suicidal, for night flying compounded the usual long list of aeronautical risks, which included inclement weather, the lack of mechanical reliability, and the challenges of a slowly emerging "black art" which would eventually become known as aerial navigation.

With neither natural nor artificial light to aid him, Grahame-White had to face the difficult task of keeping his wings level without the turn-and-bank instrument that would become recognized as a necessity, as well as navigating from place to place without being able to read a map or a compass. After almost two hours spent battling strong winds, he landed near Polesworth after having covered barely 40 miles. He was still far short of his goal.

In the meantime, Paulhan had taken off shortly after 4 A.M. and made it all the way to Didsbury, on the outskirts of Manchester. This was ruled to be close enough to earn him the prize for what had turned out to be the first cross-country air race. He had covered 185 miles in 4 hours, 12 minutes, of flying time, for an impressive average speed of 44 mph.

1911 Paris-to-Madrid Race

The very first organized cross-country race could easily have been the last. In May 1911, a newspaper called *Le Petit Parisien* (the little Parisian) offered the equivalent of $20,000 for a race from Paris to Madrid, Spain. The Spanish Aero Club added $10,000 to the purse, with the result that no fewer than 20 French pilots entered.

The race started at Issy-les-Molineux, in the Paris suburbs, on May 21, where an estimated 200,000 awaited the beginning of something completely new. Indicative of the recognized importance of the event, the crowd included French Premier Monte and his son, Antoine, along with the minister of war, Henri Maurice Berteaux, and future air race sponsor Henri Deutsch de la Muerthe. Those and other dignitaries were escorted by a troop of cavalry to a special VIP viewing area near the runway.

Louis-Émile Train took off and circled the field while checking his engine. Unhappy with the way it was running, he headed back toward the runway to land. But a troop of cavalry had gathered on the runway, forcing him to abort his landing. He swerved, the engine failed to respond and his airplane stalled and crashed into the VIPs. The minister of war was killed instantly, and the premier and his son were trapped under the wreckage. The elderly premier suffered a broken leg, but the others were all right.

The race was stopped, though the pilots who had already taken off continued, as there was no way to recall them. The next day the race was resumed, as danger and crashes were accepted as a necessary part of pioneer flying. Jules Vedrines was the eventual winner, being the only one to fly all the way to Madrid, while the favorite, Roland Garros, made it most of the way before hitting power lines, when his engine quit, causing him to crash into a river.

The death of a major political figure could easily have been used as the basis for outlawing all air races. But as auto races had established a precedent for a high degree of danger, resulting frequently in injury and death, this was apparently seen as an expected outcome of any risky activity.

1911 Circuit of Europe Air Race

In fact, the enthusiasm quickly led to what was called "the greatest aeroplane race the world has yet seen," by *The Aeroplane,* an influential British weekly. There were at least 51 pilots and airplanes entered, even though the race was scheduled to start less than three years after Wilbur Wright had shown the Europeans how to fly. Its route involved two crossings of the English Channel, a mere two years after Louis Bleriot demonstrated that it was possible to do so without drowning or at least getting thoroughly soaked.

The course of the June 18–July 7, 1911, Circuit of Europe Race stretched almost 1,000 miles through France, Belgium, The Netherlands, back to Belgium and France, to England and finally back to France. In less-than-ideal weather, this could be a daunting task even today in a small plane, yet few of the contestants had done much cross-country flying. Aerial navigation remained a vague concept, engines demanded as much luck as gasoline, and most airplanes of the day lacked even the most basic of flight instruments.

What brought out Europe's best aviators, along with a lot of those who were better qualified to be spectators, were the supreme mental and physical challenges, and what awaited the winner: public adulation, self esteem, recognition by one's peers—and, by the way, a major share of the $91,500 purse.

Most of the airplanes were no better suited to a long cross-country grind than were their pilots. Engines ran when they felt like it. Controls were unbalanced, as flutter was thought to be just something hummingbirds and butterflies did. Navigational equipment was limited to compasses and to maps which might or might not show useful smoke stacks and church steeples, sure to be hard to find among a bewildering clutter of look-alike villages and river bends. As for the conveniently straight, paved roads that future pilots would often follow, this was but a few years after the invention of the automobile, and roads were twisting, unpaved and unmarked.

For the relatively short English portion of the race, the Automobile Association had thoughtfully laid out large white arrows on the ground, directing the pilots from one turning point toward the next. The route across the Channel was marked by small boats from England and warships from France every few miles. The rest of the course looked about the same as it had a century before, when controlled flight was still a foolish, if not heretical, dream.

The Start

Forty-two pilots took off from Vincennes, just east of Paris, on Sunday, June 18, in a flurry of chugging and sputtering and rattling and wobbling. They headed for Liege, Belgium, via Reims, scene of 1909's first-ever airplane race, and the ancient health resort of Spa. Fewer than half of them completed the 192 miles of the first stage on the first day, most dropping out due to crashes or major mechanical problems — or maybe to a sudden jolt of reality.

As should have been expected so early in the history of powered flight, placing a lot of pilots under severe pressure to make long flights in minimum time and on schedule was certain to produce a host of problems. They began even before the start of the race, when Lieutenant Princetau took off from Issy, south of Paris, intending to follow the route of the race as one of several official Army observers. He died when his Bleriot promptly caught fire, crashed and burned with him trapped inside.

Lemartin, also in a Bleriot, died instantly when he smashed into a tree as he was starting the race. And Landon, flying a de Pischoff, crashed fatally at

Chateau-Thierry, barely 50 miles along the route of the first stage. Had the organizers cancelled the race at this point, few would have been surprised, though it might have produced a mini-revolution led by spectators and fans and the curious. They didn't call it off, and they were rewarded for their courage by a race which produced a steady stream of minor crashes and minor injuries, but not a single additional fatality.

Only two pilots completed the race without replacing such vital components as engines, wings and fuselages. Most of the winners enjoyed heavy support from engine and airframe manufacturers, with some of the crews changing engines and even complete airplanes several times during the race.

Interest in absolutely anything related to airplanes was exploding across Europe, and so the race attracted huge crowds at every stop. According to one British observer at Vincennes, "I guess the crowd at at least 100,000. All the organization of the police was shamefully bad. The crowd were fairly docile, and though they broke through once or twice, they were easily pushed gently back by cavalry." From other accounts, the crowd ranged from 200,000 to 400,000. And as many as 200 may have been injured when they poured onto the field and had to be chased back by the 6,000-member mounted police force.

According to one newspaper report, "Automobiles, cabs, tramways, railway trains, auto-taxis and autobuses were taken by assault, while a vast multitude on foot and bicycles thronged every route leading to the military maneuver ground. Thousands of enthusiasts even camped out all night, in spite of a pouring rain."

Despite the widespread view that we in the 21st century live in unusually violent times, it is hard to imagine a modern motor sports event in which two competitors were killed and as many as 200 spectators injured just as the race was getting underway, and yet the race continued! But such was the determination of flyers and the general public to be involved in this fascinating new adventure, that major risks to life and limb were apparently accepted as the price of progress. To add to the mystique of this still-new realm (or perhaps because of its none-too-savory reputation), two of the pilots raced under assumed names.

Some of the pilots were well prepared, having surveyed the course in advance, and then were accompanied by cars loaded with spare parts, tools and mechanics. Others seem to have done little preparation beyond checking the sparkplugs and kicking the tires. Faced with unfamiliar terrain and constantly changing weather, no one could be said to have been truly ready for such a long grind. But once it began, many of the pilots were determined to finish even if it involved ignoring the few good lessons they had learned in their short flying careers.

From *The Aeroplane*:

> In the early morning of Monday, [Jimmy] Valentine [in a Deperdussin monoplane] started ... back to Reims. He arrived at the aerodrome with his whole

machine practically falling to pieces. It appears that in smashing his propeller [when he pancaked into a field the previous day], the shaft which carried it bent, consequently when he started, the whole propeller had a "wobble" which threw it right out of balance. The unbalanced forces tore at the front of the machine 'till they wrenched the whole engine and its steel bearers loose in the woodwork ... in another few miles the whole of the power-plant would have dropped out, and the machine would have fallen from the sky.

Luck, a major component in air racing, needn't always be bad.

Leaders after the first stage of 192 miles from Vincennes to Liege, Belgium, were Vidart in a Deperdussin, followed by future World Speed Record holder Jules Védrines in a Morane, Charles Weymann, of Haiti, in a Nieuport, and Lt. De Conneau (alias "Beaumont") in a Bleriot. Vidart's time was three hours, 10 minutes, and his average speed of 61 mph wasn't all that far behind the existing world air speed record of 81 mph. He had a lead of at least 28 minutes over the others, and for this received the 1st Stage prize of £1,600 ($8,000). All the leaders flew monoplanes, in an era known mainly for biplanes.

Eventually, 18 pilots got to Liege, out of 42 starters. A few of those who didn't make it in time to embark upon the 2nd Stage on schedule straggled along behind, flying the additional stages unofficially.

Stage Two

The 2nd Stage was delayed a day due to *really* bad weather, and then was started on Wednesday, June 21, extending for just 37 miles from Liege to Spa and back. It was still a long enough leg to enable a few pilots to get themselves into difficulties. Barra (Maurice Farman biplane) and Amerigo (R.E.P. monoplane) both strayed across the nearby border into Germany, where they were reportedly greeted with enthusiasm on the part of the residents who would all too soon be enemies. Verrept (Morane monoplane) landed due to fatigue and took a nap in a peasant's cottage; awaking refreshed, he flew back to Liege.

Fifteen of the 18 starters completed Stage Two, with Jules Vedrines being the Stage winner for the $2,000 prize, followed closely by Vidart. The latter's overall lead of 28 minutes was cut to 24½ minutes by Vedrines. At the low end of the scale, a string of crashes and mechanical failures had already removed 60 percent of the starting pilots and airplanes. At the high end, the race was becoming increasingly competitive.

Stage Three

On Thursday, June 22, the remaining competitors took off on Stage Three, from Liege, and headed for Utrecht, in The Netherlands, with a compulsory stop at Venlo (still in The Netherlands, but only two miles from the German frontier), for a total of 123 miles. The finish was the closest yet, with Louis Gibert the leader in 2:04:25, Roland Garros in 2:10:21.4 and Rene Vidart in 2:17:29.

Jules Vedrines landed hard at Maestricht and smashed his Morane monoplane. He then appropriated the similar airplane of his teammate Verrept and proceeded to wreck that one while attempting to take off. He finally got to the finish line more than 20 hours after the stage winner.

Stage Four

After two days of enforced idleness due to yet more bad weather, the next stage began on Sunday, June 25: 90 miles from Utrecht to the Belgian capitol, Brussels. For unknown reasons, the official stop watches were started a day and a half before the pilots finally got permission to take off, and so their times are highly misleading. "Beaumont" won in 37 hours, 21 minutes, Kimmerling was second in 37:35, and Vedrines was third in 38:01. Their more accurate flying times were 2:12:04, 2:30:38 and 2:56:57.

Among the non-finishers were Maurice Tabuteau, who started a day late and then wrecked his airplane; and Vidart, who landed short with mechanical problems and arrived in Brussels by car.

Stage Five

On Wednesday, the 28th, after a day for more needed rest and repairs, the remaining competitors headed off from Brussels to Roubaix, just 53 miles away. Védrines took off in yet another airplane, this time a clipped-wing Morane with a new 70 hp Gnome engine. He beat the runner-up by almost 14 minutes (:58 to 1:11:40 for Roland Garros). Garros explained that he was forced to slow down to follow the slower "Beaumont," as he had forgotten his map, actually flying figure eights at times while waiting for a fast airplane to come along and lead him to the next stop. Once he saw Védrines pass by, he increased his speed and chased after him, letting the faster pilot lead the way.

Problems unimagined by modern racepilots continued to plague the pioneers. Vidart was forced to land and ask directions, while Gibert lost his goggles and had to land to get new ones. Wijnmalen, flying an unfamiliar new Farman without the type's usual front elevator, admitted that he periodically looked back to make certain the rest of his airplane was still there, having nothing visible in front of him but sky and ground.

Stage Six

The next stage, on Thursday, June 29, was a leg of 56 miles from Roubaix to Calais, on the English Channel. There was great concern over starting the stage, as the winds at Roubaix were 40 mph, and at Calais 60 mph. They did start, though at times some of the airplanes appeared to be hanging in the air or even being blown slowly backward.

Winner of the stage was Védrines in 1 hour, 16 minutes and 20 seconds, closely followed by Vidart in 1:32:08, "Beaumont" in 1:44:39, Gibert in 1:45:41 and Kimmerling in 1:56:57. The Circuit of Europe was evolving from a highly questionable experiment into a first-class race.

The overall standings showed "Beaumont" in the lead with a total time of 48:08:41. Second was Garros in 51:48:55 and Vidart in 64:21:15. Védrines' two crashes in one day had knocked him completely out of contention for the grand prize, though he was still eligible for the individual stage prizes.

The race was then suspended for several days to give the pilots a rest and to enable some of them to attend the Gordon Bennett Race at Eastchurch, England. That already classic event was won by Charles Weymann, an American living in Haiti who had retired from the Circuit of Europe Race in 5th place at the end of Stage Three, in order to prepare for the more prestigious pylon race.

Stage Seven

This stage was from Calais, France, across 22 miles of water to Dover, near where Louis Bleriot landed in 1909. From there, the 11 surviving contestants flew to Shoreham and finally to Hendon, north of London. In the words of the correspondent for *The Aeroplane,*

> The first man to land at Dover was Védrines, but, much to everyone's joy, Gibert, on the R.E.P., beat him on time by 14 seconds, and so takes the Dover 100-guinea ($525) cup. Védrines has made himself very unpopular among those following the "Circuit" by his disgusting behaviour and foul language.

Considerable attention was paid by the press to the amount of time it took various pilots to cross the Channel. While World War I was still several years off, some of the German and British newspapers were said to have made references to an "invasion," not merely a sporting event. The growing possibility of war was obviously on peoples' minds.

Védrines then easily won the legs to Shoreham and on to Hendon, with his total time for the stage being 2 hours, 56 minutes. Next quickest were Vidart at 3:27, Kimmerling at 3:28 and "Beaumont" at 3:32. Nine of the 11 who left Calais managed to make it to Hendon, though it took more than 12 hours for several of them, including Gibert, who got lost south of London near Croydon, which would soon be on its way to becoming London's main airport.

Stage Eight

The return trip via Shoreham and Dover to Calais was another romp for Jules Védrines, without question the fastest. He won the first leg to Dover by more than 20 minutes over Gibert and Vidart, and the over-water leg to Calais by three minutes over Gibert and four over Kimmerling. In the view of *The*

Aeroplane's reporter, "As usual, Védrines made himself objectionable, and ... the Royal Aero Club's Commissioner at Dover had to threaten to expel him and his machine from the aerodrome unless he behaved himself."

Stage Nine

On the next leg, from Calais to Paris for the finish of the race, Védrines became just another pilot having difficulties with the troublesome new 70 hp Gnome rotary engine. Vidart won the stage in 2 hours, 33 minutes, 56 seconds and Gibert was second at 2:36:40, while a forced landing at Amiens cost Védrines so much time that he finished in last place, at 13:44.

The final results, covering all nine stages and almost 1,000 miles (a lot more for some of those who got lost) showed "Beaumont" the winner in 58 hours, 38 minutes. More than 3½ hours back was Roland Garros in 62:17. Vidart was another nine hours behind, at 62:17, while the "great" Védrines was more than a full day behind the winner, with a total of 86:35.

The bulk of the prize money—£12,100 or $60,500—went to the experienced and well organized Jean "Beaumont" Conneau. Next, with a total of £3,800 ($19,000), came Jules Védrines. No one else won more than £1,200 ($6,000). Had the more modern concept of spreading the money more evenly to include 2nd, 3rd, 4th and lower places been used, there would have been greater incentive for those not heavily supported by manufacturers.

Only eight of the 42 starters completed the race, with Gibert the only pilot to do so with his original engine. This suggests that the Circuit of Europe Race was something less than a rousing success. But this was 1911, less than eight years after the invention of the airplane and less than two years after the invention of air racing.

It was the biggest mental, physical and mechanical challenge yet faced by the growing collection of European aviators. Engines and airframes were severely tested, and most of them failed. Not so for the stamina and determination of many of the pilots, who performed well beyond expectations. Most surprising, the first six finishers all flew French monoplanes: two Bleriots, one Deperdussin, one Morane, one Sommer and an R.E.P.

Circuit of Britain Race

Rather than spending months analyzing the human and mechanical failures in the Circuit of Europe Race and then planning the next such event to eliminate the sources of many of them, the brave aeronauts were back at it a mere two weeks later. The *Daily Mail* Circuit of Britain Race, announced a year earlier when such a journey was far beyond the abilities of more than a few pilots, was set to begin on July 22 from Brooklands, site of the world's first paved auto racetrack, in the southwest suburbs of London. The first prize of £10,000 ($50,000) was just too much to ignore.

Twenty-one pilots started the race, which would stretch for 1,010 miles around Great Britain, with 13 compulsory control stops and five days in which to finish back at Brooklands. Fewer than a third of the starters finished, evidence that little had been learned from the most recent long race.

In first place, with his second straight win, was Lt. de Vaisseau Conneau ("Beaumont") in a Bleriot, who finished in 22 hours, 28 minutes for an impressive average speed of 44.9 mph. Emile Vedrines was second in a Deperdussin, and James Valentine was third in another Deperdussin. The only British airplane to finish was the Cody Biplane, flown to fourth place by Samuel F. Cody.

In its own way, this race was as challenging as its French predecessor, but once such a task had been achieved, it no doubt seemed to much of the general public that the second race was something of an anticlimax.

1913 Circuit of Britain Race

While many short cross-country races of 30 to 60 miles were run during the 1912 European season, there was nothing of the magnitude of the previous events. Finally, on August 16, 1913, a new Circuit of Britain Race was announced for seaplanes over a 1,540-mile course around England, Scotland and Wales. Of only four entries which were received, just one started, Harry Hawker in the Sopwith Circuit Seaplane. But his first start was unsuccessful and the second, while covering two-thirds of the total distance of the race, ended when engine trouble resulted in a very hard, damaging landing.

1914 London-Paris-London Race

The last cross-country race of any consequence before war started was the London-to-Paris-to-London Race, which started and finished at Hendon Aerodrome. It was to be completed in one day — July 14.

Of 15 pilots entered, only seven started and just three of those finished. The winner by almost two hours was the lone American, Bleriot pilot Walter Brock, who thus completed the hat-trick of winning the three most important European races of the year. Far behind was Roland Garros, also in a Bleriot and later a World War I flying ace and the man for whom the most important French tennis stadium is now named. The only other finisher was Eugene Renaux (accompanied by a Miss Unwin), who struggled back to Hendon the next day.

Others who failed to complete the 502-mile course included Lord Carberry, who landed his Bristol monoplane in the English Channel on his way home, and Harry Hawker, who withdrew prior to the start after landing his Sopwith in a tree. The race may have provided some of the inspiration for the movie *Those Magnificent Men in Their Flying Machines.*

1914 Circuit of Britain Race

The 1914 Circuit of Britain Race, for which nine entries had been received and which was scheduled to begin August 10, fell victim to the start of World War I. Also scrubbed was the planned Around-the-World Race, to be held in conjunction with the Panama Pacific International Exposition, at San Francisco, for flights between May 15 and December 4, 1915. In view of the long overwater stretches required by such a race, and the primitive state of aerial technology, the cancellation no doubt saved the lives of at least a few pilots.

In the days before the first of two terrible world wars, racing was the most exciting, productive and dangerous way to use an airplane. With long grinds like the Circuit of Europe and the Circuit of Britain, men had ample opportunity to test themselves and their machines. Added to this were the handicap races run at places like Hendon and Brooklands almost every weekend and for steadily growing purses and crowds. The pressure of competition produced improvements in engines, fuels, structures and streamlining at a rate far greater than otherwise would have happened. These few years established air racing as aviation's premier proving grounds and spectator sport.

Chapter 3

Weekly Handicap Races in England

One of the most durable, if little-known, traditions in all the world's air racing is the English handicap pylon race, a version of which began in 1912 and continues to this day in much the same form. A handicapped start permits any available airplane of almost any size, power and design to be used in speed competition without having to wait for a group of true racers having roughly similar performance to be designed and built.[1]

In a handicapped race, the slowest entry is started first, and then the next-slowest is started after a calculated number of seconds based on its known or estimated top speed. Eventually, the fastest airplane gets the starter's flag and charges into the air in pursuit of those who may have completed several laps while the pilot waited, counting the exasperating seconds as they slowly ticked past.

If the handicapping is accurate, if all the pilots display equal piloting and navigating skills, if the engines continue to run at top efficiency, and if the wind remains constant from start to finish, then the last few hundred yards of the race should produce far more excitement than almost any class race. Of course, the laps prior to the finish can also be thoroughly confusing, as it is almost impossible for the spectators to determine who is doing well and who isn't. For the competitors, it is very enjoyable competition with lots of passing and almost none of the scary (but to the spectators, truly exciting) wingtip-to-wingtip flying that characterizes class racing and discourages a lot of casual sport pilots from getting involved.

The very first handicap race was scheduled as part of the program for the Easter Meeting at Hendon Aerodrome, north of London, on April 5, 1912. Sadly, the eagerly awaited four-day event was greatly reduced in scope by high winds which forced the cancellation of the monoplane pylon handicap race, a similar race for biplanes and the cross-country handicap race from Hendon to St. Albans (a 10-mile dash) and return. Even the relay race had to be scrubbed.

Similarly, the first Brooklands Aeroplane Handicap Race, southwest of London, set for Easter Monday, April 8, fell victim to the capricious English

Claude Grahame-White's Bleriot monoplane (unknown, 1910).

weather. On April 13, a handicap race was held there, and while it was conducted according to agreed-upon rules, it was still considered "unofficial and impromptu," leaving the title of the "first official handicap race" still to be awarded.

At last, on April 14, a handicap race was organized and conducted, starting at Brooklands and running to Chertsey Bridge and back, then once around the hangars and on to the corn mill for a total of nine miles. The winner of the Raikes Trophy was T.O.M. Sopwith in a Bleriot, followed by E.V.B Fisher in the Flanders F.3, and C.P. Pizey in the Bristol Boxkite, a reproduction of which can be seen at Old Warden Aerodrome, flying on very calm summer evenings.

Men were determined to race, and they did. They were not about to be stymied by the lack of well marked courses, or of actual racing airplanes, a technical committee, teams of trained pylon judges, or fancy, red-and-white checkerboard pylons. The racing was competitive, it was safe and it was fun. All this added up to success, as witnessed by the decision to hold more such races every weekend. What more could have been asked of any experiment?

On the very next weekend, there were handicap races at both Hendon and Brooklands, though the airfields were just 20 miles apart. At Hendon, in front of an estimated 15,000 spectators, the first of the great air displays was held on Saturday, April 20. In the cross-country handicap—for two laps of a course to Harrow Church and back (steeples make fine impromptu pylons)—Bentheld

3. Weekly Handicap Races in England

A 1912 Deperdussin's engine is being inspected prior to a handicap race (National Air and Space Museum).

C. Hucks won the Grahame-White Cup #3 in his Gnome-powered Bleriot. On the same day, at Brooklands, Pizey won the Cross-Country Handicap Race in (actually "on," since his airplane was as wide open as a bicycle) his Bristol Boxkite.

Following each race, the chief handicapper re-calculated each airplane's handicap to reflect the actual speed that had been recorded. The result was that race finishes gradually got closer and thus more entertaining. Some airplanes underwent modifications aimed at improving their chances of winning, including engine tuning and elementary efforts at streamlining such as the covering with cloth or sheet aluminum of some parts of the structure that had previously been exposed to the elements.

While such techniques gradually developed into sophisticated practices as the sport matured, the pre-race adjustment of handicaps ensured that the less advanced airplanes retained an equal chance to win. Improving the breed took a back seat to the crowd-pleasing and pilot-pleasing assurances of close competition.

Yet another method for encouraging participation was also a recognition of the growing popularity of handicap racing with the spectators: the prize money was increasing significantly. By the third month of racing in 1912, cash prizes as high as £100 ($500) were being awarded, along with more elaborate, expensive and usually more prestigious trophies for achievements in the increasingly familiar realm of the air that was receiving greater public attention. Air racing trophies began to take their place alongside trophies for such traditional sports as hunt racing and sailing.

Races were also getting longer, blurring the line between pylon and cross-country events. A reasonable definition of the former is any race consisting of more than one lap of an identical course.

Pilots continued their weekly battles with each other and with the weather, eventually competing in more than 100 races and record attempts from April to late November, despite the need for pilots to bundle up against the steadily dropping temperatures. Typical was the Grand Speed Handicap at Hendon on November 2, a six-lap race won by Marcel Desoutter, who flew his 50 hp Gnome Berliot monoplane to a victory which brought him the London Aerodrome Silver trophy #12. The final race of the long season was on November 24 at Brooklands: the two-lap Speed Handicap was won on a Henry Farman biplane by John Alcock, later to gain fame as the pilot on the first non-stop flight across the Atlantic Ocean.

As odd as it may seem in view of the preponderance of biplanes during the 1914–1918 world war, half the 1912 races were won with monoplanes. The debate raged over the importance of the monoplane's reduced aerodynamic drag compared with the biplane's greater structural strength. The final decision was yet to be made.

After a pause of a couple months, racing resumed at both major sites, the first for 1913 being the February 22 Grand Speed Handicap around the Hendon Aerodrome pylons. A year of learning was starting to produce better and closer racing. First and second places went to French pilots and French biplanes: E. Richet in the 110 hp Canton-Unné Breguet, followed by Pierre Verrier in a 90 hp, Renault-powered Maurice Farman. In third was Englishman Harold Blackburn flying the #33 Blackburn Mercury, a monoplane trainer which would soon be developed into a long line of military airplanes bearing the Blackburn name.

The highlight of Hendon's Easter Meeting was the eight-lap Speed Handicap, which produced a tie for first place between Collardeau in the Canton-Unné and Verrier in the Maurice Farman. To break the unprecedented dead-heat, a four-lap fly-off was run, with the *Daily Express* Gold Medal going to Collardeau.

A long string of planned races was cancelled by high winds even more than rain, but the string was finally broken by the Fifth London Aviation Meeting in mid–May, 1913. The six-lap race around the aerodrome pylons—for the Shell Trophy and £112 ($540) total purse—was won by Lewis Turner on a Caudron biplane.

Two weeks later, the Hendon Empire Day Meeting was highlighted by a series of races for the Withers Cup. The finals was for eight laps and produced the first American winner since Glenn Curtiss at Reims in 1909: Walter Brock, flying a Deperdussin monoplane powered by a 35 hp Anzani engine.

3. Weekly Handicap Races in England

Hendon's second summer meeting, on the July 19–20 weekend, saw Robert Slack fly eight laps of the 1½-mile pylon course to win the London Aerodrome Silver Trophy No. 16 in a Maurice Farman equipped with landing skids and an enclosed nacelle (later to be called a cockpit) for the pilot.

Pylon racing action finally moved away from London and the Home Counties to Burton-on-Trent, a major brewing center on the outskirts of the industrial Midlands. Among the features of the early August meeting was the Around-the-Island (formed by two arms of the River Trent) race for the Marquis of Anglesey Cup. The six-lap pylon race was won by E. Ronald Whitehouse flying a Handley Page H.P.5 E. Second was Freddy Raynham in an Avro 500, and third was Sydney Pickles in a 60 hp Anzani-powered Bleriot.

The popularity of short-course pylon racing grew to the point that major events were being held every weekend:

September 6 — Hendon 4-lap Cross-country Handicap, won by Philippe Marty in a Morane Saulnier.

September 13 — Hendon 8-lap Speed Handicap, won by Louis Noel in the Grahame-White Boxkite.

September 20 — The second Aerial Derby, 95 miles around London, was won by Gustav Hamel in his 80 hp Gnome Morane-Saulnier with its wings clipped from 30'6" to 20'.

September 25–27 — In Hendon's first International Air Contest, the British Team of Grahame-White and Hamel won the Hendon Trophy and £1,000 ($5,000) on points.

The season ran on to December 20, when Marty won the four-lap Cross-Country Handicap in his Morane-Saulnier.

For an air racing enthusiast living just north of London, 1913 would have been a year to remember, with enough action to satisfy anyone. Then, after a winter "break" of three weeks, it started up again on January 10 with a four-lap cross-country handicap race won by Pierre Verrier.

The frequency of air race meetings dropped, at least partly because they had been held too frequently and the spectators were becoming jaded. More interest was being focused on important international events such as the Gordon Bennett and Schneider Cup Races.

Of the British races, the most significant 1914 race was the Third Aerial Derby, which was held June 6 after a two-week postponement. The starting field — Hendon — and the course were the same as for 1913. Eleven pilots started, including R.H. Barnwell in the 1914 Schneider Cup–winning Sopwith Tabloid. He and Schneider winner Howard Pixton in another Tabloid pulled out due to fog. The winner was the lone American, Walter Brock, whose Morane-Saulnier monoplane averaged 71.9 mph.

The long race of the year was a handicap event from Hendon (London) to Buc (Paris) and return for 509 miles. Seven started, all but one being French.

The winner was, once again, American Walter Brock at 71.5 mph, for which he received £800 ($4,000)

Semi-weekly events at Hendon continued until August 3, with the Lord Desborough Challenge Bowl of three laps around the 4-mile course to Bittacy Hill and back. It was won by R.J. Lillywhite in the Grahame-White "Bi-Rudder Bus."

One more major race was on the schedule: the Circuit of Britain Race for the *Daily Mail* £5,000 ($25,000) prize, set to begin August 10. But even before then, the first phase of World War I had begun, and England was being drawn into the fray at an accelerating rate. That race was cancelled, and no more were to be held for almost five years, during which time aviation became a major world enterprise.

The first era of air racing thus established short-course pylon racing as a spectator sport, as well as a proving ground for new ideas. While the accident rate remained unacceptable, it was considerably lower in 1914 than it had been back in 1909 and 1910 when racing started.

Chapter 4

The 1909–1913 Gordon Bennett Cup and Speed Records

1910— Belmont Park, New York — October 29

One of the most important of the many long-lasting contributions of that first air race at Reims in 1909 was the quick-to-develop concept of a series of races, usually held annually, for the same prestigious perpetual trophy. As a general rule, the country whose pilots won three times (in some cases it had to be three times in succession) would take permanent possession of the trophy, signifying the end of the series. The first of these — officially called the International Aviation Cup, but generally known as the Gordon Bennett Cup — was presented by American newspaper magnate James Gordon Bennett, the eccentric publisher of the New York *Herald*.[1]

After Glenn Curtiss won the trophy at Reims, the next year's race would automatically be held in his home country, the USA, where it was the highlight of the first important American air meet. The selection of Belmont Park, a few miles northeast of what is now John F. Kennedy International Airport on Long Island, as the location was a fine idea, but the dates chosen in late October were unfortunate in that they all but guaranteed cold, windy weather which would be to the great detriment of both pilots and spectators.

Regardless, the turnout of pilots and airplanes was outstanding for just the second year of this series. The physical plant could hardly have been better, with the ornate grandstands, club house, headquarters building and other facilities already built for the use of the Belmont Park horse-race track.

To accommodate air racing, which shared the spotlight with a variety of other flying events, the organizers laid out two pylon courses which turned out to be a miniature version of the modern layout for today's Reno Air Races. The short course was a symmetrical six-pylon oval measured at 2½ kilometers (1½ miles), while the long course had nine pylons and stretched out for 5 kilometers (3.1 miles). As at Reno, the two courses shared the home stretch, directly in front of the grandstands, where a great crowd of mostly Americans would get their first look at airplanes in a hurry. The Gordon Bennett Race would be for 20 laps of the 5-km. course — 100 km. (62 miles).

For a full week before the feature race — generally recognized as the world air racing championship — pilots from France, Great Britain, the USA and even Switzerland competed for elaborate trophies and a share of $63,000 in cash prizes in order to be declared the best, at least temporarily, in the disciplines of duration, distance, altitude, passenger carrying and speed, along with special tests involving flights out to specified points and return.

But it was the Gordon Bennett Trophy Race that carried maximum prestige. No doubt for dramatic effect, it was held back until the next-to-last day. Among the favorites was Walter Brookins (USA), flying a brand new biplane Wright Racer, the smallest airplane in the meet and one of the most powerful, with a 60 hp, straight-8 Wright engine. Also expected to do well were Alfred Leblanc (France) and Claude Grahame-White (England), both flying larger Bleriot monoplanes powered by the new 100 hp, 14-cylinder Gnome rotary engine. Reigning Gordon Bennett Trophy holder Glenn Curtiss was expected to defend the title he won in 1909, but his little 60 hp monoplane wasn't quite ready, not being in shape to make its first test flight until a day after the 1910 race meet had come to a close.

While these and a few other racers were modified versions of standard models, only one could be considered custom-built for racing, as the need for such airplanes was barely beginning to come into focus. The Hamiltonian,

Charles Weymann's Nieuport, which he flew to victory in the 1911 Gordon Bennett Race (unknown, 1911).

4. The 1909–1913 Gordon Bennett Cup and Speed Records

flown by Charles Hamilton, was seen as the great American hope. It was as small and clean as any at the meet, and with an 8-cylinder, 110 hp engine built by auto-racing expert Walter Christie, might have presented a serious challenge to the Europeans. Unfortunately, Hamilton started his only official Gordon Bennett flight a few minutes after the final deadline, and had to be disqualified.

The only other potentially fast American racer was the Baby Wright, flown by Walter Brookins. For some unknown reason, it was flown only in distance and altitude events, and so had no chance to show its speed. The airplane, having been restored to its original form, is now on display in the Musée de l'Air at Bourget Aeroport, north of Paris.

The first to try for the Gordon Bennett was Grahame-White, who left the ground at 8:42 A.M. on Saturday, October 29. He immediately joined up on the long course and began clicking off the first of the required 20 laps for a total distance of 100 km. (62 miles). Flying fast and steady, he turned in speeds for laps 6 through 20 that were all faster than the existing world records for those distances. The Englishman finished his required laps in 1 hour, 1 minute, 4.74 seconds, to average 61.04 mph.

The crowd went wild, having seen what the organizers had promised (still not that common an occurrence in 2009): faster flying than had ever before been accomplished. But Grahame-White's perch atop the majestic mountain of speed lasted all of 20 minutes, when Frenchman Alfred Leblanc charged onto the course in a similar Bleriot shortly before Grahame-White finished his 6th lap. The crowd then got to see true air racing, as Leblanc put everything into a drive to overtake his main competitor. By the 19th lap, he was leading his cross–Channel rival by more than five minutes.

And then Lady Luck took charge. Leblanc's fuel line became disconnected, and quickly released his remaining supply of gasoline into the air instead of into his engine. The engine ran dry and stopped, while the pilot searched for an open field in which to make an emergency landing. While he was doing so, his attention was briefly distracted and he flew squarely into a telephone pole, wrecking the airplane, but fortunately not its pilot. While Leblanc's records for every distance up to 90 km. went into the record book, the mark for 100 km., along with the $5,000 first prize and the priceless Gordon Bennett Trophy, went to Claude Grahame-White. The trophy winner was recognized as the winner of the race, though LeBlanc became the new "fastest man in the air," having been clocked at 67.84 mph on one lap.

The race for the Gordon-Bennett Cup was not over. Less than nine minutes after Leblanc entered the course, he and Grahame-White were joined by yet a third pilot, Alec Ogilvie, who was flying a little 30 hp Wright Roadster. The two Englishmen and one Frenchman tore around the course as no trio of pilots had ever done. Ogilvie's fastest laps were not that much slower than the others', but he had to stop for almost an hour to replace a sparkplug which had blown out. John Moisant, an American flying a 50 hp Bleriot, eventually placed second, though more than 56 minutes behind the winner, due in great measure to his 42-minute stop for repairs.

1911— Eastchurch, Kent, England, July 13

As 1910 winner Grahame-White was from England, the site of the 1911 race would be east of London on the desolate Isle of Sheppey, along the south shore of the River Thames estuary. This race would be the longest yet, for 25 laps around a 6-km, kite-shaped, four-sided course, totaling 150 km. (93 mi.).[2]

The third running of this increasingly prestigious trophy race produced the first, tentative efforts to streamline airplanes in order to reduce their wind resistance and thus increase their speed. While the vital importance of streamlining seems overpoweringly obvious today, in the first years following the invention of the airplane, hardly anyone had flown fast enough to justify the extra effort.

Bleriots now appeared with their entire rear fuselages covered with cloth, whereas the rear structure of the airplane had always been visible to all. Edward Nieuport had three of his new mid-wing monoplane designs entered, all with fully enclosed fuselages. Only the Wright airplanes remained open, as they had no fuselage to enclose, and the proud Wrights were understandably hesitant to change the basic design with which they had first shown the world that heavier-than-air flight was possible.

A second design development, which would have major implications for the future of air racing, was the reducing of the span and area of a standard wing by chopping off some part of either wingtip, also for the purpose of increasing speed. The first to make use of this appealing but sometimes naively applied technique was Gustave Hamel, the 22-year-old son of a Royal Physician. Eighteen inches was removed from the tip of either wing of his Bleriot monoplane, resulting in a span of just 22 feet, rather than 25. Removed at the same time was much of the portion of the wingtips which flexed or warped to produce lateral control, later universally accomplished with hinged ailerons.

The entries: Chevalier in a Nieuport IIN with a 30 hp, 2-cylinder opposed Nieuport engine; Gustave Hamel in a Nieuport with a 100 hp Gnome rotary engine; Alfred Leblanc in a Bleriot XI with a 100 hp Gnome; Edward Nieuport in a Type IIC of his own design and construction, using a 70 hp Gnome engine; Alec Ogilvie in a Baby Wright Racer with a 2-stroke N.E.C. engine, and Charles Weymann in a Nieuport IIC with a 100 hp, 14-cylinder, two-row Gnome.

The excitement began at the very start of the race. After several reasonably successful practice flights in the clip-wing Bleriot, Hamel made his official start and, according to C.G. Grey in *The Aeroplane*, "He made a small circuit, and then shot across the starting line going great guns. He reached the first pylon, took it very close with a sharp turn heavily banked, slipped sideways, dived, made a frantic effort to pull the [nose] of the machine up, but was too late, and hit the ground about a hundred yards from the pylon."

Hamel was thrown clear, rolling and bouncing across the ground to a point some 30 yards past the tangled, smashed remains of his airplane. He was carried off the field unconscious, but was later found to have suffered nothing worse than bumps and bruises. The disadvantages of clipping wings beyond the point where they can provide sufficient lift and control in a steeply banked turn would continue to have an impact on air racing for far too many years to come.

A few minutes after Hamel's crash, Chevalier took off in his slick little Nieuport with less than a third of the horsepower of the Bleriots. He hummed right along for lap after lap, then encountered serious engine trouble and was forced to land in a rough field near the end of his 11th lap. It was quickly determined that one of his two cylinders had blown completely off the engine, resulting in an absence one would think the pilot might have noticed. He made a second attempt on an identical airplane, but was forced down at almost the same point, thus ending his day.

Next to attack the course was Charles Weymann, son of the American ambassador to Haiti, whose Nieuport sped around the course clearly faster than anything that had previously been seen. He completed the 25 laps in 1:11:36.2 to set a Gordon Bennett record of 78.11 mph.

Alec Ogilvie was next in his low-powered Baby Wright Racer, whose two-stroke engine produced a screeching sound unlike anything else. He flew steadily at just over 51 mph except when Leblanc, who took off in time to join him on the course, passed him on the inside and below, a technique that was later outlawed as it did not give the pilot who was being passed sufficient warning of what was about to happen. Ogilvie, who said he needed full control to keep from being turned upside down by the propwash swirling off Leblanc's Bleriot, completed the 150 km. to place 4th.

The next-to-last starter was Leblanc, who flew cautiously and made his turns wide so as not to risk repeating Hamel's accident. Nevertheless, he finished only two minutes behind Weymann, at 75.91 mph. Edward Nieuport completed the half dozen in the starting field, flying smoothly but not quite fast enough to catch Weymann and Leblanc, the latter less than a minute ahead of him in the final standings.

Streamlining played a significant role in the speeds, but horsepower produced the margin of victory, as the first three airplanes had such similar airframes.

1912 — Clearing, Illinois, September 9

The fourth race in this series was particularly noteworthy for the total victory by the French team in the absence of any competitors from England and

Andrey Frey's Hanriot being wheeled out of his hangar for the 1912 Gordon Bennett Race (unknown, 1912).

even the host country — and for a major step forward in the art, if not pure science, of streamlining. The race, for 30 laps of a 6-pylon, 6.66-km. course (totaling 200 km. or 126 miles) was held southwest of downtown Chicago, about where Midway Airport now stands.³

Teams were expected from the USA, France and England, while Belgium, the Netherlands and Switzerland had each promised at least one pilot and airplane. Substantial growth in the series was expected.

The host country thought it had a potential winner — the *American Defender* — which had a sleek, compact fuselage, Bleriot-style landing gear, shoulder wing and two small vertical tails in place of the usual single surface. It was to be equipped with a two-row, 160 hp Gnome rotary engine, the largest yet built. It was developed by W. Sterling Burgess of the Aero Club of Illinois, along with Glenn L. Martin, who would soon reach the heights of American aircraft design and manufacturing.

The British contingent was to have included 1910 Gordon Bennett winner Claude Grahame-White, Gustave Hamel and George Dyott, though it wasn't clear which airplanes they would fly. Two Belgians, flying 120 hp Etrich "Swallow" airplanes, were entered. Jan Wynmalen, of the Netherlands, withdrew at the last minute, while it was never quite certain that Edmund Audemars would represent Switzerland.

4. The 1909–1913 Gordon Bennett Cup and Speed Records

In the event, only the men of the French team arrived at Clearing, but they made quite a splash with their beautifully streamlined Deperdussin and Hanriot monoplanes, each with a 140 hp Gnome engine. Horsepower, plus such innovations as a full metal cowl surrounding the engine and a large propeller spinner controlling the flow of air around the engine, made it clear that only mechanical problems could prevent the French from totally dominating.

The race began at 9:40 on the morning of September 10 when Jules Vedrines took off in his "Dep," and proceeded to whip around the course 30 times in 1:10:56. His average speed of 105.06 mph was an American and Gordon Bennett record and, for all practical purposes, not merely the start, but also the finish of the meet.

Maurice Prevost followed in an identical Deperdussin, taking two minutes longer, but also breaking the 100 mph mark. Andre Frey, in the Hanriot, dropped out on lap 24, blaming engine trouble; he had been averaging 98 mph.

The huge crowds that had witnessed previous Gordon Bennett races were nowhere to be seen. According to *Aero and Hydro* magazine,

> Probably not more than 1,500 people saw the race. Those who went to the field in any other way than by automobile, or a specially chartered train, suffered a long walk and the extreme inconvenience of spasmodic street car service. Two hours was a quick trip to or from the field by trolley. Consequently the people who did see the race were veritable enthusiasts and no greater gathering of aero celebrities has been on the same acreage in the history of aviation in America.

Those who got to the field saw a limited amount of flying, for all the emphasis was on the Gordon Bennett race, with little besides the occasional arrival or departure of an aerial visitor to break the silence. The lack of a domestic threat to the French team no doubt played a role in discouraging a lot of those who might otherwise have made the trip.

During the formal awards presentation ceremony for the Gordon Bennett Cup, an announcement was made by Jacques Schneider that would soon propel airplane racing to a new level, both technically and publicly.

1913 — Reims, France, September 29

The site of the race was the same as it had been for the first, but so much else had changed. There were events for speed and for altitude, but none for distance or duration. The Gordon Bennett Race was in a bright spotlight, thanks to several successful runnings. The total entry list was way down, with speed planes only from France. There was a minimum-speed race, and the altitude contests included events for pilot-only, and for those carrying one and two passengers. Eugene Gilbert, even without oxygen, coaxed his Morane monoplane up above 19,000 feet.[4]

For the Gordon Bennett, there was only the French team, consisting of

Maurice Prevost, Eugene Gilbert and Crombez in nearly identical Deperdussin monoplanes powered by 160 hp, twin-row Gnome rotary engines. Emile Vedrines, brother of the 1912 winner, flew a Ponnier of similar size and layout.

Speeds clocked during the French team trials made it apparent that records would be broken, and the crowd was not disappointed. Ten times around the 10-km. 6-pylon oval course produced a 4th place speed for Crombez of 106.73 mph, almost 2 mph quicker than the 1912 winner's record. Gilbert turned in a 3rd place speed of 118.51 mph, Vedrines 2nd place at 122.53 mph, and Prevost became the first man to be officially timed at faster than 200 km/hr as he finished at 124.78 mph.

Three of the four flew Deperdussins, adding to the prestige of the mark's one-two finish in 1912. But Armand Deperdussin, who had financed the company, as well as several airfields, was nowhere to be seen, having just been jailed for having paid for his airplane design and manufacturing ventures with money embezzled from a previous enterprise in which he had been involved.

Regardless, the efforts by M. Deperdussin and others in what would later gain fame as SPAD, the producer of many thousands of World War I pursuit planes, created airplanes that were the fastest in the world, thanks to the first organized effort to stimulate airplane design and construction through racing. Had their streamlining developments been utilized during that war, Allied airplanes would have easily out-sped their German and Austrian rivals.

The only actual racer from the pre-war Gordon Bennett Cup series that has survived is the aforementioned Baby Wright Racer. While none of the ultimate Deperdussin monoplanes exists, a nearly identical air show version of the

Maurice Prevost's Deperdussin being manhandled into starting position for the 1913 Gordon Bennett Race, which he then won (National Air and Space Museum).

1913 "Dep" has been restored and is on display in the Musée de l'Air at Bourget Aeroport, north of Paris.

Before the date of the planned 1914 Gordon Bennett Race had come around, Europe was knee-deep in the "War to End All Wars." Designers, builders and pilots shifted their concerns away from all-out speed toward improving armament, camouflage and combat maneuverability.

Chapter 5

The 1913–1914 Schneider Cup for Seaplanes

The clear purpose of the pioneering James Gordon Bennett Cup Race series was to accelerate the pace of progress in the design, construction, power and piloting of all types of aircraft. It achieved its purpose fully in its first few years.[1]

When Jacques Schneider announced his intention to underwrite a series of annual competitions for his new Schneider Cup, it was his goal to stimulate progress specifically in seaplanes. In those early days, there was a serious shortage of useful landing fields located near major population centers, a shortcoming he felt was retarding progress. Since almost all large cities abutted large lakes, wide rivers or oceans, seaplanes looked to him and a lot of others as the most direct route to a glorious future full of larger and faster flying machines.

By offering cash prizes, a soon-to-become classic trophy and growing public attention to spur improvements to seaplanes, he hoped to turn racing advances into practical techniques that would make commercial seagoing aircraft able to carry larger loads over greater distances at higher speeds and with increased reliability. It was a large gamble, as the first flight of a seaplane had been made by Henri Fabre near Marseille in March 1910, and there were few of them currently being flown.

So that the machines raced in this series would be true seaplanes, and not "racing freaks," a novel series of sea-worthiness trials was prescribed:

First, each seaplane had to be taxied across the starting line and then flown around a short course of 5-to-10 miles.

Second, during this preliminary lap, each seaplane had to be landed twice, each time taxiing half a nautical mile at a speed of at least 12 knots before taking off again. Third, after completing this test, each had to land and taxi to a buoy where it would remain moored for six hours with no one aboard. No repairs or alterations were permitted during this time, and the seaplane had to remain afloat. Once it had been demonstrated that it was a true watercraft, it could proceed to the speed portion of the contest.

Monaco — April 16, 1913

The initial Schneider Race was held as part of the annual two-week Hydro-Aeroplane Competitions, and was organized by the Aero Club of France. The site was the Mediterranean Sea, just offshore at Monaco. The course was 10 km. (6.2 mi.) in circumference and would be flown for 28 laps, equal to almost 175 miles.

Seven seaplanes were to have represented France and one the U.S., with no entries from other countries. Only four passed the sea-worthiness tests: Charles Weymann from the U.S. in a 160 hp Gnome-powered Nieuport; Frenchmen Maurice Prevost in a 160 hp Gnome-powered Deperdussin Monaco, which was twice the size of that manufacturer's little Gordon Bennett Racers; Gabriel Espanet in a 100 hp Gnome-powered Nieuport; and Roland Garros in an 80 hp Gnome-powered Morane-Saulnier. All four seaplanes were originally land-based monoplanes to which twin floats had been added, rather than being purpose-built racing floatplanes or flying boats.

The pilots started at irregular intervals for practical reasons, which meant that more than two were rarely in the air at the same time. Prevost was the first to start, and he completed the 280 km. in 2 hours, 50 minutes, 47 seconds, for

Gabriel Espanet's Nieuport X. He dropped out on lap 25 in the 1913 Schneider Cup Race after averaging 63 mph (source unknown).

Charles Weymann rounds a turning point in the 1913 Schneider Trophy Race prior to dropping out on lap 8. He was flying the #5 Nieuport monoplane.

an impressive average speed of 52.4 mph. But the officials eventually determined that he had failed to cross the finish line correctly and insisted that he take off again and finish officially, which added almost an hour to his time and dropped his official speed to 45.75 mph.

All the while, Espanet was clipping off lap after lap at better than 60 mph and looked like a sure winner, at least until lap 25, when his oil line broke, his engine began to overheat and he was forced to land. Weymann, the lone American, failed to take off at the prescribed time when he found water in his engine. He fixed it and took off late. With his total time being included in the records, his actual flight time, which was shorter than Prevost's, could not bring him victory.

With only one of the nine original entries flying the full distance, the race could have been considered less than a rousing success. But as this was the world's first seaplane race, no one was hurt, and no seaplane was wrecked, it had to have met the organizers' hopes, if not their dreams.

Monaco — April 20, 1914

It was assumed that a year of experience would result in pilots and airplanes that were better prepared than they had been for the inaugural race,

5. The 1913–1914 Schneider Cup for Seaplanes

when hardly any pilot finished in good order. Certainly there was more interest, with 10 qualifiers, including four from France, two, each, from England and the U.S., and one, each, from Germany and Switzerland.

Most pilots again flew float-equipped standard monoplanes, aside from the Swiss, Burri, in an F.B.A. flying boat, and Howard Pixton, of England, in a purpose-built Sopwith "Schneider" biplane. One of the Americans, William Thaw, showed up with a Curtiss A-1 Triad flying boat, similar to the U.S. Navy's first airplane. Dissatisfied with it, he substituted a Deperdussin like the 1913 winner's. Charles Weymann flew a Nieuport. Ernst Stoffler, of Germany, started out with a big Aviatik Arrow biplane, damaged it, and borrowed another Deperdussin for the race.

The course was the same as the first year's, though the two landings had to be made during the first lap of the race. Sadly, the race was almost as unsatisfactory as that of 1913.

The race was again against the clock, though it began in good form with the first four starters in the air simultaneously. Pierre Levasseur and Gabriel Espanet, of the French team, were first off in their Nieuports, followed by Burri

Howard Pixton taxies his Sopwith Schneider past the Monaco waterfront (British Aerospace Corp.).

and Howard Pixton and briefly joined by Lord Carberry. The first four sped round and round for more than half the distance before problems began to arise. Espanet dropped out with engine trouble on his 16th lap, and Levasseur did the same on his 17th. Burri ran low on gas on his 23rd lap, landed, refueled and re-entered the course, now well behind the others.

Pixton, meanwhile, flew as if he owned the course, averaging 81 mph for the first 5 laps and increasing his speed until he was roaring along at almost 90 mph by the 15th lap, when one of the cylinders of his 100 hp Gnome rotary engine cut out. Still, he flew faster than anyone else, finishing in a time of 2 hours, 13 seconds for a speed of 86.4 mph. Burri, thanks to his pit stop, took 3 hours, 23 minutes to complete the race, averaging just 51.4 mph, though even this was faster than the previous year's winner had achieved.

Observing Pixton's completely unexpected speed, Weymann, Thaw, Stoffler and Garros decided that the prize money for lower placings wasn't worth the effort and never bothered to take off. Maurice Prevost, seeing that one of the French team pilots was not going to fly, headed for the starting line as the first alternate entry, but his engine quit on the way. Then, Levasseur borrowed Weymann's Nieuport, took off and flew eight laps before retiring.

Of the 10 qualified pilots, only two completed all 28 laps, while none of the others, even after swapping airplanes, accomplished much. Two years into the Schneider Cup series, there was precious little to show for the effort. But before anything could be done to perk things up, World War I interfered and put all thoughts of flying for fun far into the background.

Section Two: Between the Wars

Chapter 6
The Last Gordon Bennett Race, 1920

September 28, 1920— Etampes, France

After World War I had ended and while life in Europe was struggling to return to normal, the James Gordon Bennett Cup Race series was resumed. As the French had won the last two races with ease, it was assumed that they would win again and permanently retire the trophy. The most serious obstacle in their path was the most streamlined airplane anyone had seen, or would see for years to come.[1]

The race would be for three laps of a 100-km. course located south of Paris, from Etampes to Gidy and return. The total of 186 miles made it the longest closed-course race to date.

The surprise of the meet came from America, in the form of the radical Dayton-Wright RB-1. The silver bird had a smooth, teardrop-shaped fuselage with neither windshield nor landing gear sticking out into the breeze. The top of the fuselage lacked any protuberances, the only view from the cockpit being through small windows on either side, which would prove of questionable value in a race. The landing gear retracted into the sides of the fuselage where it could produce almost no aerodynamic drag. Even more futuristic was the variable-camber wing with its leading and trailing edge flaps, intended to permit shorter take-offs and landings without reducing the top speed. Despite considerably less power than any of its rivals (merely a 200 hp Hall-Scott straight-6), its lower wind resistance was expected to lead to much higher speed.

Completing the American Team were three one-of-a-kind racers: the army's Verville VCP-R biplane and the private Curtiss-Cox *Texas Wildcat* biplane and *Cactus Kitten* shoulder-wing monoplane. As only three airplanes could race for any one country, the last-named was never uncrated at the race site. Both Curtiss-Cox racers were powered by 340 hp Curtiss C-12s, and the Verville by a 600 hp Packard 1A-2025, liquid-cooled V-12.

France entered two Nieuport 29V military pursuits modified for racing and flown by Sadi Lecointe and Georges Kirsch, along with a SPAD 20bis5 modified pursuit to be flown by Bernard de Romanet. The sole British entry to arrive on time was a Martinsyde Semiquaver, not much larger than a modern Pitts Special aerobatic biplane. All four would be powered by well-proven 300 hp Hispano Type 42 V-8s. The other British entries were the Nieuport & General *Goshawk*, which straggled in on the day of the race, and the Sopwith 107 *Rainbow*, which was withdrawn shortly before the race when the manufacturer went out of business. The *Texas Wildcat* crashed two days before the contest, leaving the U.S. with just two entries.

First to start was Georges Kirsch in a Nieuport 29V at 1:37 P.M. His first lap was made at a world 100 km. record speed: 173.6 mph, but this slipped all the way to 136 mph on the second, and he dropped out on the final lap as his sparkplugs had become increasingly fouled by oil.

Next off was Bernard de Romanet in the SPAD S.20bis5. Two laps at 160 mph were followed by a ½-hour pit stop for adjustments to his lubrication system, and so his average for the distance was down to 112.86 mph.

Sadi Lecointe took off just two minutes later and by the end of his second lap had set a world closed-course record for 200 km.: 170.6 mph. A slightly slower third lap resulted in a final average speed of 168.768 mph.

The futuristic American entry took the starter's flag shortly after 2 P.M., but pilot Rinehart was never able to retract his drooped leading edge flaps due to a jammed control cable. He didn't complete the first lap.

Sadi Lecointe and his record-setting Nieuport (unknown, 1920).

6. The Last Gordon Bennett Race, 1920

A modified military pursuit flown by Georges Kirsch of France in the 1920 James Gordon Bennett Trophy Race (J.H. Robinson).

Rinehart's teammate, Schroeder, took off in the powerful Verville racer which had not been flight tested at the race site. It lasted less than a lap, retiring with an overheated engine. As illogical as it may seem today, the drag-producing cooling system was often reduced in capacity in a forlorn effort to increase speed, while naively hoping that the inevitable effects of overheating could be delayed until the race was over.

The final starter was Frederick Raynham in the quaintly named *Semiquaver*. While his first 50 km was the fastest yet for that distance in the race—177.6 mph—he got no further, having been defeated by a broken oil pump. In fact, four of the six starters dropped out due to engine-related failures.

Lecointe, of France, was the winner, with a speed of 168.7 mph, more than 40 mph faster than the pre-war Gordon Bennett record. He thus retired the trophy to France, where it is on display in the Musée de l'Air, at Le Bourget Aeroport, in the northern outskirts of Paris.

The only airplane known to have survived from the race series is the Dayton-Wright, now fully restored and on display in the Henry Ford Museum in Dearborn, Michigan, west of Detroit. It is not known why the promising machine was never flown after its abortive racing effort, as its technical advances

Howard Reinhart's Dayton-Wright Racer, whose advanced technology wasn't enough to win the 1920 Gordon Bennett Race (National Air and Space Museum).

could have played a major role in accelerating the progress of modern aerial transportation. It would be many years before such smooth surfaces, retractable landing gears and variable-camber wings became accepted.

The James Gordon Bennett Trophy was the first of the awards for a major international racing series to be retired, and represents an increase in speed of 3½ times, or 120 mph, in just 11 years.

Chapter 7

Streamlining and Power Light Up the 1919–1923 Schneider Cup Series

Post-War Schneider Cup Races

It had been more than five long, hard years since the last Schneider Cup Race. During the interim, France, Italy and the U.S. had soundly defeated Germany and Austria in the bloodiest war in history. More than 200,000 pursuits, bombers, scouts and trainers had been built, compared to no more than a few thousand airplanes of all types during the decade before the war. Engines had become more powerful and more reliable. Airframes had been built stronger to withstand the greater g-loads experienced in aerial dog-fights. Pilots by the thousands may have died in action, but more than enough of them survived the war to populate a new era in peacetime aviation.[1]

Airplanes, in general, were beginning to assume a more important role, with the first rumblings of commercial airlines and of economical personal flying. Tales of derring-do in the skies over wartime France—almost always exaggerated and sanitized—became the basis for a rapidly growing interest among young people, who saw themselves as daring pilots in leather helmets and white silk scarves. The sky, no longer a battlefield, was becoming a place of romance and adventure.

September 10, 1919—Bournemouth, England

The course of this first important post-war race was a triangle of 37 km. (23 mi.) around Poole Bay, west of the Isle of Wight along England's south coast. It would be flown for 10 laps, making it the longest Schneider Race yet.

There were four entries from the host country. Vincent Nicholl was in the prototype Fairey III–A Royal Navy bomber, powered by a 450 Napier Lion engine, and with its biplane wings clipped from 46' to 28' expressly for racing. He dropped out on lap 1 due to the heavy fog. Harry Hawker was in a new model Sopwith

Schneider, with a 400 hp Bristol Jupiter engine. He, too, lasted less than a lap because of the dangerously limited visibility. Basil Hobbs, in a Supermarine Sea Lion I flying boat with a 450 hp Rolls-Royce Lion, struggled through one lap and then dropped out. H.A. Hamersley, in the little Avro 539 Schneider with a 250 hp Siddeley Puma, was held in reserve. His mount was later raced as a landplane.

France entered three seaplanes which had been modified from wartime pursuits, though none of them got to the starting line. Sadi Lecointe's SPAD S.20, with a 300 hp Hispano-Suiza 42, failed to pass the mooring tests because its floats leaked. Jean Casale's Nieuport 29, with a similar engine, was damaged too severely to start. And Henri Malard, flying an identical seaplane, was forced down in the English Channel on his way to the race site and floated for 24 hours before being rescued.

Guido Janello, from Italy, was the only pilot to fly the correct number of laps, but he made one turn on each lap around the wrong marker boat, having been confused by the fog, and thus failed to fly the correct course. He has been credited with a completely unofficial 110 mph. In recognition of his valiant attempt to complete the race, the honor of staging the next race was awarded to Italy, though the trophy was not.

September 20–21, 1920— Venice, Italy

The three previous Schneider Races had shown little indication of developing stability, as no more than half the entrants started, and no more than half the starters finished. If the series was to become the important force for technical progress its originator intended, the ability of seaplanes to pass their water tests and then fly more than 200 miles at high speed would have to be demonstrated soon, or the world would lose interest.

Unfortunately, the 1920 race only added to the gloomy outlook. Eight of nine entered craft were withdrawn as untested or unsatisfactory before they could become serious contenders. In fact, only Italy's Luigi Bologna attempted (successfully) to pass the navigability trials in his 550 hp Ansaldo V-12-powered Savoia S.12bis flying boat.

On the day of the "race," he completed all 10 laps of the 37.1-km. triangular course in 2 hours, 10 minutes, 35 seconds for a record-setting 105.971 mph. For the Italians, at least, things were looking up. The spectators could be excused if they lacked equal enthusiasm.

August 6–7, 1921— Venice, Italy

Encouraged by the 1920 race, the Italian Air Ministry went all-out, conducting elimination trials to pick its three-pilot team from a field of 12, most

7. The 1919–1923 Schneider Cup Series

of whom flew Savioa S.13 or Macchi M.7 flying boats. The only foreign entry to arrive was Frenchman Sadi Lecointe in his Nieuport-Delage 29, with its 300 hp Hispano-Suiza 42. A hard landing during qualifying trials buckled the float structure, it began taking on water and was withdrawn.

The race was scheduled for 16 laps of the triangular course for a total of 394 km. or 245 miles. For the very first time, a Schneider Cup Race would be genuinely competitive.

Giovanni De Briganti was first off the water in his Macchi M.7bis flying boat and began clipping off laps at a record pace — almost 118 mph. A few minutes later, Arturo Zanetti joined him on the race course, whipping his Macchi M.19 around at almost 130 mph. Soon they were joined by Piero Corgnolino in a Macchi Naval M.7, averaging 120 mph. The crowd massed along the bank was seeing some of the finest air racing yet, as one seaplane followed another with wondrous noise and, for the time and despite the built-in drawbacks of flying watercraft, unprecedented speed.

Zanetti kept up his impressive pace through lap 11, well in the lead at 129.7 mph, until the crankshaft on his 600 hp Fiat A.14 V-12 broke, flammable liquids poured out, and the seaplane caught fire. He set it down quickly and expertly as the flames began to spread, and jumped into the water to save himself. Then, on the final lap, Corgnolino, averaging 119 mph, ran out of gas barely a mile from the finish line and splashed down safely.

De Briganti, despite having the slowest of the three seaplanes, managed to stay in the air and sped across the line in 2 hours, 4 minutes, 40 seconds to average a Schneider Race record 117.859 mph. The prestige of the Schneider

The Savoia S.13 flying boat flown to an unofficial win by Guido Janello in the 1919 Schneider Cup race. The only pilot to complete the race, held in dense fog, he turned around the wrong pylon on every lap (Smithsonian Institution).

series got a big boost and the crowd finally got some excitement, though perhaps not as much as the pre-race publicity had promised.

August 10–12, 1922 — Naples, Italy

The new course was a 28.5-km. triangle, to be flown for 13 laps, equaling 370 km or 230 miles. The entry list was the shortest in years, made up of three Italians, two French and one British pilot, all with flying boats.

The two dismantled French C.A.M.S.36 boats were being shipped to Naples by train when a rail strike interrupted service and they became stranded. The sole British entry — Henry Biard — brought a Supermarine Sea Lion II, with a 425 hp Napier Lion W-12 engine, which had been converted from a naval craft into a racer. The Italians presented three. Alessandro Passaleva was in a Savoia S.51 sesquiplane with a 300 hp Hispano V-8, Arturo Zanetti was in a Macchi M.17bis with a 240 hp Isotta-Fraschini V-6, and Piero Corgnolino had a Macchi M.7bis with the same engine.

The race began at 4 P.M. and within minutes all four flying boats were in the air. Biard was first off and immediately began flying laps at close to 150 mph, leaving the others well back. He kept this up through the seventh lap, when he was slowed by traffic, which he eventually passed on the way to a finishing time of 1 hour, 34 minutes, 51 seconds, equal to a speed of 145.721 mph. Just two minutes back was Passaleva, even though his laminated wooden propeller was starting to come apart, setting up a fierce vibration and threatening to fly to pieces. Yet he finished at 142.649 mph, followed by Zanetti at 132.757 mph and finally Corgnolino at 124.030 mph. All four finishers broke the existing Schneider speed record.

The long-promised close competition had finally materialized, with all four starters completing the course with a minimum of mishaps. The impact of growing government support of national entries was also beginning to be felt, and would soon revolutionize the Schneider series.

September 27–28, 1923 — Cowes, England

An Englishman having won the last race, the 1923 event would be moved to Great Britain. It was held along a 69-km. (42.8-mile) triangle over the estuary of the River Solent, between the south coast of England and the Isle of Wight. Five laps would equal 344.5 km. or 214.1 miles.

This seventh running of the Schneider would see the first true racing seaplanes, and the first serious effort by the U.S., along with the first appearance of purpose-built military racers. Major improvements to engines and fuels and to the science of streamlining re-directed the race series away from trying to produce benefits to commercial seaplanes to a search for all-out speed. As a

7. The 1919–1923 Schneider Cup Series

Lt. David Rittenhouse's CR-3, with the pilot standing on the foreground float (National Air and Space Museum).

result, the gap between seaplane speed records and landplane speed records would begin to shrink.

The maximum effort by the Americans included four custom-built float biplane racers, though no more than three from any country could compete. The Wright NW-2 (525 hp Wright T-2 V-12) blew its engine on a trial flight and crashed. The Naval Aircraft Factory TR-3A (240 hp Wright E-4A V-8) backfired and sheared its starter while preparing to race.

This left a pair of Curtiss CR-3s, which would change the face of the Schneider Cup Race. For power, they used the new 470 hp Curtiss D-12, a liquid-cooled V-12 engine with advanced design features that would soon be copied by major manufacturers in other countries. In place of the traditional-but-clumsy Lamblin "lobster pot" radiators, the CR-3 used wing surface radiators that produced far less wind resistance. Converting horsepower into thrust was a very efficient Curtiss-Reed one-piece forged aluminum propeller.

The streamlining was not so much novel as more complete than had previously been seen. The engine cowl, in particular, was a masterpiece of design, fitting tightly around the engine and flowing smoothly into the oval cross-section fuselage. All the wing and floats struts had streamlined cross-sections and neat fairings where they were attached to the wings.

The CR-3's were at the very front line of aeronautical technology, thanks to the generous support of racing by the U.S. Navy. Number four, flown by David Rittenhouse, had started out as the CR-1 in which Bert Acosta won the

Lt. Rutledge Irvine's Curtiss CR-3 being beached via its dolly after the 1923 Schneider Cup Race (unknown, 1923).

1921 Pulitzer Trophy Race, then became the CR-2 for the 1922 Pulitzer, before getting floats and becoming an R2C-2. Number three also began as a CR-1 and became a CR-2 for the 1922 Pulitzer and then a CR-3 for Rutledge Irvine to fly in the Schneider.

There were four French entries. The Blanchard-Bleriot monoplane failed to arrive. The Latham L.1 was damaged in transit. The C.A.M.S. 36bis was damaged at the start of the race, and the C.A.M.S. 38, which was similar except for its pusher propeller, was raced by Maurice Hurel, who dropped out on lap two when its 300 hp Hispano V-8 seized. The Italians were nowhere to be seen, as their country was in turmoil caused by the recent forceful take-over of their government by dictator Benito Mussolini and his fascists.

That left the British. The slick little Blackburn Pellet flying boat, with a 450 hp Napier Lion engine, sank during mooring trials, without injury to Reginald Kenworthy, but its promising future was not to be. The Supermarine Sea Lion III (the improved II) was flown by Henry Biard to third place at 157 mph. Its hull is on display in the Science Museum, located in the South Kensington district of London.

The Curtiss CR-3's romped to victory, Rittenhouse in first place at 177.266 mph, more than 30 mph faster than the existing record. Not far behind was Irvine at 173.347 mph. The Europeans caught on quickly. It was clear that unless they followed the Americans' lead toward higher power, minimal size and improved streamlining, they would stand no chance in future races.

Chapter 8

The 1920–1925 Pulitzer Trophy Races Stimulate American Military Racer Development

Pulitzer Trophy Race Series

Less than two months after the final James Gordon Bennett Trophy Race had been completed in France, America entered the game with the first of a series of races for the Pulitzer Trophy, also presented by a newspaper empire to stimulate circulation at least as much as aeronautical progress.[1]

November 25, 1920— Mitchell Field, L.I.

The course—to be flown for four laps—was originally a 33-mile triangle from Mitchell Field to Lufberry Field to Damm Field, immediately to the east of Garden City, Long Island, New York. Problems experienced in marking the course resulted in it being reduced to 29 miles, though the full impact of this did not become apparent until the race was over.

The entry list was extensive, with no fewer than 38 pilots and airplanes ready to taxi to the starting line. Most pilots were in standard World War I military airplanes, as hardly any high-performance civilian airplanes yet existed. The list included 17 U.S.-built Army deHavilland dh.4 bombers, 6 Navy Vought VE.7 pursuits, 4 British S.E.5 pursuits, 3 Italian Ansaldos and 2 Thomas-Morse scouts.

The closest to a true racer was the Verville-Packard VCP-R, which was modified from a prototype VCP-1 pursuit by the Army Air Service's Engineering Division, with improved streamlining and double its original power (600 hp Packard V-12), and would be flown by civilian Corliss Moseley. It was first raced two months earlier in the Gordon Bennett Race, but retired early with engine trouble. The only other entrants with enough power even to simulate racers were the two Thomas Morse MB-3 prototype army pursuits, with 325 hp Hispano V-8s, to be raced by Harold Hartney and Leigh Wade, and a pair

Corliss Moseley's Verville-Packard VCP-R, in which he won the 1920 Pulitzer Trophy Race (J.H. Robinson collection).

of Curtiss-Kirkham 18-T-1 triplanes flown by William Haviland and W.D. Culbertson.

First off was Hartney, a Canadian, who sped to an average of 148.19 mph, the fastest so far by any non–European in a closed-course race. Culbertson, in a tri-plane, whipped off a first lap at 157.5 mph, then broke a connecting rod after completing the first three laps at an average of 147.3 mph. In the other three-winger, Haviland managed only a single lap at 138.3 mph before carburetor problems forced him down. In one of the Thomas Morse scouts, Wade flew a first lap at 137.9 mph, then a wing wire broke and he managed to land before this led to more serious damage.

Moseley experienced no such troubles, completing the four laps in 44 minutes, 29.57 seconds for an official average of 156.54 mph, with a fastest lap at 158.20 mph. His speeds, as well as those of all the others, were first computed on the basis of a 33-mile course length and were significantly higher. When the distances to and from a re-located pylon were taken into account, the length of the true course was shown to be just 29 miles and the speeds were reduced accordingly.

November 3, 1921— Omaha, Nebraska

The entry list was down to 12, with but 6 starting the race, which consisted of 5 laps of a 30.7-mile (50-km.) triangular course.

8. The 1920–1925 Pulitzer Trophy Races

The most interesting of the new airplanes was the CR-1, first of what would be a long line of advanced design Curtiss military racers which featured excellent streamlining and screaming Curtiss liquid-cooled V-12 engines that became the inspiration for an entire generation of airplane power plants. The CR-1 was a classic open-cockpit biplane, but gave away nothing to the new crop of monoplanes.

Two other special-built racers were the Curtiss-Cox *Cactus Kitten* and *Texas Wildcat*, the former a triplane and the latter a shoulder-wing monoplane, both with Curtiss V-12 engines. The *Wildcat* was withdrawn, as its landing speed was higher than the Pulitzer's 75 mph upper limit. The *Kitten* would be raced by Clarence Combs.

Two Thomas-Morse military racers—an MB-6 biplane and an MB-7 highwing—used 300+ hp Wright-built Hispano V-8 engines. Completing the lineup was a pair of Italian Ansaldo biplanes. The SVA-9 was a standard World War I pursuit, while the A.1 Ballila had been modified with a 400 hp Curtiss V-12.

The first to enter the race course was the flamboyant, talented Bert Acosta, who circled the course five times in the CR-1 to average 176.75 mph, 20 mph faster than the existing Pulitzer record. The combination of the cleanest airframe and probably the best racepilot would prove to be too much for the others to match, let alone exceed. Three minutes later, Lloyd Bertaud took off in the more powerful Ansaldo A.1 and turned in a speed of 149.71 mph.

Three more minutes and it was the turn of Combs in the difficult-to-fly *Cactus Kitten*, which managed to complete its only race, placing a strong second at 170.34 mph. After a five-minute gap, James Curran started in the standard

Clarence Coomb's Curtiss-Cox Cactus Kitten, flown to second place in the 1921 Pulitzer Trophy Race (U.S. National Archives and Records Administration).

Ansaldo, but retired on lap three with damaged rocker arms. The next-to-last starter was John MacReady in the Thomas-Morse MB-6; he averaged 160.72 mph for third place, and would pilot the first non-stop transcontinental flight less than two years later. A late starter was Harold Hartney in the other Thomas-Morse, who crashed on lap 1 when his fuel pump failed; he was injured but recovered.

October 14, 1922 — Selfridge Field, Michigan

The third running of the Pulitzer attracted the largest and finest collection of purpose-built military racers ever seen. This led to unusually close competition, which made it one of history's great closed-course air races. Fifteen airplanes started the race (5 laps of the 31.1-mile course), of which 13 were specially developed racers. All 11 that crossed the finish line were true racers.

The starters: one Verville R-1 by Corliss Moseley; two Curtiss CR-2s (improved CR-1s) by Harold Brow and Al Williams; three Verville-Sperry R-3s by Eugene Barksdale, St. Clair Street and Fonda Johnson; two Loening R-4 monoplanes by Ennis Whitehead and Lester Schulze; Two Thomas Morse R-5s by Clayton Bissell and Frank O'Driscoll; two Curtiss R-6s to be flown by Russell Maughan and Lester Maitland; and a single Wright NW-1 sesquiplane by Lawson Sanderson, a Thomas Morse M.B.7 by Francis Mulcahy and a Bee Line BR-1 by Steven Calloway.

The sleek Curtiss racers were completely dominant. Maughan in an R-6 won at a record 205.86 mph, and Maitland in the other R-6 was 2nd at 198.85 mph. Brow in one of the CR-2s was 3rd at 193.70 mph, while Williams in the other CR-2 was 4th at 188.00 mph. In 5th was Barksdale in an R-3 at 180.74 mph, while Sanderson in the NW-1 was averaging 186 mph when forced out on the 4th of 5 laps. All the Curtiss racers used Curtiss D-12 engines, while the others used a mixture of Packard V-12s and Wright-built Hispano-Suiza V-8s.

The first seven finishers broke the old Pulitzer record, Maughan by almost 30 mph. The ability of the army and navy to respond rapidly to the challenges of competition with major advances in performance was made inescapably clear. It was a case of the emotional rivalry: the army versus the navy, and manufacturer versus manufacturer. The Pulitzer Trophy carried enormous prestige, while the cash prizes were minimal. No civilian racer would attain their speeds until the 1931 Thompson Trophy Race.

October 6, 1923 — St. Louis Flying Field, St. Louis, Missouri

The 4th Pulitzer Race was for 4 laps of a 31.1-mi. (50-km.) triangular course to the northwest of what is now Lambert Field. The entry list was down from the previous year's 15 to just 7, led by two new Curtiss R2C-1s, which were much improved R-6s with engines boosted from 375 hp to 500 hp. They would be flown by veteran navy racepilots Al Williams and Harold Brow.

The completely new pair of Wright F2W-1s generally resembled the successful Curtiss machines, but used 780 hp Wright T-3 V-12s that could trace their origins back to the World War I Liberty engine. They would be flown by Lawson "Sandy" Sanderson and Steven Calloway. The two Curtiss R-6s that took 1st and 2nd in 1922 were back, to be raced by Walter Miller and Johnny Corkille. A sole Verville-Sperry R-3 from 1922 would be flown by Alex Pearson.

Curtiss again stole the show, with Williams winning at 243.67 mph and adding 38 mph to the Pulitzer and American closed-course racing records. He had already set a World 3-km. straight-dash record at 259.15 mph. Close behind in 2nd place was Brow at 241.78 mph, as six of the seven starters finished and all broke the existing record by at least 10 mph.

October 4, 1924 — Wilbur Wright Field, Dayton, Ohio

The steep drop in enthusiasm on the part of the American military was very much in evidence, as the four entries included three veteran racers and one modified prototype army pursuit. After several years of safe flying, the law of averages caught up with the Pulitzer Race. During the full-power diving start, the Curtiss R-6 of Burt Skeel disintegrated, killing the pilot who had won the previous year's Mitchell Trophy Race.

The diminished interest of the military in public racing produced the only Pulitzer Race in which there was no speed record. Harry Mills won in the low-wing Verville-Sperry R-3 at 216.55 mph. Wendell Brookley was 2nd in one of last year's Curtiss R-6 at 214.41 mph, and the only other finisher was Rex Stoner in the PW-8A pursuit at a mere 167.93 mph.

October 10–12, 1925 — Mitchell Field, Long Island, New York

This was the last National Air Races to be held on a military base, another indicator of the shift of interest toward civilian competitions. While the navy was represented by two brand new Curtiss R3C-1 (cleaned-up R2C-1s), the army fielded a single P-1 pursuit and three PW-8B pursuits, none of them more than slightly modified for racing.

First place, at a World Record speed of 248.98 mph, went to Cyrus Bettis,

Al Williams' Curtiss R3C-1 (U.S. Army Air Service, 1925).

in one of the R3C-1s, followed closely by Al Williams in the other R3C-1 at 241.70 mph, for a clean sweep. The best of the pursuit planes was Leo Dawson's P-1 at 169.9 mph, more than a lap of the 31-mi./50 km. course behind. The high speeds were achieved even though the rules had been changed to forbid diving starts.

The Pulitzer Trophy Race series thus ended after six years during which the winning speeds rose from 157 mph to 249 mph. The army and navy learned some major lessons about streamlining and horsepower that would eventually lead to better military airplanes. But the death of Skeel and the increasing conservatism of military leaders directed the limited research funds provided by Congress toward more obviously military purposes. Not even the widespread positive impact on the American people could dissuade them from retiring from competition.

The major long-term impact of the Pulitzer was not in streamlining, though that was certainly impressive. It was in engines. The Curtiss D-12 led directly to powerplants that were built in the tens of thousands by both sides in World War II. The American Allison V-1710 was used in the Lockheed P-38 Lightning, the Bell P-39 Airacobra and the Curtiss P-40 Tomahawk and Kittyhawk. The British Rolls Royce Merlin powered Hawker Hurricane and Supermarine Spitfire fighters, and Avro Lancaster and deHavilland Mosquito bombers, as well as the P-51 Mustang, which used the V-1650 Merlins built on license by the Packard Motor Car Co. Additionally, the Daimler-Benz 600-series engines which powered Nazi Germany's Messerschmitt 109 and 110 fighters were directly descended from the Curtiss V-12s.

The roars that began around the Pulitzer pylons were multiplied in the skies above London, Berlin and all parts in between.

Chapter 9

The 1922–1929 Kings Cup Races: Jolly Competition in a Garden Party Setting

Races over long closed courses were pioneered by the Aerial Derby, beginning in 1912 with an 81-mile race around London, which started and finished at Hendon Aerodrome, north of London. It was won by T.O.M. Sopwith (soon to gain fame with his World War I Camel pursuit) in a Bleriot XI at 58 mph. By the early 1920s, interest in the Aerial Derby had waned, while the once-popular Circuit of Britain races were not resumed immediately after the war.[1]

September 14–15, 1922 — Croydon

In 1922, the Circuit of Britain Race was restarted. It began at Croydon, London's first airport, south of the city. It stretched north for 405 miles via Birmingham and Newcastle, finishing its first day at Glasgow, Scotland. On the second day, the pilots who had not already been forced out by engine troubles flew back to Croydon via Manchester and Bristol. Most of the 21 starters flew civilianized World War I airplanes, old and new deHavilland biplanes, along with a couple of current airliners that had been temporarily excused from their daily duties. This and future races had staggered starts based on each airplane's estimated top speed.

Eleven pilots finished the 805-mile grind, with winner Frank Barnard placing first at 123.6 mph in a passenger-carrying deH.4 of the Instone Air Line. The winner's trophy was presented by King George V, and very quickly the event became known as the King's Cup Race, starting a tradition which continues to this day.

July 13–14, 1923 — Hendon

The course was the same as for the first race, except for the new start and finish points on the north side of London, which shortened it to 794 miles. Most of the 17 pilots entered in the handicap race flew staid deHavilland biplanes, with five of them in readily available, demilitarized deH.9 World War I daylight bombers.

The winner, at 149 mph, was Frank Courtney, later to emigrate to America and become a well-known free-lance test pilot. He flew the same "hush-hush" prototype Armstrong Whitworth Siskin military trainer he had flown in the 1922 race. In second place was long-distance pilot Alan Cobham in a deH.9 and in third was future Schneider Cup Race pilot Hubert Broad in a cleaned-up deH.9.

August 12, 1924 — Martlesham and Felixstowe

The third Kings Cup race was open to both landplanes and seaplanes, the former starting at Martlesham, and the latter at the Royal Naval Air Station at Felixstowe. The course crossed the sea to the Isle of Man, with all aircraft finishing on England's south coast at Lee-on-Solent. The course, to be flown in one day, measured 950 miles and had three observed turning points but no compulsory stops. The entry list was the shortest yet — 10, of which 6 finished — though both previous winners raced, and there was a greater variety of aircraft.

Alan Cobham won in *Galatea*, the deH.50 prototype which he would later fly to North Africa and back in just over one day. In second was Norman Macmillan in a float-equipped Fairey III Royal Navy bomber, while in third was Alan Butler, long-serving chairman of deHavilland Aircraft, in a deH.37.

July 3–4, 1925 — Croydon

The longest race in Kings Cup history consisted of 804 miles north to Scotland and back in a counterclockwise direction on the first day and then clockwise on the second. Making the entry list particularly significant was the appearance of the two deHavilland Gypsy Moth prototypes, the beginning of lightplanes in the British Isles. Engines ranged from the tiny 700 cc. Blackburne V-twin to a 485 hp Bristol Jupiter radial. A majority of pilots flew civil airplanes, the mark of another trend.

The race began in dense fog and was plagued by bad weather the entire time, with the result that only four of the 14 starters completed the 1,608-mile grind. Frank Barnard repeated his 1922 victory, this time in a Siskin V, at 141.7 mph. Placing second was H.W.G. Jones in the only Siskin IV at 142 mph, and in third was H. Deming in a deH.37 at 120 mph.

July 9–10, 1926 — Hendon

The race was for 1,464 miles and involved flying one lap of a 732-mile figure-eight course on each of two days. Sixteen pilots entered, 14 started and only 4 finished. The winner, in a deH.60 Gypsy Moth, was Hubert Broad at 90.4 mph, second was E.R.C. Scholefield in a Vickers Vixen single-engined Amy bomber at 142 mph, and third was H.W.G. Jones in a Martinsyde A.D.C.1 at 152 mph. Among those dropping out was 1922 winner Frank Barnard in the Bristol 99 Badminton, a small, special-built racing biplane with a 525 hp Bristol Jupiter engine.

DeHavilland deH.71 Tiger Moth racer flown to speed records by future Schneider Trophy Racer Hubert Broad (Hawker Siddeley Aircraft).

July 30, 1927 — Hucknall, Nottinghamshire

The race was almost cancelled when half the entrants rebelled against what they considered unrealistically high handicap speeds which would rule out any chance of their winning. While nine of them formally withdrew before the start, this still left 16 pilots, including the first two women to race for a Kings Cup. Thanks to weather that was foul even by British standards, only six completed the 540-mile race which included three separate courses.

The winner was Wally Hope at 92.8 mph in a deH.60 Gipsy Moth, followed by W.J. McDonough at 102.8 mph in a Westland Widgeon, and E.R.C. Scholefield in a Vickers Vixen III at 141.6 mph.

July 20–21, 1928 — Hendon to Brooklands

It was a big race, with 36 starters setting out from Hendon on the first day's 541-mile leg to Glasgow, Scotland, and 24 of them heading back south the next day on a 556-mile leg. Twenty-three finished at Brooklands, the site of the world's first paved auto racetrack, in London's far southwest suburbs. Almost all flew purely civilian airplanes, though the great majority of pilots had previously flown in the military. The most unusual entry in this (or any race) was a Cierva autogiro.

Wally Hope became the first pilot to win the Kings Cup in successive years, averaging 105.5 mph in a later-model Gipsy Moth. Placing second was Cyril Uwins at 127 mph in the Bristol Type 101, an unsuccessful military prototype. Third place went to Miss Winifred Spooner, at 83.5 mph in a Gipsy Moth. Guy Warwick crashed in his little A.N.E.C. Missel Thrush, becoming the series' first fatality.

July 5–6, 1929 — Heston to Henlow

Of the 60 pilots who originally entered, 41 started the 1,169-mile race which roamed all around England in two legs. While the percentage of civil aircraft continued to rise, there were two pilots in currently active Royal Air Force Gloster Grebe fighters, and one in an elderly World War I–vintage S.E.5 pursuit.

The winner, in one of the Grebes at 150 mph, was Richard "Batchy" Atcherly, whose crazing flying would become a popular favorite at major air displays. Second went to L.G. Richardson in a deH.60 Moth at 100.2 mph, and third to Wally Hope in his third Gipsy Moth, at 91 mph.

The first eight Kings Cup Races encompassed much of England as well as parts of Wales and Scotland, bringing a view of the sport's action within range of millions, and helping to popularize cross-country air racing. And while the handicapping system discouraged creative speed-increasing modifications, the program gave opportunities to a wide swath of the population.

Chapter 10

The 1927 Dole Race Disaster: On to Hawaii and into the Pacific

Pioneering in any field of endeavor involves an element of risk, be it physical, financial or personal. As long as the risk is tempered by a reasonable amount of knowledge and judgment, it stands a chance of producing true progress, whether in nuclear physics, literature or airplane racing.[1]

The Dole Race from Oakland, California, to Honolulu, Hawaii, on August 16–17, 1927, was an unfortunate example of taking a big risk without first looking very closely at the possible consequences. It was the first attempt at a long-distance race entirely over water, and followed by just a few weeks the first time that the 2,400-mi. route had been conquered, and even then by a very brave crew in a sturdy, three-engined Fokker. It was a route that obviously had to be flown non-stop as there was nowhere to land along the way.

But the world had suddenly fallen madly in love with long-distance flying. In short order, Charles Lindbergh had pulled off his epic 3,600-mi. solo flight in mid–May 1927, from New York to Paris, and then in June, Clarence Chamberlin and Levine flew 3,900 miles from New York to Germany in a single hop. To a lot of people, it no doubt seemed that taking off and flying for thousands of miles over open water before landing must not be terribly difficult — but they were about to learn otherwise.

The first serious attempt to fly non-stop from the U.S. west coast to Hawaii came on August 31, 1925, when two U.S. Navy pilots — John Rodgers and Byron Connell — flew a PN-9 flying boat to within a few hundred miles of their goal before running out of gas. They then used fabric from the lower wing as a makeshift sail and let the wind propel them to within 10 miles of Hawaii before finishing the trip on the end of a towline.

Interest in long-distance over-water flights had long centered on the Atlantic Ocean, with several crews dying in attempts before Charles Lindbergh succeeded, and others vanishing afterward. The next obvious challenge was westward across the Pacific. And thanks to pineapple millionaire James Dole, a purse of $35,000 was offered for a race from California to what would eventually become America's 50th state.

Inspired by the amazing outpouring of praise that engulfed Lindbergh, scores of builders and pilots jumped at the opportunity to snatch a piece of that hero worship and the $25,000 first prize. Within a few days of the official announcement, enough pilots had indicated their intentions to enter so that success was assumed, though not assured.

What was given entirely too little attention was the far greater difficulty that was involved in navigating to a small group of islands, whereas Lindbergh had an entire continent as his target. The lack of reliable engines, radios and instruments apparently bothered few of the entrants, who had been caught up with the anticipation of ticker-tape parades and pretty girls begging to kiss America's newest heroes. That the effective distance would be increased by the prevailing winds from the west was also ignored by too many.

The original idea was to permit a pilot to take off at any time during the year following the opening day. But it soon became clear that everyone intended to be on the starting line at the very first opportunity, thus converting a series of more easily controlled individual flights into something much more like a true race.

Rules governing the airplanes that could be entered were vague, stressing airworthiness, something that is hard to determine for an airplane whose first test flight might be the trip from the workshop to the starting line. As for basic design parameters such as wing loading and resistance to g-forces, they apparently were up to the designers and builders. Any type of engine could be used, though almost everyone chose the Wright J-5-C, a 9-cylinder radial of 788 cu. in. that developed 200–220 hp. Why was it so popular? Probably because that was the engine that got Lindbergh across the Atlantic.

The first airplane and crew to make news was the Tremaine *Hummingbird*, piloted by George Covell, which crashed fatally on its first test flight, August 10.

One of the first to arrive at the starting field was the Fisk CF-10 *Spirit of Los Angeles*, an all-wood triplane that James Giffen piloted right into San Francisco Bay on its arrival, August 11. All three crewmembers escaped without injuries from an airplane already considered unsuitable for the long trip to Hawaii.

The next day, Arthur Rodgers, a Royal Flying Corps ace in World War I, crashed to his death on the first test flight of the Bryant *Angel of Los Angeles*. The twin-boom airplane had a 3-cylinder, 120 hp Bristol Lucifer engine at either end of the central pod.

Three crashes that took three lives in three days should have alerted everyone, especially officials of the sanctioning National Aeronautic Association and the Department of Commerce, to a developing tragedy and the ineffectiveness of the rules-making and rule-enforcing procedures. But such was the atmosphere surrounding the great spectacle that everything was allowed to proceed as planned.

10. The 1927 Dole Race Disaster

The big day arrived with eight crews and their airplanes ready to go in front of a crowd estimated at 75,000. First off was Bennett Griffin in the TravelAir 5000 *Oklahoma*, which was so heavily loaded with fuel that it needed a hard push from the ground crew to get rolling. After an agonizingly slow start, it finally left the ground and slowly gained altitude as it headed westward. The race had officially begun. No one could have realized that neither Griffin nor his airplane would ever be seen again.

The next in line was Norman Goddard in a modified Goddard Sport called *El Encanto*. He tried to pull it off the runway, but it immediately settled back, dug one wheel in, ground looped and ended off the runway with too much damage to continue.

Third was Livingston Irving in the Breese *Pabco Pacific Flyer*. After a long run, the heavy machine briefly rose, only to drop back, doing minor damage. It was soon towed away to allow the next contestant to make an attempt.

John Frost seemed one of the best prepared, having acquired the shiny, new prototype Lockheed Vega, called *Golden Eagle*, with a design which would usher in a new era in fast, efficient airline flying. The Vega was easily the fastest airplane in the field, and quickly was lost to view, its engine humming smoothly. After a truly dreary start, the outlook for a successful race appeared to have brightened.

Next came the airplane that was clearly the crowd favorite. The exten-

Pabco Pacific Flyer in which Livinston Irving crashed on take-off for the Dole Race (National Archives and Records Administration).

sively modified Buhl Airsedan *Miss Doran* was named for the wide-eyed but increasingly nervous Mildred Doran, a 22-year-old school teacher, who was to be its once-eager passenger. The biplane took off with apparent ease, then soon returned for repairs to its rough-running engine. It then headed off again over San Francisco, its bay and the beginnings of the Pacific Ocean.

Martin Jensen was next in the Vance Breese *Aloha*, followed by veteran Art Goebel in the TravelAir *Woolaroc*, neither of which had any obvious problems.

William Irwin was the sixth to take of successfully, in his Swallow *Dallas Spirit*, but he returned to the starting field with a large quantity of fuselage fabric ripped away. Repairs would take too long to permit them to remain competitive, so they withdrew. The next day, while awaiting word from those who had not been heard from since their departure, Irwin took off to search and was never seen again. The vast ocean claimed another victim.

Only Goebel, of those on their way, had a radio with which to make periodic position reports, the others depending on accidental visual spotting by the members of ships' crews. It turned out that most of the reports were in error, including those of the *Miss Doran*, which joined the growing list of those lost without a trace.

Meanwhile, on Hawaii, the anxious "reception committee" grew to many

Martin Jensen flew this Breese *Aloha* to second place in the Dole Race and was the only other to finish (National Archives and Records Administration).

10. The 1927 Dole Race Disaster

All three members of the crew of the Buhl Airsedan *Miss Doran* died when it crashed into the Pacific Ocean during the Dole Race (National Archives and Records Administration).

thousands. Finally, after more than 26 hours, the TravelAir of Art Goebel and his navigator, Bill Davis, first appeared as a dot in the distance, then steadily grew into the welcome shape of one of the airplanes they had been awaiting. The greeting was tumultuous, adding to the exhaustion of the bedraggled aviators until they were finally allowed to sneak away for showers and some rest.

Back at the airport, the crowd continued to watch the eastern horizon for any sign of the other airplanes. They watched and they waited until it became obvious to even the most optimistic that all of them would long since have run their fuel tanks completely dry and crashed into the sea. The enormity of the tragedy was coming into focus: with the three airplanes lost during the long flight from the mainland with seven aboard must be added to two airplanes and three men killed on test flights. Two airplanes made it all the way, while 10 died trying.

"Experts" fired off blame in all directions. It was the weather, it was a lack of proper testing, it was the loose rules. When things had cooled down it could be seen that the very idea of a non-stop race over 2,400 miles of water was the source of all the trouble. Only one crew and airplane had ever achieved this against the prevailing winds, and so to expect airplanes prepared under racing conditions to do it was foolish, to say the least.

Many years later, a group planning an around-the-world race for helicopters contacted the author for suggestions. Upon being informed that the Hawaii-to-California leg of the race was farther than any helicopter had yet flown non-stop under any conditions, they quickly, quietly and wisely dropped the idea.

Chapter 11

The 1925–1928 Military-Oriented U.S. National Air Races

America's National Air Races began in the early 1920s, though at least one of the annual events acquired that title retroactively, when it had become a mark of prestige. Regardless, the long series of major events which led directly to the first "true" National Air Races at Cleveland in 1929 paved the way for important milestones in American aviation.

This Church Midwing, powered by a converted Henderson motorcycle engine, was raced at Cleveland in 1929 (author).

1923 — St. Louis Field, St. Louis, Missouri, September 30 to October 6

It was called the International Meet, and was held at what soon became known as Lambert Field, after a three-day delay due to heavy rains. In addition to some major trophy races, the organizers had arranged for aerial demonstrations and static exhibits of very large and very small new airplanes, along with stunt flyers, the bombing of an imitation fort by military planes, and parachuting.[1]

The most important race on the program was the 1923 Pulitzer Trophy Race, won by Al Williams at 243.67 mph and described in Chapter 8. Second in importance was the Mitchell Trophy Race, for four laps around the 31-mile (50-km.) course. The winner was Burt Skeel, who averaged 146 mph in a Thomas Morse MB.3, then died a year later during the diving start to the Pulitzer Race.

1924 — Wilbur Wright Field, Dayton, Ohio, October 2–4

It was held at a small airfield northeast of Dayton and not far from where the Wright Brothers had made their 1904 flights. The Pulitzer Trophy Race was the feature of the event, with Harry Mills winning in a Verville-Sperry R-3, as recounted in Chapter 8. In the Mitchell Trophy Race, Cyrus Bettis won with a standard Army Curtiss PW-8 pursuit plane at 176 mph. and thus earned for himself a slot in the starting line-up for the 1925 Pulitzer Race.

A series of events for very light, low-powered, custom-built racing planes entertained the crowd, but was mainly a discouraging display of mechanical failures which proved that 80 cu. in. converted motorcycle engines produced entirely too little power for even the smallest of airplanes.

1925 — Mitchell Field, Long Island, New York, October 9–12

The National Air Races returned to Long Island, where cold winds cut the attendance from a projected half million to barely 50,000 for the four days. While civilian entries outnumbered military entries 122 to 41, the military races again took the spotlight.

The only major race was the final Pulitzer, won at a record 249 mph by Cyrus Bettis in a Curtiss military racer. Army Lt. T.K. Matthews won the Mitchell Trophy Race for pilots flying Curtiss PW-8 pursuits, at 162 mph.

In the Town & Country Club Race for civilians, "Casey" Jones, one of the most popular and busy racing pilots of his day, won at 128.4 mph in a Curtiss Oriole, over 8 laps of the 12-mile course.

1926 — Model Farms Field, Philadelphia, Pennsylvania, September 4–13

This year's races saw a move in the direction of popular support, with lots of events for civilian pilots in civilian airplanes, though the military again dominated, this time with standard production airplanes. Among the military events, the Mitchell Trophy Race for pilots from the Army's 1st Pursuit Group was won by Lieutenant Eliot in a Curtiss P-1 Hawk at 160 mph. The Kansas City Rotary Club Trophy Race for all three military services saw Navy Lt. George Cuddihy win in a new Boeing FB-3 pursuit at 181 mph.

The Town & Country Club Trophy Race, for light commercial airplanes, was won by James Ray in a sesqui-wing Arrow at 136.4 mph for 8 laps of the 12-mile course. In the Glenn Curtiss Trophy Race for biplanes with engines having less than 510 cu. in., Basil Rowe won in a Thomas Morse Scout at 109.6 mph.

1927 — Felts Field, Spokane, Washington, September 21–25

The Pacific Northwest air meet was called the best held in the U.S. to date. It would have actually shown a profit, had not a few ticket sellers slunk off into the night with their pockets full. The program showed signs of the shape which would make the National Air Races famous in a few years.[2]

The Non-Stop New York-to-Spokane race was a valiant effort, but the three starters landed far short of their goal. The best was Eddie Stinson (of later manufacturing fame), who got as far as Missoula, Montana, in a Stinson monoplane. A similar airplane, flown by Duke Schiller and Eddie Bohn, landed in Billings, Montana.

The two-class New York–Spokane Derby, which permitted stops, saw Charles "Speed" Holman collect $10,000 by winning the faster Class A in a

Clyde Cessna's Cessna CM-1 was flown in the Gardner Trophy Race with a 225 hp Wright J-5 engine (Peter M. Bowers).

Laird Commercial biplane, while in Class B, $5,000 was won by C.W. Meyers in a Waco 10 biplane.

The Free-for-All Pylon Race for Low-powered Airplanes, for the Western Flying Trophy, was won by Eugene Detmer in a TravelAir. In the free-for-all race for 2-, 3- or 4-place airplanes, the Seattle Chamber of Commerce Trophy went to J. Ray in a Pitcairn Sesqui-wing. Each took home $1,000 for first place.

The fastest of several military-only pylon races was for the Seattle Spokesman-Review Trophy, and was won by E.C. Batten in an experimental Curtiss XP-6A pursuit at 201.2 mph.

1928 — Mines Field, Los Angeles, California, September 8–16

The national scope of the National Air Races (and Aeronautical Exposition) was solidified with a move to Mines Field (now Los Angeles International Airport). The "pre–Bendix" non-stop New York–Los Angeles Race drew eight starters, all of whom flew factory-built airplanes from Stinson, Bellanca, Lockheed and Cessna. While no one managed to complete the 2,470-mile race and so it was officially ruled a non-event, Dole Race winner Art Goebel made it as far as Prescott, Arizona, in his Lockheed Vega. In second was George Haldeman in a Bellanca, who got as far as Albuquerque, New Mexico.

A far more successful race over the same course permitted stops. The winners, among 40 finishers in three classes, were John Livingston, flying a Waco 10 biplane in Class A in 22 hours, 56 minutes and 59 seconds; Earl Rowland, flying a shoulder-wing Cessna, in Class B in 27:00:31; and Robert Cantwell, flying a Lockheed Vega monoplane in 24:09:01.

In the pylon racing portion of the program, the Civilian Unlimited Free-for-All trophy went to Robert Cantwell in his Vega at 140.30 mph, followed closely by Art Goebel at 139.73 mph and then Lee Schoenhair at 117.98 mph.

Up to this point, air racing had been the preserve of army and navy pilots and airplanes. It was within the military services that the money could be found for big engines, and the engineering talent that was already employed to design modern airframes. Civilians were slogging along with inefficient commercial airplanes and flimsy private planes. It was far from an even contest, and so the fans could be excused for preferring the all-alike military races which offered more speed, drama, noise and often closer competition than races for civil airplanes that had been built for very different purposes than racing around the pylons or across the country.

But now, with a half dozen years of experience, of learning what should be done and, perhaps more important, what should not be done, it was time to find a permanent home for the National Air Races, a place where it could grow into more than just a showcase for the military's aeronautical prowess.

Chapter 12

The 1929 U.S. National Air Races and the Thompson Trophy Race

August 24–September 2, 1929
Cleveland National Air Races

One of the greatest leaps forward in air racing history began with a perfectly ordinary listing in the long printed schedule: "Event #26 — Free-for-all Speed Contest." By the time the 10-lap race around a 5-mile triangular course was over, the very nature of the sport had changed.[1]

The 1929 Cleveland National Air Races was a 10-day extravaganza which included a dozen cross-country races, two dozen closed-course pylon races, a relay race and several Australian pursuit races. There were efficiency contests, along with spot landing contests for both pilots and parachutists. There were demonstrations by the military's latest pursuit planes and scouts and bombers, mixed in with the fascinating sight of autogiros and dirigibles and just about everything else that could be coaxed into the air.

For 10 days, Cleveland Municipal Airport (now Cleveland-Hopkins International) was the unquestioned center of American aviation. Under the outstanding leadership of brothers Clifford and Phil Henderson, the meet drew an estimated 500,000 paid spectators. In addition, uncounted (and non-paying) tens of thousands more watched from outside the airport on the west side of Ohio's largest city, then an all-grass flying field, in great contrast to today's sea of concrete.

In downtown Cleveland, the Aviation Exposition filled the new Public Hall with displays of airplanes and engines and everything that makes them work, laid out for all to see, close up and at their leisure.

Opening day, Saturday, August 24, was exactly that: a day for opening ceremonies, massed military flights, parades, fireworks, band music and finally nighttime stunt flying combined with fireworks. The activity began at 2 P.M. and lasted past midnight. If there were any doubts about the magnitude and stature of this first major airplane meet in Cleveland, they should have been silenced by the elaborate ceremonies. But as yet there had been no airplane racing.

12. The 1929 U.S. National and Thompson Trophy Races

Lewis Love's Davis V-3 was raced in 1930 (Truman C. Weaver collection).

Sunday was "All Ohio Day" and began at 1 P.M. in deference to those who wished to attend church services in the morning. There was music by the Cleveland Chamber of Commerce Band and by the Cleveland City Band. So far, nothing approaching the excitement of a pylon race had been detected.

At last, around 1:30, 10 pilots were flagged off for Event #8 (events were never meant to occur in numerical order). It was scheduled for eight laps around the five-mile race course. Among the all-civilian competitors were future greats Art Chester in #84, a TravelAir biplane, and Steve Wittman in the #97 Pheasant H10 biplane in which he had taught himself to fly. What should have been a thrilling start for the racing portion of the grand program quickly turned into a comedy of errors.

Some of the pilots correctly flew around the five-mile course, while others picked out a couple of the wrong pylons around which to make their first turns and found themselves flying around the 10-mile course! The air races management decided that this exceeded the limits of acceptable individuality and so the race was declared "no contest" and re-scheduled for August 28.

In the opinion of John T. Neville, writing in *Aviation* magazine for Sept. 7, 1929,

> The remarkable difference in racing skill among the pilots of unquestionable general ability became apparent in the very first lap....
>
> Some of them ... flew just wide enough as they approached the pylon, started their bank at just the right time, and swept around the turning mark with but a few feet to spare. Others made every conceivable error, the commonest fault being to fly directly at the pylon and start the turn too late, sweeping far beyond the mark, as much as two or three hundred yards in some cases, before the turn was complete.
>
> Some pilots ... especially those flying cabin machines with but little reserve of power, flew very low and then became uneasy about turning their planes up on their wingtips, edging around the turns with but thirty or forty degrees of bank.

It wasn't only the spectators who had a lot to learn about airplane racing.

Fortunately, they and the pilots would have plenty of opportunity to learn and to enjoy and to remember.

The first race to be completed, and the only full race of the second day's program, was Event #23, the National Guard Race, for seven laps around the 10-mile course. It was open to army pilots flying presumably standard, Liberty-engined military observation planes: Douglas O-2H and Curtiss O-11 open-cockpit, fabric-covered, strut-braced biplanes having fixed landing gear. While now they would be considered collectors' items, then they were the best that could be had.

The first three airplanes across the finish line — all O-11s — were dropped down in the standings on the basis of their previously calculated handicaps. After the apparent winner, Lt. Philip Love, had been disqualified for improperly improving the streamlining of his *stock* airplane, the first-place trophy and $500 were awarded to John Gill, even though he had looked to the crowd like the fifth-place finisher. Air racing is not always as simple and obvious as it claims to be. Officially in third place was Lt. Wilson V. Newhall, who would reappear in 1946, racing a sleek World War II Army surplus Bell P-63 Kingcobra.

A few minutes after one o'clock, the participants in the All-Ohio Derby — all civilians — took off for a publicity-oriented cross-country race around the state that was estimated to entail five hours of flying over two days.

The Women's Air Derby from Santa Monica, California, to Cleveland was the first such event ever held, and was aimed at recognizing the growing importance and capabilities of women pilots. Before the event had concluded, many of the air race officials were probably wondering if scheduling this had been such a smart move. Almost as soon as the rules and prize money (the most for any race this year) had been announced, five of the top women pilots in the country announced they would boycott the race! They were unhappy that admission was limited to airplanes having engines of no more than 810 cubic inches of piston displacement, since several of them owned and flew airplanes having larger engines.

The boycott failed and 20 pilots started the race on August 18, almost a week before the last of the bunting had been draped on the grandstands at Cleveland. Over Arizona, altitude record-holder Marvel Crosson disappeared, only to be found later near the wreckage of her TravelAir biplane, her unopened parachute nearby. The cause of this tragic accident was never determined.

Then there were cries of sabotage, first by German pilot Thea Rasche, whose deHavilland Gypsy Moth was forced down in southeastern California, and then by the husband of Claire Fahey, who force-landed near the Mexican border on the second day. Investigations found nothing to support the charges, and the final results of the race were eventually declared official.

Louise Thaden won Class D (for airplanes with 510–810 cu. in. engines) in her TravelAir biplane, crossing the country in just over 20 hours (not including numerous required stops), to win the top prize of $3,600. Gladys O'Donnell was second in her Waco 10, arriving more than an hour later. In Class C (275–510 cu. in.), Phoebe Omlie won $600 in her Monocoupe with a trip that took more than 25 hours, followed by Edith Folz in an Eaglerock Bullet, trailing her by 16 hours.

The Women's Air Derby received intensive coverage from the press, due to its novelty, to the many mishaps experienced and overcome by the pilots, to the expected and unexpected obstacles encountered, and to the controversies surrounding the race. Other events, which produced far closer competition, were lost in the glare of the attention paid this first women's transcontinental race.

On Tuesday, August 27, America saw its first pylon race exclusively for women, who had been officially excluded from other closed-course races by the National Air Races management. This tradition of separating the genders would remain in effect for most of the succeeding 40 years. The race, for 10 laps of the 5-mile course, was won at 112.38 mph by Phoebe Omlie in her Monocoupe. She was initially disqualified for having cut a pylon, but she protested, claiming she had then circled the pylon, which was the penalty in those days. The protest was graciously supported by the second- and third-place finishers, and upheld. She was awarded a duplicate $500 first prize. In first place was Mrs. Jessie Keith-Miller in a Fleet 2 biplane at 98.73 mph, and in second was Lady Mary Heath (Great Lakes 2T-1A Trainer) at 96.17 mph.

Soon afterwards, the winner of the Portland (Oregon)-to-Cleveland Derby for civilians finished the four-day grind. Theodore Wells, flying a TravelAir D-4000 biplane, completed the course in 14¾ hours. Second was famed air show pilot "Tex" Rankin, flying a Waco Taperwing in just under 15½ hours. Only two of the nine starters failed to finish, one of them being Charles "Speed" Holman, whose racing career was just getting started.

The next pylon race — Event #2 — was a direct descendant of the 1924 Lympne Lightplane Races in England, being limited to engines of 100 cu. in., with most pilots choosing to use modified motorcycle engines. It was for 10 laps of the 5-mile course, with a race-horse start in which the airplanes are lined up side-by-side at the end of the runway and all start at the same time. Three civilian pilots took off, but only Eddie Heath, flying a Bristol Cherub–powered Heath Super Parasol, finished, at all of 62.91 mph. Dropping out were famed stunt pilot Freddy Lund (flying a Henderson-powered Low Wing Sport) and Jack McMillan (in a Henderson-powered Heath Super Parasol). As was demonstrated in England, the small, converted motorcycle engines failed to measure up.

The race lasted almost 48 minutes, far longer than modern crowds would tolerate for airplanes flying barely 60 mph round a 5-mile course. During the final four laps of the race, there was only one airplane left on the course, putt-

putting past the crowd once every five minutes. In 1946, the 45-minute Thompson Trophy Race, which packed much more crowd appeal, was nevertheless found to be boring by a lot of spectators. But in 1929, the future fans were much more forgiving. Everything that happened at Cleveland in 1929 was new and different and exciting.

Wednesday, August 28

Wednesday was American Legion Day and began with the take-off of seven civilian pilots in two divisions of the Philadelphia-to-Cleveland Derby, the route of which would take them first to Hartford, Conn., then to Boston, Albany, Syracuse and Buffalo. On the departure from Boston, competitor E. J. "Red" Devereaux crashed, killing himself, his wife and his mechanic. This brought to four the number killed in the air races, though all of them, unpredictably, on cross-country flights, rather than in the presumably more dangerous pylon races. The winner of Division D was Errett Williams, flying an Alexander Eaglerock Bullet. The Division F winner was J. Wesley Smith in a Bellanca CH300.

The day's first pylon race was the re-run of the OX-5 race postponed from Monday, when the pilots couldn't agree on which course to fly around. This time, everything worked well, with 10 civilian pilots starting and 7 finishing. The winner, at 104.54 mph, was George Shealey in a TravelAir 2000, with William Winkle second at 100.74 mph in a Brunner-Winkle Bird. Future star Art Chester was fourth in a big TravelAir biplane.

The format of Event #9, a race limited to civilians on the 5-mile course for airplanes limited to 510 cu. in. engines, is not clear from the available records. There was a surprisingly long entry list, which forced the management to split the 23 pilots into two preliminary heat races and a finals, or maybe two divisions of the finals. What is clear is that the ultimate winner, who had to fly either once or twice, was Verne Roberts in a Monocoupe, at 129.18 mph. In second was Ray "Spud" Quinby, in another Monocoupe at 128.09 mph.

Yet a third pylon event was held —#5— for lightplanes limited to 275 cu. in. Eddie Heath won by almost a minute in his Bristol Cherub–powered Heath *Baby Bullet*, at 109.46 mph. In second place was H.A. Speer in the Nicholas Beazley Barling at 105.93 mph. One of the pilots who failed to finish was Ted Lundberg, who flew a novel Driggs Skylark, powered by a converted English Rover automobile engine.

The Oakland (California)-to-Cleveland Derby, for civilian-flown airplanes with engines of no more than 800 cu. in., was far longer than most of the other cross-country events, and yet had a much closer finish. Loren Mendell, flying a Buhl Cabin Monoplane, edged out W.J. Barrows, in a Fairchild 71 by a mere 3½ minutes at the end of almost 18 hours of flying. The spectators at Cleve-

12. The 1929 U.S. National and Thompson Trophy Races

land Airport could see only the finish of this and other cross-country races, but air races manager Cliff Henderson knew they were vital to his goal of achieving nationwide publicity, stature and attention. After all, it was the Cleveland *National* Air Races, not some cow pasture air show.

The next two days were full of races for men and races for women; races around the pylon courses and races to and from cities in neighboring states; races for civilian airplanes in various displacement-limited categories, along with races for army and navy airmen flying nearly-identical pursuits and attack planes; and even novelty races such as relays involving landing and swapping pilots after every few laps.

The first seven days of the 1929 Cleveland National Air Races were a carefully calculated build-up to the program for the finale three-day Labor Day weekend, when the biggest crowds were expected.

The first event of day eight was #7, for 16 army pilots flying Curtiss D-12-powered Curtiss P-1 Hawks, a standard pursuit plane. For 80 miles around the 10-mile course for the prestigious John Mitchell Trophy, it was won by a margin of only 1½ seconds by 2nd Lt. P.B. Wurtsmith in #44 at 152.17 mph. In second place was 2nd Lt. A.L. Moore at 152.04 mph. In third, barely 0.4 seconds back, was 2nd Lt. K.E. Rogers at 152.01 mph. It was the closest finish to date in a National Air Races. Even though all the airplanes were identical, the fans got a taste of what pylon racing is supposed to be about: close competition in which the pilots' skill makes the difference between winning and trailing behind.

Then came Event #4, for U.S. Marine Corps attack-plane pilots. If it was actually flown for the announced 10 laps of the 10-mile course, the officially published times do not match the published speeds. The results show that Lieutenant Boyden won the race with a time of 30:46.4, Lieutenant Bryce was second in 30:59.4, and Lieutenant Belcher was third in 31:13. It was obviously a highly competitive event, thanks to what one reporter called "some of the best flying of the races."

Sunday, "All Nations Day," was another big day with five closed-course races and the finish of another cross-country race.

But this time, the cross-country grind was considerably more than advertised, and would soon lead to one of the classic air competitions of the 1930s and 1940s, the Bendix Transcontinental Derby. The Non-Stop Derby stretched 2,070 miles from Los Angeles to Cleveland. First prize of $5,000 went to Henry J. Brown, who covered the distance in 13 hours, 15 minutes, 7 seconds in his Pratt & Whitney Hornet–powered Lockheed Air Express. Second, in a time of 13:51:10.8, was Lee Schoenhair in a P&W Wasp–powered Lockheed Vega. Of the other two starters, Roscoe Turner (Vega) landed well after the 6 P.M. deadline, while John Wood crashed fatally in another Vega near Needles, Calif., not long after take-off.

The day's first pylon race was Event #17, for open-cockpit airplanes having no more than 800 cu. in. Sixteen civilian pilots started, with the winner being Charles "Speed" Holman at 150.61 mph in a Wright J4–powered Laird biplane. More than a half minute behind at 147.33 mph was Ted Wells in a TravelAir 4000 biplane

In the very best tradition of show business—and do not linger under the illusion that the National Air Races was a purely sporting event—the best was saved for last. Labor Day was about to lay claim to more than the traditional picnics, parades and political speeches.

Event #3 was for civilians flying experimental airplanes, which the rules defined as having in their design "a substantial deviation from the conventional." One can only wonder what such a rule would produce in the 21st century, in view of the remarkable creativity on display at the Experimental Aircraft Association's annual AirVenture Fly-In at Oshkosh, Wisconsin.

In this case, four airplanes took the starting line:

#32, Doug Davis' Chevrolair–powered TravelAir Mystery Racer.
#47, Eddie Heath's Bristol Cherub–powered Heath Baby Bullet.
#144, H.A. Speer's Nicholas Beazley Barling NB-3, with its British-built Armstrong Siddeley Genet engine.
#71, H. S. Myhres' Wright–powered Simplex Racer.

Five laps of the 5-mile course later, the winners were Doug Davis at 113 mph in Class C (up to 510 cu. in.), and Myhres at 147 mph in Class D (510–800 cu. in.).

Next came Event #21, open to multi-engined airplanes, each carrying a 1,000-lb. payload for 5 laps of the 10-mile course. While a bit short of rip-roaring action, it did more than most events to display the practical side of larger airplanes. Two of the pilots—Waldo Waterman, later to gain fame for his roadable airplanes, and William Brock—flew tri-motored Bach Air Yachts. M. Milton flew a Fokker F10 tri-motor. Waterman won at 136.41 mph, followed by Brock at 134.46 mph and Milton at 123.00 mph.

Event #10 was the Cleveland-to-Buffalo Efficiency Race for all types of commercial airplanes—200 miles along the south shore of Lake Erie. Scoring was based on speed, payload and fuel used. Top scorer, out of 30 entrants, was George Haldeman, whose Bellanca CH-300 achieved 131 mph while carrying 1,625 lbs. of payload and using just 51.9 gallons of gas. Close behind was J. Wesley Smith, in a similar airplane, with 125.42 mph, 1,520 lbs. and 45.3 gallons used.

And then it was time for Event #26, the "Free-for-All," which was open to any type of airplane—standard or modified—piloted by a civilian or military man. It was the only event in the National Air Races in which participants would be allowed to use hot or "doped" fuel containing "picric acid, ether or similarly highly explosive liquids." By just about anyone's standards, it would be an Unlimited Class race, though the term would not be used officially in pylon racing for another 35 years.

The prizes included $1,500 and a trophy: peanuts today, but enough in 1929

12. The 1929 U.S. National and Thompson Trophy Races

R.G. Breene's #80 Curtiss P-3A was a standard U.S. Army pursuit plane flown to second place in the 1929 Thompson Cup Race (Truman C. Weaver collection).

to spark a revolution. Perceptive observers would have noted that the trophy was called "The Charles E. Thompson Cup." But no one could have suspected what the future held in store for an award with a very similar name.

There were 11 entries, 7 starters and 6 finishers. One was from the U.S. Army, one from the U.S. Navy and all the rest were flown by civilians. Such a mixture was unprecedented, and would be the key to the rapid elevation of this event to legendary status.

The military racers were:

1. Curtiss F6C-3, gray-and-yellow, a standard U.S. Navy carrier-based pursuit biplane, powered by a 400 hp liquid-cooled V-12 Curtiss D-12 engine, to be flown by Lt. Cdr. Joseph Clark.
2. Curtiss XP-3A, the modified second prototype of a limited-production U.S. Army pursuit biplane design. The racer was powered by an air-cooled radial 410 hp Pratt & Whitney R-1340 Wasp engine, and streamlined with a special engine cowl and propeller spinner. It would be flown by the Army's Lt. R.G. Breene.

The civilian airplanes:

1. TravelAir Speedwing "Bug," orange-and-white. A specially-built biplane with racing wings and NACA cowling around its 240 hp Wright Whirlwind radial engine, to be flown by I.M. McConaughey.
2. TravelAir R, a red monoplane, powered by a brand new 225 hp air-cooled Chevrolair six-cylinder in-line engine developed by the Chevrolet Brothers, of Indianapolis, Ind. The pilot was C.E. Clark, who failed to start.
3. The Simplex Racer, white-and-red, a radical design with a lower

Cmdr. J.J. Clark's Curtiss F6C-3 in which he placed 4th in the 1929 Thompson. Highly modified, it crashed in the 1930 Thompson Trophy Race (National Air and Space Museum).

wing that could be removed to convert the biplane into a high-wing monoplane. Powered by a 225 hp Wright J-6 Whirlwind radial engine, it was to be flown by H.S. Myhres.
4. Pitcairn PA-4 Special, powered by a 225 hp Wright J-6 Whirlwind, and to have been flown by Chares Faulkner. It failed to start.
5. Curtiss Falcon, a biplane powered by a Curtiss Conqueror V-12, to have been flown by H.L. Atkinson. It did not start.
6. Laird LCR-300, a biplane powered by a 225 hp Wright J-6 Whirlwind, and piloted by Eric Wood, the fourth entrant who failed to start.
7. Cessna AC, a monoplane powered by a Comet engine, to be raced by C.D. Bowyer.
8. Lockheed "Speed Vega" 5, a standard commercial monoplane, powered by a 450 hp Pratt & Whitney R-985 Wasp Jr. The pilot would be future racing hero Roscoe Turner.
9. TravelAir Model R "Mystery Racer," black-and-red. An all-out racing monoplane, powered by a Wright R-975 engine, specially boosted to 400 hp. The pilot was Doug Davis.

Public and press interest was focused on the "Mystery Racer," so-called because it had been built behind locked doors, and was kept in a closed hangar at Cleveland except when it was being flown. It was a product of a small Wichita, Kansas, manufacturing firm headed up by Walter Beech, Clyde Cessna and

12. The 1929 U.S. National and Thompson Trophy Races

Lloyd Stearman, men with great foresight, whose names would eventually be carried by one out of every 10 airplanes built in the world.

The men had been moderately involved in air racing for several years, and decided on an all-out effort to draw attention to their company and its products. The design was laid down almost a year ahead of time, but construction didn't begin until late June 1929. As racing airplanes were a lot less sophisticated than they are today, rapid construction was not uncommon. In fact, the Model R was finished and ready to fly in eight weeks.

Inspired by the sleek monoplanes of the 1928 Schneider Cup Race, and designed by Herb Rawdon, the Model R had a wire-braced wing, but otherwise was as streamlined as anything yet seen. A low-drag windshield, wheel pants, a tight cowling and well-designed fairings set it apart from the others, as much as did its purely racing purpose.

Pilot Doug Davis, a native of Atlanta, Georgia, had a surprising amount of flying experience for his 24 years. He had impressed the TravelAir Company sufficiently to earn their trust and thus his job.

As race-horse starts had not yet become a staple of pylon racing, the seven airplanes were flagged off separately at short intervals for the five-lap dash around the 10-mile triangular course. First to get the starter's flag was Navy pilot Clark in the Curtiss biplane, followed by Roscoe Turner and then Army Capt. Breene. Davis was the fourth off, and immediately began shortening the distance between himself and those who had preceded him into the air.

On lap two, Davis unintentionally cut inside a pylon. By the rules of the day, he was required to circle it immediately, which he did. But he turned so tightly that he momentarily blacked out from the g-load. Being uncertain he had actually circled the pylon, he flew around it a second time. This gave the other pilots a "free" one-mile advantage over Davis, which should have put him out of contention.

But his TravelAir turned out to be so much faster than any of the other airplanes, including the two military pursuits, that he began catching up immediately. On his third lap, he was reported to have clocked an unprecedented 208 mph. To make certain he wouldn't cut any more pylons, Davis cautiously flew a slightly wider course than many of the others.

The order of finish of the first four starters remained the same to the end. But when their times were adjusted for the staggered start, Doug Davis was the clear winner by 40 seconds:

1. Doug Davis	15:23.6	194.90 mph
2. Lt. R.G. Breene	16:03.4	186.34
3. Roscoe Turner	18:21.3	163.44
4. Cmdr. J.J. Clark	19:32.0	153.38
5. H.S. Myhres	19:43.0	152.15
6. I.M. McConnaughey	20:39.7	145.20
7. C.D. Bowyer	dropped out on lap 2	

The *New York Times* headlined it: "Commercial Plane Beats Army, Navy." The *Cleveland Plain Dealer*, which should have had a clearer picture of the significance of the race, called it: "Georgia Hall of Fame Adds Pilot," while giving far bigger play to Dr. Hugo Eckner, and the monster Zeppelin he had flown over from Germany.

As first-time air racing operations go, the 10-day Cleveland meet was an overwhelming success, drawing enormous crowds and nationwide attention to Cleveland and to American aviation. There were fatal accidents, to be sure, but none during pylon races and none in view of the spectators at the airport.

Of course, there were shortcomings. The official results of some events weren't posted until as much as two days after the event, and so some of the prize money was delayed. Rules were modified during the races, but this sort of questionable behavior is not unknown today.

Still, the fans loved it, and aviation acquired a showcase of huge potential. The total purse paid approached $80,000, an astronomical amount in 1929. With 12 months to polish and tune the things that were done right, and to correct those that weren't, designers and builders and pilots could look forward to great times.

Chapter 13

The 1925–1931 Schneider Cup Races: Rampant Nationalism

Once the Europeans had seen what heavy government financial support could produce in the way of speed through sophisticated streamlining and more horsepower, they had little choice but to follow suit. Moreover, the roaring success of America's twin-float Curtiss seaplanes was expected to lead to cleaner and more powerful developments in that country, as well, and thus would present a steady threat to the Europeans.

It soon became apparent that one year was not long enough to design, build and test completely new seaplanes. And while several potentially competitive designs were under development, they would not be ready for the 1924 Schneider Race, scheduled for October 27 over the Chesapeake Bay, southeast of Baltimore, Maryland.

The Curtiss CR-3 that Rutledge Irvine had flown to 2nd place in 1923 was flown over the proposed 50-km./31-mile course by Lt. Ralph Oftsie, who proceeded to set several National Aeronautique Association (FAI) speed records. But as no others could be expected, the race was postponed a year rather than be a non-competitive win for the American team. The gesture of sportsmanship was widely applauded at the time, but would eventually be seen by some as a missed opportunity.

1925 — Baltimore, Maryland, October 2

Interest in the U.S., Great Britain and Italy was great, though not all of it was realized. The race course was a slightly modified version of the one for the postponed 1924 race, though the facilities offered the teams were far below Schneider Cup standards, with flimsy tents serving as hangers.[1]

The Italians had more modern racers in the works, but arrived at Baltimore with a pair of Macchi M.33 shoulder-wing flying boats that were clearly out of date, even though they used American Curtiss V-12 engines purchased soon after the 1924 race and used as the basis for future racing and then military engines.

The British brought four racers, two of which were the most modern yet seen: twin-float monoplane Supermarine S.4s, powered by 530 hp Napier Lion three-bank W-12 engines. They had been designed by R.J. Mitchell, who would use the knowledge gained in his work on racers to create the immortal Spitfire, of Battle of Britain fame. The other two were tiny Gloster III float-equipped biplanes, powered by the same engines. As entry forms for just two had been filed, one of each was scratched when they were damaged during trials.

The Americans were more than ready to defend their title, with four improved versions of their recent Pulitzer Trophy winners, called the Curtiss R3C-2. To get rid of the considerable heat developed by their 500 hp Curtiss V-12 engines, the upper surfaces of their wings were covered with surface-evaporation radiators, which had much less wind resistance than old-style radiators. A full team of three would be flown by Navy officers George Cuddihy, Ralph Oftsie and Army officer Jimmy Doolittle.

On race day it quickly became apparent that the Americans had figured out what it would take to win. Each of the R3C-2s tore around the course at record speed. But on the 6th lap, Oftsie's engine broke its magneto drive and he landed, having averaged 219 mph for the first five laps. One lap later, Cuddihy's engine caught fire due to an oil leak, and while he put the fire out with an extinguisher, he was forced to retire after having averaged 221 mph.

This left Doolittle, who was already well ahead and continued to run at top speed, eventually winning at 232.573 mph. This broke the old Schneider record by no less than 55 mph. Having won the race in one of the army's *very few* seaplanes, Doolittle was paraded around on a float as an army "admiral." It was only the first of his many encounters with fame.

In second place, almost 10 minutes back, was Hubert Broad in a Supermarine S.4 at 199.170 mph. The only other finisher was Giovanni de Briganti, in a Macchi M.33, at only 168.453 mph.

Had the U.S. not cancelled the 1924 race, which it would have won easily, the Schneider Cup would now be on display in some major American museum. Instead, it would remain in competition.

1926 — Hampton Roads, Virginia, November 12–13

The 9th Schneider Cup Race was America against Italy, Curtiss against Macchi. In the end, power and streamlining told the story. The American team of Christian Schilt, William Tomlinson and George Cuddihy flew improved versions of the sleek biplanes which had been victorious in the previous two races, while the Italian team of air force pilots Mario de Bernardi, Adriano Bacula and Arturo Ferrarin flew the brand new Macchi M.39. The Italian machine was a logical development of the American ideas, with at least 200 more horsepower, and a single wing in place of the Curtiss' two.

De Bernardi was an easy winner, averaging 246.50 mph for 7 laps around the 50-km. (31-mi.) course. Two and a half minutes behind him was Schilt, at 231.36 mph in the previous year's winning seaplane. In 3rd was Bacula at 218.01 mph. With more horsepower and less drag, the Italians kept the U.S. from retiring the trophy. It was the last time a group of Americans would compete.

1927 — Venice, Italy, September 26

The British returned to the fray, having spent their brief "retirement" perfecting the monoplanes that were not ready in 1926. The Supermarine S.5 and the Gloster IVB had advanced streamlining and 875 hp Napier Lion W-12 engines. The new Italian Macchi M.52s were cleaned-up M.39s with 1,000 hp Fiat V-12 engines. The British racers were clearly faster, Sidney Webster winning in an S.5 at 281.66 mph, Oswald Worsley 2nd in an S.5 at 272.91 mph, and S.M. Kinkead a close 3rd at 272.53 mph until dropping out on the next-to-last lap. Of the Italians, Frederico Guazetti was fastest at 257.78 mph until he pulled out on lap 6, while de Bernardi had been even faster — 263.1 mph — but went out on lap 2.[2]

1929 — Isle of Wight, September 6–7

With another two years to prepare, both the British and the Italians were able to make major improvements on their basic designs. The Supermarine S.5

Giovanni Monti's Macchi M.67 was forced out of the 1929 Schneider Cup Race with an over-heated engine (*Aeroplane and Astronautics* magazine).

had become the S.6A with a 1,900 hp Rolls Royce R engine, which would become the late–World War II Griffon. The Macchi M.52 had become the M.52R and the M.67, the latter with a new 1,800 hp W-18 engine from auto maker Isotta-Fraschini. While increasing horsepower usually does not increase speed very much, when it is increased by such amounts, it is bound to have an impact.

In the race—for 7 laps of a 50-km. course between the English south coast and the Isle of Wight—the S.6As were supreme. The #2 flown by Henry Waghorn averaged 328.63 mph, breaking the previous year's record by 47 mph. Richard Atcherly would have placed 2nd at 325.54 mph had he not been called for cutting a pylon. In 2nd place was Tomaso Dal Molin, at 284.2 mph, and in 3rd, DeArcy Greig, the third member of the British High Speed Flight, at 282.11 mph. Now, Great Britain was in position to retire the trophy with one more win.

1931— Isle of Wight, September 6–7

What turned out to be the anticlimactic final Schneider Cup Race could just as easily have been the most exciting and hotly contested. At least five new types of seaplanes were under development, all of them with the potential to win.

Three were from France: the Bernard HV.220 was the final step in a series of increasingly fast low-wing monoplanes, and was powered by a 2,000 hp Lorraine Radium V-12. The Dewoitine D.412 was of the same design philosophy and probably would have used the same engine. The Nieuport-Delage 450 was yet another twin-float, low-wing seaplane powered by an Hispano W-18, that was originally meant to have a 1,200 hp but probably would have used the Radium as that was the largest available engine. But none was ready for the 1931 race, and soon the need had passed. No trace of any of the seaplanes has been found.

The Italians had been testing five Macchi M.C.72s, vastly improved M.67s with two Fiat V-12 A.S.5 engines coupled into the radical A.S.6, packed into the nose—in tandem. The front engine drove a two-bladed, fixed-pitch propeller turning in one direction, and the other drove its prop in the opposite direction, via a drive shaft that went through the front engine's hollow drive shaft. This constituted the first use of co-axial, contra-rotating propellers which eliminated the adverse effects of torque produced by a single propeller turning in one direction and trying to make the airplane roll in the opposite direction.

Two of the potent machines—rated at a then-world record 2,800 hp— were lost in fatal training accidents, leaving three. One was used by Francesco Agello in 1933 to set a World Seaplane Speed Record of 433 mph for 3 km., and then by Guglielmo Cassinelli for a 100-km record of 391.72 mph. Another was flown in 1933 by Pietro Scapinelli on a 30-minute flight at 385 mph to win the prestigious Bleriot Cup. The fifth was flown in 1934 by Agello to set the still-existing 3 km. record at 440.681 mph, and is on public display in the Italian

Air Force Museum at Vigna di Valle, north of Rome. All three would probably have been available for a 1933 race, and would no doubt have been favored to win.

Had the British been as good sports in 1931 as the Americans had been in 1924, the series would have continued, full blast. But in view of the many obstacles they had cleared, including the need for a last-minute injection of money from a private source, and the need to boost the horsepower of the Rolls Royce R engine without necessitating a complete redesign, it was felt that the race should go on.

With no foreign opposition, the necessity to fly more than a single seaplane was not there. John Boothman was chosen to fly one of the new Supermarine S.6b with its 2,650 hp R (for Racing) engine. For seven laps around the triangular 50-km. course he roared, taking sharp turns at speeds never before considered, even though the only pressure he was under to get the maximum performance was his own. Boothman's average speed of 340.08 mph was not that much faster than the 1929 record, but could have been considerably more if the Italians or French had been there to push him.

John Boothman's Supermarine S.6b carried him to victory in the final, 1931, Schneider Cup Race at 340.08 mph (Vickers Ltd.).

Jimmy Doolittle won the 1925 Schneider Cup Race in this Curtiss R3C-2 (National Air and Space Museum).

Three weeks later, on September 29, George Stainforth flew the same machine to a new absolute World Speed Record of 406.99 mph, the first time any human had officially traveled over 400 mph. The S.6b has long been on display in London's Science Museum, along with the Schneider Cup, which Great Britain had retired.

The long series of Schneider Cup Races had produced amazing progress in engines, fuels and streamlining, much of which led to better airplanes of all types. But the dwindling prospects for seaplanes were not improved. Soon, the need for long water "runways" was eliminated out by the appearance of hard-surface runways and by the development of variable-pitch propellers which act like multiple-speed gears in a car. Low pitch and low gear are used for initial acceleration, and high pitch and high gears for high speeds. Seaplanes never reached the levels of usefulness hoped for by M. Schneider, and today can be found in small numbers, mainly as fire bombers and sport aircraft.

Chapter 14

The 1930–1934 National Air Races: GeeBees and Wedell Williams

The first half of the 1930s introduced the world of air racing to men like designers and builders Ben Howard and Clayton Folkerts, Jimmy Wedell and Steve Wittman, Art Chester and Keith Rider, and to pilots like Jimmy Doolittle and Roscoe Turner and Harold Neumann. It would prove to be the high-watermark of the Golden Age of Air Racing.

1930 Chicago National Air Races

The second of the classic National Air Races was held August 23 through September 1 at Curtiss-Reynolds Airport (later the Glenview Naval Air Station), near Glenview, Illinois. It was located north of Chicago, and about five miles from the shore of Lake Michigan.[1]

The Henderson brothers were again in charge, with R.W. "Shorty" Schroeder as contest chairman. Backing the event was the Chicago Air Race Corp., comprised of such local business luminaries as newspaper magnate Robert R. "Bertie" McCormick, publisher of the *Chicago Tribune*; John Hertz (of car-rental fame), and drugstore chain founder C.R. Walgreen. Despite the devastating effects of the Great Depression, which had hit Wall Street late the previous year, enough funding was arranged by these men to launch a huge advertising campaign after setting aside $100,000 for prize money.

The selection of Chicago was made by the National Aeronautic Association (NAA), which, as the American representative of the International Aeronautics Federation (FAI), was the governing and sanctioning body of the races. It followed a lively bidding war for the emerging giant of public aviation events. Other cities showing interest included Miami, Portland (Oregon), San Antonio, St. Louis and Washington, D.C. The last-named had hoped to use the National Air Races to stimulate sufficient local interest in aviation to make possible the construction of a major municipal airport. As it turned out, the construction of Washington National Airport was delayed for almost a decade.

The schedule was much better planned than in 1929, with 34 crowd-pleasing pylon races and only 7 cross-country races. The pylon events were neatly divided into displacement classes: 110 cu. in., 275 cu. in., 350 cu. in., 450 cu. in., 650 cu. in., 800 cu. in. and 1,000 cu. in. Most, in turn, were divided into two or three subdivisions: Men's Open (for airplanes with open cockpits), Men's Cabin (for airplanes with closed cabins) and Free-for-All (open to any style). In addition, there were 500 cu. in. and 800 cu. in. Open and Cabin races for women pilots.

Fewer races were scheduled for military pilots, for sportsman/amateur pilots, and for pilots of transports, multi-engined airplanes and amphibians. Capping all of this pylon activity were the feature races: the Mrs. R. McCormick Trophy Race for women, and the Thompson Trophy Race for men. All racing would be around a dangerous (because of the steep 120° turns) three-pylon, five-mile course.

Like almost every air race program, and unlike all other motorsports events, there was a lot more to see than just racing. Aerobatics or stunt flying played a major role, as did formation flights by army and navy air squadrons, and demonstrations of some of the more unusual flying machines of the day. It made for a complete flying display, as one of its major purposes was to educate the American people and stimulate their support for, and personal involvement in all phases of aviation.

The resounding victory by Doug Davis in the custom-built TravelAir Mystery S over the military's best in the 1929 Thompson Cup Race triggered an explosion of activity among creative designers and builders who were eager to display their talents and ideas in this exciting new public arena called the National Air Races. The first results of this were clearly evident in the hangars and on the field.

TravelAir Mystery S

Two new airplanes emerged from the lively little factory in Wichita, Kansas, a city that would soon become the world center of personal airplane manufacturing. The new racers were #26, red-and-yellow, sponsored by the Shell Oil Co. and flown by Jimmy Haizlip, and #13, red-and-white, sponsored by the Texaco Oil Co. and flown by Frank Hawks. Both were powered by the nine-cylinder, air-cooled 420 hp Wright R-975 Whirlwind radial engine.

Wedell-Williams

Pilot and born-engineer Jimmy Wedell, of Patterson, Louisiana, had two different racers which generally resembled the TravelAirs. Jimmy flew his red-

and-silver #17, *We Will Jr.*, powered by a 110 hp supercharged Cirrus straight-four. He also flew the black-and-white #92, initially a two-seat sportplane powered by a 450 hp Pratt & Whitney R-985 Wasp Jr.

Howard

Ben O. Howard's first racer, the #37 DGA-3 *Pete*, was built with Gordon Israel. It weighed less than half as much as some of the others, and thus needed far less power: a 90 hp Wright-built, British-designed deHavilland Gypsy straight-four. It was painted silver with black markings. The airplane later survived being converted into a sportplane, then was restored to its original configuration for display in the Crawford Aviation and Auto Museum, Cleveland, Ohio.

Benny Howard's Howard *Pete*, third place winner in the 1930 Thompson Trophy Race, has been restored to like-new condition (John Garrett).

Cessna

The firm that eventually produced more than 150,000 light personal airplanes got its first taste of public attention with a pair of small racers. Stan Stanton flew the GC-1, *Miss Blackwell*, red-with-black-trim and powered by a 110 hp, 310 cu. in. Cirrus engine. Bill Ong was the principal pilot of the red-black-and-white GC-2, a slightly smaller airplane with a 110 hp, 422 cu. in. Warner radial engine.

Keith Rider

Another airplane that was the first in an important racing series, the blue-and-white B-1 was designed and built by Keith Rider. Smaller than most, it was powered by a 366 cu. in., four-cylinder, in-line, air-cooled Menasco C4, and was flown by John MacReady, who had been the co-pilot on the first non-stop flight across America, in 1923.

Flagg

The *Phantom I* was designed and built by Claude Flagg and raced by Danny Fowlie. It was black and gold, with white numbers, and powered by a 90 hp, seven-cylinder, geared Pobjoy Niagara radial engine.

Heath

Two of many small, efficient airplanes designed and built by Eddie Heath were entered. The *Baby Bullet* was silver with black trim, and a 32 hp Bristol Cherub engine. The *Cannonball* was black and yellow, with a 65 hp, four-cylinder Heath engine.

Laird

The *Solution* was a scaled-down version of the popular Laird commercial biplanes, and was raced by Charles "Speed" Holman. It was black and gold, and powered by a 450 hp Pratt & Whitney R-985 Wasp Jr. Matty Laird's first true racer was built in three weeks! It had one brief test flight, then was flown across Chicago from the factory to the race site with only a few minutes remaining before the start of the Thompson Trophy Race. Of such are legends (and gray hairs) made. It was eventually restored for display at the New England Air Museum, Hartford, Connecticut.

Cross-Country Races

The schedule of cross-county races included two for women. The Class A Pacific Derby from Long Beach, California, to Chicago, was won by Gladys O'Donnell in a Waco biplane in 15 hours, 13 minutes, 16 seconds. The Class B Dixie Derby from Washington, D.C., was won by Phoebie Omlie in a Monocoupe in 11:42:21.

For the men, there was the Class A Pacific Derby from Seattle, Washington, won by John Blum in a Lockheed in 18:24:31. The Class B Pacific Derby from Brownsville, Texas, was won by Johnnie Livingston in his Monocoupe in

14. The 1930–1934 National Air Races

Art Chester's Chester "Jeep," raced and won for several years during the 1930's, then was restored by the EAA Museum staff (Robert Pauley).

16:10:29. The Class A Atlantic Derby from Miami, Florida, was won by A. W. Killips in a Waco in 11:53:23. The Class B Atlantic Derby from Hartford, Connecticut, was won by J. Wesley Smith in a Monocoupe in 8:24:37.

The featured cross-country event was the Men's Non-Stop Derby from Los Angeles, Calif., which would lead directly to a classic event, the next year's inaugural Bendix Transcontinental Derby. The official results:

1. Wiley Post	11 Lockheed Vega 5B, NR-105W	9:09:04	192.326 mph
2. Art Goebel	62 Lockheed Vega 5, NR-7954	9:39:13	182.315
3. Lee Schoenhair	36 Lockheed Vega 5A, NR-308H	9:53:57	177.793
4. Roscoe Turner	25 Lockheed Air Express, NR-3057	9:58:41	176.387

Closed-Course Races

These classes were open to any type of airplane which had an engine no larger than the stated limit, hence some airplanes flew in several different displacement-class events. The big winners among the men included Eddie Heath in both his special-built *Baby Bullet* and a standard Heath Parasol. John Livingston dominated several races in the first factory clipped-wing Monocoupe, while Ben Howard introduced the first in a series of pure racers, his open-cockpit *Pete*.

Leading the women were Mary Haizlip, flying an Inland Sport; Phoebe Omlie, flying a Monocoupe, and Gladys O'Donnell, flying both a Waco and a Monocoupe.

With all of this as prelude, the big races entered the spotlight on the final day.

Mrs. R. McCormick Trophy Race

Scheduled for 10 laps of the 5-mile course, it attracted the fastest women pilots from previous races. The official results:

1. Gladys O'Donnell	105 Waco ATO, NC-8558	20:00.8	149.90 mph
2. Mary Haizlip	17 Cessna GC-2, NR-404W	20:12.8	148.42
3. Opal Kunz	7 TravelAir 2000, NC-6040	20:34.9	145.76

The Thompson Trophy Race

Following the huge impact of the 1929 Thompson Cup Race, a new trophy was commissioned by Thompson Products Co., the purse was enlarged, and one of the most famous series in air racing history was launched. The first race was for 20 laps of the 5-mile course and open to men flying any type of airplane — period. There were no limitations on airframe design or dimensions, engine size, type of fuel or anything else. It was meant to encourage new and better ideas; this kind of thinking would eventually lead to what would be called the Unlimited Class.

The pre-race favorite was Marine Capt. Arthur Page, flying last year's factory-standard Curtiss F6C-3 biplane pursuit, which had been extensively and expensively modified by Curtiss for the navy into the XF6C-6, a sleek parasol-monoplane racer with a 700 hp. Curtiss D-12 engine. It appeared to have more than enough power and streamlining needed to win with ease.

Captain Page was waved off first, "race horse" starts still being somewhere in the future. Ten seconds later, the next pilot got the starter's signal, then another 10 seconds passed for the third, and on it went until all seven were away and screaming around the course. On lap three, Frank Hawks began to experience fuel starvation with his TravelAir's Wright engine, and dropped out. On lap eight, Errett Williams pulled his Wedell Williams up and out, leaving five.

Page had steadily pulled away from the pack, averaging a reported 219 mph through lap 16 of 20, and establishing a commanding lead. Then something went wrong. Either he encountered carbon monoxide poisoning (the widely accepted explanation) or developed magneto problems that forced him to bank wide around the home pylon. He gradually descended and hit the ground with his left wing. The airplane folded up in a cloud of dust. The badly injured pilot was rushed to the hospital, where he died the next day. In a very short time he had gone from being on the verge of a historic victory, to being a tragic figure.

Meanwhile, Holman, who had been in second place, found himself leading, though in a tight battle with Haizlip. The final results:

1. Charles Holman	77 Laird "Solution" NR-10538	29:43.0	201.91 mph
2. Jimmy Haizlip	26 TravelAir Mystery N482N	30:01.8	199.80
3. Ben O. Howard	37 Howard DGA-3 "Pete" NR-2Y	36:51.3	162.80
4. Paul Adams	81 TravelAir Speedwing NR-612K	42:03.8	142.64
— Capt. Arthur Page	27 Curtiss XF6C-6 A.7144	out lap 17	
— Errett Williams	92 Wedell Williams NR-536V	out lap 8	
— Frank Hawks	13 TravelAir Mystery NR-1313	out lap 3	

Despite the sobering effects of Page's death, the races were another rousing success, confirming hopes that the National Air Races would be a fixture on the schedule for many years to come. It was the unified goal of pilots and designers and builders, as well as mechanics and a horde of new fans. Model airplane builders, in particular, flocked to the flurry of new designs.

1931 Cleveland National Air Races

Cleveland was selected as the site of the National Air Races for the next 10 years—1931 through 1940—according to an announcement on December 22, 1930, by Senator Hiram Bingham, president of the National Aeronautic Association. The New York Times reported that Senator Bingham said that the establishment of a permanent home for the races would make it possible to place greater emphasis on the annual development of improved types of airplanes, an increase in the efficiency in the administration of the races, improved control of the racing events, and the construction of permanent accommodations for the spectators.[2]

The previous 10 National Air Races had been held in 10 different cities, but only the last two—Cleveland and Chicago—produced a financial profit. Sen. Bingham added that NAA could terminate the contract if the Cleveland Chamber of Commerce and associated agencies sponsoring the races were unable to live up to the financial provisions.

With this great show of confidence, accompanied by the pointed motivation to do well, the Cleveland organization charged ahead with elaborate plans to create a permanent presence on the north side of Cleveland Airport with wooden grandstands and an air race administration building.

For 1931 there would be two new events of major long-term significance on the program. The Bendix Transcontinental Derby, with a purse of $15,000 and a bronze trophy that would soon become famous, replaced the Non-Stop Los Angeles to Cleveland Race of previous years. A series of Shell Speed Dashes over a one-mile straight course would serve as qualifiers for the men's Thompson and women's Aerol Trophy Races.

As a sign of the changing times, the National Air Races would offer only a single race exclusively for military pilots flying military airplanes. The combination of a steep drop in the army's and navy's interest in racing, and the rapid increase in the number and variety of custom-built pure racers, made it possible to plan a 10-day air racing extravaganza in which the military would concentrate on massed fly-bys and demonstrations more appropriate to their normal operations. As long as the spectators had seen little besides identical military planes that looked alike and sounded alike, they didn't complain. But once they had tasted the variety of shapes, colors and sounds of original-design racers, they were hooked.

Trans-Continental Races

Also gone were the shorter cross-country races which had served to stimulate interest around the Midwest. This time, there would be just two long-distance events, the Transcontinental Handicap Air Derby from Santa Monica, California, which was divided into Men's and Women's Divisions. And the Transcontinental Free-for-All Speed Dash from Los Angeles, which would soon be known everywhere as the Bendix Trophy Race.

The handicap race was judged not on all-out speed, but by how much each pilot exceeded the predicted speed for his or her airplane, expressed as a percentage. This was determined by pre-race speed runs in which each airplane was flown by a non-competing pilot. Either division would split $6,000 prize money, while the overall winner would also receive a Cord front-wheel drive cabriolet automobile, priced then at $2,500 and valued today at no less than $175,000.

Winner of the Women's Division, with 109 percent of her predicted speed, was Phoebie Omlie in a Warner-powered Monocoupe, who received $3,000 and the car. In second, winning $1,800, was Mary Haizlip in a Lambert-powered Monocoupe, who achieved 99 percent of her predicted speed. In third was Martie Bowman in a Warner-powered Inland Sport, who earned $1,200. Ten pilots finished the race.

In the Men's Division, winner D. C. Warren scored 103.5 percent in his Gypsy-powered deHavilland Moth, and earned $3,000. Second place went to Lee Brusse in the Kinner-powered Waco Model F at 102.1 percent, for $1,800. And placing third was Eldon Cessna in his Warner-powered Cessna Racer, earning $1,200 for scoring 101.4 percent. Seven of the 10 finishers exceeded 100 percent of their predicted speed, and even the 10th-place finisher, H.G. Myers, scored 99 percent.

The featured transcontinental race was for the Bendix Trophy. There were eight starters, two of whom flew racers and six who flew various factory-built Lockheed monoplanes: Orion, Altair, Vega. One of the racers—Walter Hunter

14. The 1930–1934 National Air Races

in the TravelAir Mystery, in which Doug Davis won the 1929 Thompson Cup Race — got only as far as Terre Haute, Indiana, before dropping out.

The other custom-built racer was the brand new Laird *Super Solution*. It bore a family resemblance to last year's *Solution*, but was slightly longer, much cleaner and had a Pratt & Whitney R-985 Wasp Jr. that produced 535 hp. Perhaps the most important change was the pilot, winner of the 1925 Schneider Cup Race in a Curtiss R3C-2 floatplane, Jimmy Doolittle, who was becoming recognized as the greatest speed pilot of the era.

Doolittle smashed all relevant records with a 2,046-mile dash in just 9:10:21 for a speed of 223.04 mph, earning him $7.500. He finished more than an hour ahead of runner-up Harold Johnson in a Lockheed Orion ($4,500), and more than 1½ hours ahead of third-place Beeler Blevins ($3,000) in another Orion.

In the first Thompson Race, a custom-built racer had whipped the best the military had to offer, while in the first Bendix Race, a "special" whipped the best that the manufacturing industry could field. It was another defining moment for air racing. Parts of the *Super Solution* have survived and are in the

Jimmy Doolittle's GeeBee R-1 carried him to 1st place in the 1932 Thompson Trophy Race and became the permanent symbol of speed in the air (Roger Huntington).

National Air & Space Museum, while one flying reproduction and one non-flying reproduction have been built. The official results:

1. Jimmy Doolittle	#400 Laird *Super Solution* NR-12048	9:10:21	223.04 mph
2. Harold Johnson	#64 Lockheed Orion NR-12220	10:14:22	199.82
3. Beeler Blevins	#112 Lockheed Orion NR-988Y	10:49:33	188.99
4. Ira Eaker	#50 Lockheed Altair NR-199W	10:59:45	186.07
5. Art Goebel	#129 Lockheed Vega NR-7954	11:55:48	171.50
6. James Hall	#125 Lockheed Altair NR-15W	12:51:16	159.17
— Loe Reichers	#11 Lockheed Altair NR-998Y	Did not finish	
— Walter Hunter	#31 TravelAir Mystery NR-614K	Did not finish	

Shell Speed Dash

The official speed for each attempt would be the average of the speeds for two runs in opposite directions over the one-mile straight course, which would cancel out any effects of wind. As NAA national records and FAI world records had to be set over a 3-kilometer (1.86-mile) course, the winner in each event would own merely a "National Air Race record." There would be separate winners for women in the 510 cu. in. and 800 cu. in. classes.

Class	Pilot	Airplane	Speed (mph)
275 Cu. In.	Merle Lambert	#74 Heath Cannonball R-10372	unknown
400 Cu. In.	Ray Moore	#132 Keith Rider R-2 NR-52Y	unknown
510 Cu. In.	Johnnie Livingston	#14 Monocoupe NR-105W	unknown
510 Cu. In.	Phoebie Omlie	#8 Monocoupe NR-8917	unknown
650 Cu. In.	Johnnie Livingston	#14 Monocoupe NR-105W	unknown
800 Cu. In.	Ray Moore	#131 Keith Rider R-1 R-51Y	unknown
800 Cu. In.	Gladys O'Donnell	#7 Waco CTO NR-21M	unknown
1,000 Cu. In.	Robert Hall	#54 GeeBee Y NR-11049	213.87
1,875 Cu. In.	Lowell Bayles	#4 GeeBee Z NR-77V	267.34
Thompson Trophy Race	1. Lowell Bayles	#4 GeeBee Z NR-77V	267.34
	2. Jimmy Doolittle	#400 Laird "Super Solution" NR-12048	255.35
	3. Robert Hall	#54 GeeBee Y NR-11049	213.87
	4. Ben O. Howard	#37 Howard DGA-3 "Pete" NR-2Y	175.68
Aerol Trophy	Maude Tait	#54 GeeBee Y NR-11049	unknown

Displacement Class Pylon Races

These were mainly for five or six laps around the five-mile pylon course, with a few of the fastest races being held on a 10-mile course. One new, higher-limit class was introduced in recognition of the number of custom-built racers using larger Wright and Pratt & Whitney air-cooled, radial engines. There were also more races for women pilots. There was even one pylon race in which both men and women could race together. This year, for the first time, the displacement class races were divided into ATC races for airplanes that had been issued formal Approved Type Certificates by the government, and Free-for-All races which were open to any airplane. As usual, an engine could be used in any class as long as it did not exceed the upper limit.

The world got its first look at a new brand of racing planes, the GeeBees. Designed and built by the five Granville Brothers, in Springfield, Massachusetts, they ranged from the single-seat Model D and E Sportsters through the two-seat Model Y Sportster, to the chubby Model Z Super Sportster, an all-out racer. All were low-wing monoplanes, with fixed landing gear covered by spats. All but the Menasco-powered Model D had radial engines.

Aerol Trophy Race

The featured women's pylon race was sponsored by the Cleveland Pneumatic Tool Co., which later would back the Greve Trophy Race. It extended for 5 laps of the 10-mile course, and could be flown in any type of airplane, with any size engine. The eight most successful women in the previous events were entered, and all finished. The leaders won $3,750, $2,250 and $1,500.

1. Maude Tait	#54 GeeBee Y NR-11049		15:59.62	187.574 mph
2. Mary Haizlip	#104 Laird LC-RW-300 NC-10591		18:09.58	165.201
3. F. Klingensmith	#62 Cessna BW NC-5834		18:42.70	160.327
4. Joan Shankle	#45 Lockheed Altair NC-13W		19:35.54	153.121
5. Phoebe Omlie	#59 Monocoupe		20:07.65	149.049
6. Bettie Lund	#119 Waco CTO NC-12099		20:20.85	147.438
7. Opal Kunz	#121 TravelAir		20:34.75	145.778
8. Gladys O'Donnell	#7 Waco CTO NC-21M		20:47.64	144.272

Thompson Trophy Race (Second Race in the Series)

1. Lowell Bayles	#4 GeeBee Z NR-77V	25:23.9	236.24 mph
2. Jimmy Wedell	#44 Wedell Williams NR-278V	26:19.0	227.99
3. Dale Jackson	#77 Laird Solution NR-10538	28:24.7	211.18
4. Robert Hall	54 GeeBee Y NR-11049	29:48.8	201.25
5. Ira Eaker	#50 Lockheed Altair NR-199W	30:29.1	196.83
6. Ben Howard	#37 Howard "Pete" NR-2Y	36:40.8	163.57
7. William Ong	#145 Laird LCR-300 NC-9419	39:12.2	153.05
—Jimmy Doolittle	#400 Laird LC-DW-500 NR-12048	out lap 7	

The winners received $7,500, $4,500 and $3,000.

The gold Wedell Williams Racer helped make the reputations of the builders and pilot Roscoe Turner (John Sunyak collection).

1932 Cleveland National Air Races

This year saw the birth of an icon, an airplane whose barrel shape and striking color scheme would make it the permanent symbol of airplane racing: the GeeBee Model R Super Sportster. More than 70 years after both original Rs had been reduced to scrap, an authentic reproduction was still able to steal the show at the world's largest aviation event, thanks to unmatched glamour and mystique. Competitively, it was another matter. While a GeeBee R was flown to first place in the Thompson Trophy Race, the type's only other achievement was being flown to 4th in the Bendix Trophy Race.[3]

The other major new type to appear in 1932 — the Pratt & Whitney–powered Wedell Williams Racers—took the top three places in the Bendix, and 2nd, 3rd and 4th in the Thompson. That excitement was able to out-shine technical accomplishment may not be fair, but it is often a fact of life.

The meet ran for 10 days — August 27 through September 5 — and offered $68,000 and several shiny new cars to the winners of cross-country races, pylon races and straightaway speed dashes.

The spotlighted GeeBee Model R was a visual shock, being fatter than anything previously raced, which left many people wondering why it was getting so much attention. But the Granville Brothers, of Springfield, MA, had already built a reputation, and this time had enlisted the help of aeronautical engineer Howell Miller. To those with some knowledge of aerodynamics, the fuselage was close to the ideal "teardrop" shape, though it provided its pilot with almost no forward visibility from his cockpit near the tail. The Bendix Trophy R-2 version, to be raced by Lee Gehlbach, used a 500 hp Pratt & Whitney R-985 Wasp Jr. engine, while the Thompson Trophy R-1 had an 800 hp P&W Wasp. It would be flown by Jimmy Doolittle, the increasingly famous winner of the 1925 Schneider Cup Race and the 1931 Bendix Trophy Race.

The main rivals of the GeeBees would be three nearly identical Wedell Williams Racers, the brainchildren of Jimmy Wedell. They were refined versions of the 1929 Thompson-winning TravelAir S, with wire-braced wings, more fully enclosed landing gear and 450–500 hp P&W Wasp Jr. engines.

The 2,043-mile Bendix Race from California attracted five custom-built airplanes: three Wedells, one GeeBee R and the Vance Flying Wing. The last-named failed to finish, Lee Gehlbach in the GeeBee placed 4th at 210.75 mph, while the Wedells swept the top spots. Jim Haizlip won at a Bendix record of 245.28 mph, designer Wedell was 2nd at 232.37 mph, just 28 minutes behind, and Roscoe Turner was 3rd at 225.99 mph. The trio of Model 44s had made its mark at the very first opportunity.

Qualifying for the Thompson Trophy Race consisted of the Shell Speed Dash, comprised of four passes over the 2-km. (1.24-mile) course. Any doubts about the efficiency of the GeeBee Model R were erased by Doolittle's average of 294 mph, an official World Speed Record for landplanes. Next in line were Jimmy Wedell at 277 mph, Turner at 267 mph and Haizlip at 266 mph. No one else was able to top 250 mph.

The start of the 10-lap, 100-mile race was at 10-second intervals, beginning shortly after 5 P.M. First to get the starter's green flag was Bob Hall in the Springfield *Bulldog*, followed closely by Doolittle. In short order, the red-and-white GeeBee had moved into first place even though it was being flown cautiously and very wide around the course. Its speed was such that Doolittle was able to lap everyone but Wedell, as he cruised to victory at a record 252.69 mph, a full minute ahead of the runner-up.

Doolittle's post-race comments made it clear that he felt the GeeBee was the worst airplane he'd ever flown, thus triggering a decades-long debate over the flying qualities of the fierce-looking Granville racer. It didn't end until the 1990s, when Delmar Benjamin's brilliant air show demonstrations in an exact replica GeeBee quieted those who called it a "death-trap."

While 1932 was the only year a GeeBee Super Sportster finished a race at Cleveland, its mystique remained. People who can recognize only one racing plane can usually spot a GeeBee Model R. Even though both of the originals were wiped out in fatal crashes, it is the permanent symbol of pylon racing.

1933 Los Angeles National Air Races

The National Air Races were temporarily shifted to Mines Field (later to become Los Angeles International Airport) and were held over the July 1–4 holiday weekend. The program was reduced in length by eliminating the pylon races for factory-built airplanes, and all the cross-country races except for the Bendix Trophy Race, which started from Floyd Bennett Field, NY. The total purse was down to $50,000.[4]

It was a disappointing year for new designs, these being limited to several 500 cu. in. machines, including Art Chester's *Jeep* and the Miles & Atwood Special.

The Bendix Race saw the first win in a major event by Roscoe Turner, who averaged 214.7 mph in the #2 Wedell Williams for the 2,470-mile grind. Jimmy Wedell was 2nd in his #44 at 206.32 mph. The other five starters, including Lee Gehlbach in the other Wedell Williams, and two commercial Lockheeds failed to finish and both the GeeBee R-1 and R-2 were wrecked.

The Shell Speed Dash — 4 alternate-direction passes over the 2-km. course — was won by Turner at an average speed of 280.347 mph, just ahead of Jimmy Wedell at 278.92 mph and Lee Gehlbach at 251.93 mph, all in Wedell Williams racers.

In the Thompson Trophy Race (10 laps of the 10-mile course) Roscoe Turner was disqualified for failing to circle a cut pylon immediately, thus depriving him of a double win and Wedell Williams of a 1-2-3 sweep. As it was, Jimmy Wedell won at 237.95 mph, Lee Gehlbach was 2nd at 224.95 mph, both in Wedells, while Roy Minor was 3rd in Benny Howard's *Mike* at 199.87 mph.

1934 Cleveland National Air Races

The success or failure of an air race can be judged in several ways. If a large crowd comes through the ticket gates and the event shows a profit, it's a success. If the races are highly competitive and safe, it's a success. If the press coverage is extensive and more positive than negative, it's a success. And if there is a lot of creativity and originality on display among the raceplanes, it has to be considered successful. Conversely, if two or more of these criteria are not met, then the hoped-for success has not been achieved.[5]

At Cleveland, it was a decidedly mixed bag, leaning toward success. While most of the signs of success were present, there were few new or significantly modified airplanes on the field, and the new ones made little impact on the outcome of races or on future designs.

Steve Wittman's V-12-powered *Bonzo* hadn't been sufficiently tested, and was kept at home.

The Keith Rider R-3 *Marcoux-Bromberg* nosed over at the start of the Bendix Transcontinental Derby, killing pilot Jim Granger.

Benny Howard's big radial-engined, high-wing *Mr. Mulligan* was damaged at the start of the Bendix Race.

The Granville-Miller-Delackner R-6 *Q.E.D.*— sort of a stretched GeeBee — started the Bendix but failed to finish before the deadline for arrivals.

The Brown B-2 *Miss Los Angeles* was flown to second place in the Thompson Trophy Race by Roy Minor.

The 2,042-mile Bendix Race from Los Angeles to Cleveland attracted only five starters, one of its poorest showings. Doug Davis, winner of the historic 1929 Thompson Cup Race, won at 216.24 mph in the #44 Wedell Williams, arriving a half hour before J.A. Worthen in the #45 Wedell Williams, whose speed was 203.21 mph. This was hardly a sign of progress.

Qualifying for the pylon races consisted of a series of runs over a straight 2-km. speed course, called the Shell Speed Dash. Tops, with an American record, was Doug Davis in his Bendix winner at 306.22 mph. Close behind were Roscoe Turner in the #57 Wedell Williams at 295.47 mph, and Worthen in the #45 at 292.14 mph.

The new Greve Trophy Race was for airplanes having no more than 550 cu. in piston displacement. It was sponsored by the Cleveland Pneumatic Tool Co., and consisted of three heats, each of 6 laps around the 5-mile course, with the winner being decided on points. The winner was Lee Miles, in the Miles & Atwood Special, with two pilots tied for second: Roger Don Rae (#131 Keith Rider *San Francisco*) and Art Chester (#15 Chester *Jeep*).

In the Thompson Trophy Race, already a classic, Roscoe Turner got his first win, flying the 100 miles at 248.13 mph. On lap eight, co-favorite Doug Davis cut a pylon in his #44 Wedell Williams, circled it as the rules required, turned too tightly, snap-rolled and spun into the ground. His brief but brilliant career ended at age 29. In second place was Minor in the Brown B-2 at 214.93 mph, almost three miles back at the finish.

Chapter 15

The 1934 MacRobertson Race: The World's Greatest Air Race?

The 1934 London-to-Melbourne Race

Any race that stretches 11,300 miles and attracts 64 entries from 12 countries must rank high on the list of "the world's greatest air races" even if only one-third of those entered started, and barely half of those finished. The longest cross-country race was sponsored by Sir MacPherson Robertson as part of an Australia anniversary celebration. No race before or since has been able to excite the world's press and public as did this one.[1]

While it was won in fine style by two men flying a specially built British long-distance racer, the second and third placers flew standard twin-engined airliners built in the U.S. Had the purpose been to demonstrate the rapidly advancing state of long-range airline flying, it would have achieved its goal in grand style.

But as the point of the flamboyant exercise was to show the world that Australia was not as far from the Mother Country as it seemed, men and women from Europe, North America and Australia began making plans to conquer the many obstacles provided by flying over some of the least friendly water and terrain one could find.

Some teams searched for a type of airplane that already had a good reputation in the exotic field of long-distance flying. Others decided on types which were familiar to them from previous, if somewhat less extensive, ventures into the unknown. Others poured through recent editions of *Jane's All the World's Aircraft* in hopes of finding an airplane with just the right combination of speed, range, navigational equipment, and of course price to give them at least a chance of negotiating the 11,300 miles without crashing or at least getting hopelessly lost.

The ideal mount for this novel challenge would be an airplane designed expressly for flying almost halfway around the world without needing extensive repairs or the replacement of vital parts, including exhausted pilots. But as no such airplane existed, and time was seriously limited, few gave much consideration to this possible solution. In fact, members of the organizing committee were still arguing over rules as late as November 1933, for a race scheduled to start in October 1934.

The route they eventually agreed upon started at Mildenhall, northeast of London, and had required stops at Baghdad, Allahabad (India), Singapore, Darwin (Australia), Charleville (Australia) and finally Melbourne. Optional stops were arranged for airplanes lacking the range to fly non-stop between the required stops. Every effort was made to provide the supplies of fuel, oil and food that would be vital to the continuation of the race. To make it appealing to those having adventurous spirits but not ideal airplanes, the race was divided into two divisions, Speed and Handicap, the latter set up so that all airplanes should have an equal chance to win.

With less than a year to design, build, test and prove a new design, work began on what would become not merely the winner, but one of the great racing airplanes of all time, the deHavilland deH.88 Comet. The design of three identical airplanes, which were to have a cruising speed of more than 200 mph and range of 3,000 miles, was started in January 1934, with barely nine months remaining before they would have to be at the starting line. To do this, the engineers proposed an airplane with a long, slim fuselage, two tightly cowled six-cylinder engines and something not yet common, fully retractable landing gear. Two pilots would be seated in tandem, under a long canopy.

The first flight of the prototype Comet was made on September 8, just six weeks before the start of the race. That meant six weeks in which to complete the testing and then complete the construction of the second and third Comets. If there had been any serious problems with the design or construction, there would not have been time to make corrections and re-test. It was all or nothing.

When the officials showed up at Mildenhall, they found a Royal Air Force base under construction and a crowd bursting out of its limited assigned space. Emblematic of the general lack of facilities was the wind sock, a device designed to show the direction of the wind. Not having a proper one, someone managed to sew together pair of pillowcases, which had to suffice.

One by one, the competing airplanes arrived. Of particular interest were the then-very-modern Douglas DC-2 entered by Royal Dutch Airlines (KLM), and a Boeing 247 airliner to be flown by air-racing great Roscoe Turner and famous exhibition flyer Clyde Pangborn. Both machines provided the comfort that the others lacked, which could prove vital during the long hours of discomfort, tension and boredom.

And there was the trio of Comets. The green #19 would be flown by Ken Waller and Owen Cathcart-Jones, the red #34 *Grosvenor House* would be flown by Charles Scott and Tom Campbell Black, and the black #63 *Black Magic* would be flown by Jim and Amy Mollison. None of the crews had much experience flying their racers, as much of the days leading up to the start were filled with last-minute adjustments and paperwork.

Douglas DC-2 was flown to second place in the MacRobertson Race by Parmentier and Moll (Harm Hazewinkle collection).

At 5 A.M. on October 20, the airplanes were taxied or pushed out toward the starting line. Few of the pilots had gotten much sleep the preceding night, but adrenalin was flowing in sufficient quantities to keep them all wide awake. It was cold and damp, with only the 30 mph wind being of any value, as it would shorten the take-off run of airplanes carrying the absolute maximum load of fuel.

First to get the starter's flag was *Black Magic*, which accelerated so slowly that many wondered if it would ever leave the ground. At almost the last possible moment, it lifted and then slowly climbed into the gray sky, bound for Baghdad, some 2,500 miles away. Ahead of the Mollisons was many hours of navigation without any of the aids we know today, without decent radios, without anything like modern flight instruments, and with little more than the minimum fuel needed to get to their first destination, and also the prospect of deteriorating weather. Add to all this the physical and mental strain of flying with little sleep, and the chances for success seemed to be dropping rapidly. This was, in effect, the first long test flight for any of the Comets.

Back at Mildenhall, the twin-engined Boeing 247D airliner was next to start, followed by the green Comet, whose just-repaired landing gear and propellers had never been tested in flight. Next came the Airspeed Viceroy, a one-of-a-kind "racing version" of the Envoy, a six-passenger British airliner. After that, it was the Comet *Grosvenor House*, and then what was considered the Comets' toughest rival: the Dutch-owned and -flown DC-2, the immediate predecessor of the immortal DC-3. Finally, the remainder of standard

15. The 1934 MacRobertson Race

Cochran and Smith's Granville-Miller-Delackner R6, the ultimate GeeBee, is on display in Ciudad Laredo, Mexico (John Garrett).

and slightly modified single- and twin-engined airplanes got their marching orders.

The Mollisons got to Baghdad in just over 12 hours, averaging exactly 200 mph, thanks to a lack of problems. The crew of *Grosvenor House*, on the other hand, drifted off course and, fearing they had insufficient fuel, made an intermediate stop at an RAF field at Kirkuk, Turkey, arriving almost two hours after the Mollisons. Scott and Black then headed for Allahabad, 2,300 miles away in India, arriving ahead of everyone else after a smooth trip. The Mollisons, however, landed at Karachi, then encountered problems with their landing gear and returned for 16 hours of repairs. They were effectively out of contention, and then out of the race shortly after their next stop, at Jabalpur, where the only fuel for refilling their tanks was of such low grade that it ruined *Black Magic*'s engines.

Scott and Black were soon off on the 2,200-mile leg to Singapore, but encountered their first serious problems. The onset of badly deteriorating weather added to their steadily increasing fatigue and soon combined to produce a near accident while landing at Singapore. But they made it down safely, and found themselves leading the KLM DC-2 crew by 1,200 miles and the American Boeing by more than 2,000 miles.

Their next leg was the 2,100 miles to Darwin, Australia, much of it over

Scott and Campbell-Black's all-conquering deHavilland deH.88 Comet *Grosvenor House* now resides at Old Warden Aerodrome in England (*Aeroplane* magazine).

the shark-infested Timor Sea. The weather worsened, forcing them down to 1,000 feet; then one engine had to be throttled back when it lost all oil pressure, which was often a warning of complete engine failure. Limping along on one engine, they struggled into Darwin, to be welcomed by thousands who had been alerted to their approach. While they were now in Australia, they still had 2,000 miles to cover to Melbourne.

Engine repairs made at Darwin were enough to get them to Charleville, where two new cylinder heads would be waiting. They placed first in the Speed Division with a time of 65 hours, 24 minutes, 13 seconds, which gave them a speed of 173 mph, in an airplane that could fly just a little faster than 200. They also placed first in the Handicap Division with a score of +1 hour, 56 minutes, 47 seconds quicker than their handicap predicted. But as they had chosen to compete only in the Speed Division, they could win only that one; the Dutch entry thus won the Handicap Division.

While all this was going on, the DC-2 had run into impossible weather shortly after leaving Charleville, with electrical storms rendering the crew's radio worthless and helping to get them lost. They managed to find a small airfield north of Melbourne, landed, and sank into the soft mud, requiring hundreds of people to pull them out. They finally got to Melbourne almost 16 hours after *Grosvenor House*, though most of that time had been spent at optional stops which they made only because they wanted their entire trip to more closely resemble normal 1930s airline operations.

Four more hours passed and Turner and Pangborn arrived in their Boeing 247 to claim 3rd place in the Speed Division. The other remaining Comet — Jones and Waller's — placed 4th. Everyone who got to Melbourne had a set of wild stories to tell about battling fierce weather, navigating from one unmarked airstrip to the next, and the ever-present fatigue. Only the Dutch crew, who flew with several passengers and bags of mail to simulate routine airline service, could claim to have had experiences for which they were properly prepared.

The MacRobertson Race was the peak of long-distance racing. The route from England to Australia seemed to symbolize the ultimate in paving the way to the sort of airline flying which we now view in a matter-of-fact way.

But this was not the end of long-distance racing. The Schlesinger race, from Portsmouth, England, to Johannesburg, South Africa, was conducted between September 29 and October 1, 1936. Of the nine crews to start, only Charles W.A. Scott and Giles Guthrie, in a Percival Vega Gull lightplane, made it all the way, in 52 hours, 56 minutes. All the others crashed or dropped out for mechanical reasons along the way, making it a test of survival more than speed.

There was a serious plan to run a race from New York to Paris in August 1937, for which 21 teams entered. Before the race could be started, however, the U.S. government, through its Department of Commerce, refused to issue the necessary licenses, due to its concern over the safety of such an enterprise.

Immediately following the cancellation, a new race was scheduled on August 20–21 from Marseilles, France, to Damascus, Syria, and back to France, ending at le Bourget Aeroport, north of Paris. Twenty-four entries were received from teams in Great Britain, France, Italy, the U.S. and Germany. The 13 starters included 8 from Italy, four from France and the MacRobertson-winning Comet. The top three places were won by Italian crews in Savoia-Marchetti S.79s, while in fourth was the Comet flown by Alex Clouston. Before any more long-distances races could be organized, the outlook for peace was dimming, and attention was becoming increasingly focused on preparations for war.

Chapter 16

The 1933–1936 Coupe Deutsch de la Meurthe and the Sleek Caudrons

Henry Deutsch de la Meurthe inherited an oil fortune, founded the Automobile Club of France and soon was offering prizes for flying, the first of which went to Alberto Santos-Dumont for ballooning accomplishments in 1901. By 1912 he was supporting air racing, with a contest for a Coupe Deutsch race circling the outskirts of Paris. It was won in 1912 by Emmanuel Helen in one of the first Nieuport monoplanes at 78 mph, by Eugene Gilbert in 1913 in a Deperdussin racer at 101 mph, and after the war, in 1920, by Sadi-Lecointe in a Nieuport 29V at 166 mph.[1]

A second series, for a 3-lap race around a 100-km. course south of Paris, ran from 1921 to 1922. Georges Kirsch won the 1921 race in a Nieuport-Delage sesquiplane at 173 mph, and the second was won by Fernand Lasne in a Nieuport-Delage at 180 mph. Neither series attracted all that much attention.[2]

M. Deutsch de la Muerthe sponsored no more races until 1933, when the best-known of his three series began as the longest closed race ever held. It involved two stages, one in the morning and the other after a 90-minute period for lunch and rest, each flown for 10 laps around a 100-km. course, starting and finishing at Etampes, south of Paris. The total distance for the one-day event was 2,000 km., or 1,243 mi. The only technical restriction on airplane design or power was the limiting of engine displacement to eight liters (488 cu. in.).[3]

The Coupe Deutsch was open to pilots and airplanes from any country, and was intended to stimulate international competition, now that the Schneider Cup had been retired by the British. With the maximum placed on the size of the engine, emphasis would pass from the Schneider's brute horsepower to the realm of streamlining, improvements in which might benefit all of aviation. On the minus side, the engine limitation would make it difficult to compare the performance of Coupe Deutsch airplanes with those developed for other races and formulas.

16. The 1933–1936 Coupe Deutsch ... and Sleek Caudrons

May 29, 1933

The entry list for the first race included a full dozen pilots, though Englishman Nicholas Comper was the only non–French pilot, and his Comper Swift sport-racer was the only non–French airplane. But, unlike most previous race series, this one attracted purpose-built racers right from the start.

From the Avions Caudron factory came three: a pair of Type 362 with fixed landing gears, 170 hp four-cylinder, air-cooled, in-line Renault engines; and a single Type 366 with a 220 hp Regnier engine of the same lay-out. All three Caudrons had long, slender fuselages, which would quickly become recognized as the make's signature.

There were two identical Potez-type 53 racers with Potez R-9B nine-cylinder radial engines of 7.9 liters (485 cu. in.) which developed 310 hp at 2,520 rpm. They also featured fully retractable landing gears, which were not yet common among any class of airplanes. Race number 10 would be flown by Georges Détré, and number 12 by Gustave Lemoine.

There were two Farman racers of similar low-wing lay-out, each with a single-wheel main landing gear below the fuselage and skids near the wingtips for balance during take-offs and landings. Number 3 had thin, wire-braced wings, a large fairing under the fuselage for the wheel, and a 400 hp Farman V-12 engine. Number 7 had a thick cantilever (internally braced) wing and a 165 hp Renault Bengali straight-four engine.

Nicholas Comper's Comper *Swift*, one of the few dozen produced that had an in-line engine (unknown).

The Comper Swift was one of very few from a limited production run to have a 160 hp Gypsy Major straight-four engine. The little high-wing sport-racer had a gross weight under 1,200 lbs.

The pair of Albert A.140s looked like Potez 53s, but were powered by 200 hp Regnier straight-six engines. Had either of them gotten as far as the starting line, they might have proven competitive.

The only other airplane entered was the Kellner-Bechereau, a low-wing design with a metal monocoque fuselage, retractable landing gear and the most powerful engine in the field, a 370 hp Delage V-12. Two weeks before the race, it was destroyed in a landing accident, killing its pilot, Captain Vernhol.

Qualifying time trials revealed the favorites in their Caudron 362s: Raymond Delmotte at 200.3 mph, and Ludovic Arrachart at 183.9 mph. Sadly, Arrachart was killed a week before the race, when his engine failed during a test flight and the racer spun in.

Only six airplanes were ready to start: the two Potezs, flown by Detre and Lemoine; Delmotte's Caudron 362; Comper's Swift; and the two Farmans.

During the staggered start, the field was reduced to five when a bumpy take-off run by Maurice Arnoux resulted in a collapsed landing gear and broken propeller on the Renault-powered Farman. At the end of the fifth lap of stage one, both Salel (Farman) and Lemoine (Potez) dropped out, leaving just three airplanes tearing around the 62-mile course.

The first stage was then completed, the pilots rested, the airplanes were re-fueled and all three took off for the second 1,000 kms. For another three hours, the airframes, engines and pilots were strained beyond anything previ-

With a 370 hp Delage V-12 engine, this Kellner-Bechereau was the most advanced airplane to be entered in the 1933 Coupe Deutsch (J.H. Robinson collection).

ously experienced in air racing. At last, Georges Détré sped across the finish line at Etampes after no less than six hours, 11 minutes and 45 seconds of maximum-speed flying, to average 200.59 mph.

Forty-two minutes later, Raymond Delmotte took the checkered flag after almost seven hours in the cramped, noisy, hot cockpit. His average, in the only Caudron to finish, was 180.9 mph. Last across the line was Nicholas Comper, having flown an airplane of his own design at 149 mph for more than eight hours of pushing the limits.

As a spectator event it was a disappointment, the final segment having displayed one airplane on an average of every five minutes, with the rest of the time free for eating fine food and drinking fine wine and discussing why one's favorite wasn't doing as well as someone had foolishly promised. But as a demonstration of high-speed, long-distance racing, it had established new standards. Engines took a terrific beating and some of them continued to produce the power for which they had been designed. Airframes somehow held together. Pilots, though understandably exhausted at the finish, had retained enough of their mental and physical capabilities to control highly specialized airplanes under the most trying of conditions.

May 27, 1934

By the time the 1934 race rolled around, eight airplanes were at the starting line, while two from Italy and three others from France had been entered but failed to show up. There were four Caudrons, one Caudron-Regnier, two new Potezs and the new Comper Streak.

The products of the brilliant design team headed by Marcel Riffard and George Otfinovsky, the Caudrons included three fairly similar versions. The Type 366 was one of last year's 360s with a 217 hp Regnier engine, two-position propeller and well-faired landing gear. The Type 450 was new, with a 320 hp Renault in-line six, and two-position prop. Type 460 was like a 450, but with fully retractable landing gear. The new propellers had one angle of pitch for quick take-off, and the other for high speed, much like a two-speed auto transmission. This simple change cut the Potez's take-off distance in half.

The Potez racers looked like those of 1933, but with important improvements. The 53-2 had a 315 hp radial engine and a fixed-pitch prop, while the 53-3 had a 350 hp radial and two-position prop. Nick Comper had a brand new low-wing racer with retractable landing gear, but a 145 hp Gypsy engine, smaller than the one he used in 1933.

Serious problems with the landing gears of the Caudron 460s forced them to fly with the wheels locked down and covered with temporary fairings that were less streamlined than the carefully prepared set on the 450.

Not long after the start of the morning's 1,000-km grind, Yves Lacombe's

Both Potez 53: #10 (right) was flown by Georges Detre to win the 1933 Coupe Deutsch (Potez).

460 developed engine trouble and he had no choice but to land. Georges Détré, in the Potez 53-2, experienced an oil leak on the final lap of the first stage, pulled out, and he, too, landed. The other six finished the first stage in good shape, rested and were ready for the second, except for Lemoine, who was having trouble with his propeller pitch-changing mechanism; he averaged 229 mph for the first stage but failed to start the second.

For another 2½ hours they sped on, pulling high g-loadings thirty more times at the pylon turns, thus subjecting their bodies and their airplanes to repeated unnatural forces. The beating took its toll. At the mid-point of the final 621-mile stage, Nick Comper called it quits, as his landing gear had failed to retract and the reduced speed was dropping him farther and farther behind. He had averaged 168 mph for the first stage. With but a single 100-km. lap to fly, failing oil pressure forced Delmotte to retire after having averaged a near-record 240 mph for Stage #1.

After a total of 5 hours, 8½ minutes, Maurice Arnoux streaked across the finish line in the fixed-gear Caudron 450 to win at a record 241.7 mph. Masotte was second in the Caudron-Regnier at 225.15 mph, and last place went to Albert Monville in the only Caudron 460 to finish, at 211.92 mph.

As an indication of what the Type 460 might have done with its wheels up in the wings, a few days later, Raymond Delmotte flew one of them with a special 9½-liter engine, to a new FAI World Record for the 3-km. straightaway sprint at 314.3 mph.

Despite the success of the Caudrons, dreams of the Coupe Deutsch becoming the landplane counterpart of the Schneider Cup Race were rapidly dim-

16. The 1933–1936 Coupe Deutsch ... and Sleek Caudrons 119

After placing well in the 1934 and 1935 Coupes Deutsch in France, one of the Caudron C.460s was sent to the 1936 Los Angeles National Air Races, where Michel Detroyat won the classic Thompson Trophy Race at a record 264.26 mph (the late Robert Morrison).

ming. Only one foreign competitor had raced, and he had been in a completely outclassed sportplane. Since three wins by one country would retire the trophy, the 1935 Coupe Deutsch would be the last, unless someone other than a Frenchman managed to win.

May 19, 1935

Advance entries for the 1935 Coupe Deutsch made it clear that 1935 would see an all–French race, with seven Caudrons and one Martinet-Regnier (originally a Caudron). The most promising newcomer was the pair of Caudron 560s, a Type 460 with the new 450 hp Renault V-12 engine. Had the engine not refused to run consistently, the 560 almost certainly would have been a winner and a record breaker. But neither of the 560s left the ground.

There was competition, to be sure, but not the sort envisioned by M. de La Muerthe. It turned out to be within the Avions Caudron organization, rather than between manufacturers or countries.

Waiting in the wings as an example of the creativity the organizers had hoped to encourage was Roland Payen's Pa-100, perhaps the first delta-winged airplane to fly. It had a large canard surface near its nose, its canopy faired into the tail somewhat like the Geebee R, and retractable mono-wheel landing gear. It flew on the power of a 180 hp Regnier engine, but was badly damaged in a landing accident before it had a chance to race.

Qualifying trials of five laps around the 100-km. course strongly suggested records would be set during the race. Yves Lacombe (C.460) was clocked at 254 mph, Maurice Arnoux (C.450) at 249 mph, and Albert Monville (C.460) at 248 mph. Only Charles Franco, flying the C.430, which was a limited-production two-seater converted to a racer, was less-than-competitive, at 196 mph.

The trio of C.460s charged into the lead, clipping off lap after lap (and record after record) at better than 260 mph. Delmotte led at the end of the first 1,000-km. stage at 277 mph, followed closely by Masotte at 274 mph. Along the way, Arnoux set a world 100-km. closed-course record on his seventh lap at 291.5 mph, then encountered lubrication problems and made a hurried forced landing in a field.

Speeds were reduced in the second stage by intermittent rains, but averages for the entire 2,000 kms. remained high. Delmotte won in a C.460 at a record 275.89 mph, almost 35 mph faster than the previous year. Lacombe, in another C.460, was second at 263.60 mph. And in third was Maurice Arnoux, who had taken over Monville's C.430 for the second stage, and then had to make a pit-stop for "adjustments," thus reducing the speed in the 1934-winning airplane to 216.67 mph.

If the Coupe Deutsch had failed to stimulate international pylon racing for land planes, it had provided a perfect opportunity for the Caudron works to show what it could do. Level speeds close to 300 mph on little more than 300 hp — at sea level — was a great accomplishment in 1935, and is almost as impressive more than 70 years later.

With no rivals in sight in Europe, Avions Caudron looked westward for some competition, and found it 6,000 miles away, in Los Angeles, where the National Air Races were held over the Labor Day weekend, September 4–7, 1936. They chose the C.460 in which Monville had placed 3rd in the 1934 Coupe Deutsch, and Lacombe had placed 2nd in 1935. Re-numbered 100, it was entered in the Greve and Thompson Trophy Races, in the latter against several airplanes having almost three times as many cubic inches.

With Michel Detroyat as pilot, it swept the Greve race for airplanes having engines of no more than 550 cu. in., with a race record 247.3 mph, well ahead of the fastest American entry, at 225.9 mph. In the classic Thompson Trophy Race, Detroyat won with ease at 264.3 mph, well over two minutes ahead of the fastest American. Accusations by many of the pilots of its unfair government subsidizing were in error, and the Yanks were chased back to their drawing boards.

September 13, 1936

After its third win in a row, the Coupe Deutsch was retired by the Aero Club de France, which promptly put it back into circulation, no doubt to the great joy of Avions Caudron. The factory acted as if there were serious rivals to be dealt with, and prepared a pair of C.461s, which were C.460s with flush canopies and

16. The 1933–1936 Coupe Deutsch ... and Sleek Caudrons

round vertical tails. In addition, it offered a C.560, which was a C.460 with the 450 hp Renault V-12, and a C.561, which combined the improvements of the two, being a machine with a flush canopy and the more powerful engine.

The only airplane entered by another manufacturer was the Lignel 20, a conventional design with a 220 hp Renault straight-four engine. It was said to have had a top speed in the neighborhood of 240 mph, which would have rendered it at best no more than an also-ran. In the event, the first Lignel didn't fly until April 1937. It was withdrawn, as were the unready C.560 and C.561, leaving the two C.461s and the reliable old C.450 in which Maurice Arnoux had won two years earlier.

Much of the race was flown in bad weather, which proved a particular problem for the C.461s, whose flush canopies restricted forward visibility in exchange for a speed increase of 12–13 mph. Raymond Delmotte, in one of the C.461s, dropped out during the first stage when an exhaust stack broke after he had been clocked at a fastest lap of 269 mph.

Arnoux (C.450) won the first stage at 257 mph, to Yves Lacombe's 252 mph in the C.450. Both then lost considerable time due to difficulty re-starting their engines for stage two. Lacombe eventually won the 2,000-km grind at 242.01 mph, taking 24 seconds less than Arnoux had in winning in 1934 in the same airplane. The latter pilot finished at 229.66 mph in the C.461.

The continued domination of Caudron racers, in the face of vanishing competition, was expected to be extended in 1937, though war clouds were darkening over Europe. Some racers had actually been built in the guise of prototypes of combat airplanes, though it is hard to imagine how many aviation experts could have been fooled.

In fact, the C.460 which had just swept the Los Angeles National Air Races was considered by the U.S. Army Air Corps as a possible basis for a lightweight pursuit plane. A test pilot, dispatched to Los Angeles by future Army Air Forces Chief Gen. "Hap" Arnold, reported back that the necessary modifications to the racer to turn it into a pursuit craft (e.g., machine guns, radios, etc.) would have led to increased weight, larger wings and then more power, which would reduce its performance to that of an airplane already being flown by the army: the Curtiss P-36 Hawk.

1937

Five Caudrons were entered in the 1937 race, scheduled for September 12. Three were to have been the new C.760, which more closely resembled a pursuit plane. They had roomier fuselages and were to be powered by the still-troublesome 450 hp Renault V-12. The other two Caudrons were the new Type 460-2 (or C.462) which were flush-canopied C.460s with a new 350 hp Renault straight-six.

The other two entries were Lignel 20s. The one with a 400 hp Regnier engine crashed in July while attempting a speed record, leaving only the one with a 220 hp Renault which hadn't been ready in 1936. In June, all five Caudrons were withdrawn, presumably because the factory was one of the few which had not been nationalized and had found itself in financial difficulties.

With only one entry still on the books, there was no choice but to postpone the 1937 race until 1938, when the chances of war would either have dissolved or come into clearer focus.

1938

For the May 29, 1938, Coupe Deutsch race, the maximum engine displacement was reduced from 488 cu. in. to 397 cu. in. (6½ liters), in hopes of attracting new designs. Other changes included a qualifying flight of five laps (310 miles) at no less than 218 mph, and a take-off over a 3' barrier, after a run of no more than 1,650 feet. The goal was more "practical" designs, or at least the discouragement of what were then known as "freaks."

Two Lignel 30 racers were entered, both to be powered by a new 280 hp Regnier straight-four engine. One was to have retractable landing gear and the other a fixed, suggesting there was still some disagreement about what are now seen as obvious advantages of retracting the wheels.

In addition, there were two Bugatti racers being built in Paris for the famed maker of high-performance cars. It still isn't quite clear which was which. But the airframes were all but identical and certainly radical. The wing was slightly swept forward. The "Y" tail had intakes in its leading edges for cooling air which would be piped forward. The structure was molded plywood-and-cork composite, which no doubt would have been invisible to radar, had the need arisen.

One of the Bugattis was to have had a single 3.2-liter Type 50 racecar engine, and the other two, for a total displacement just under the race limit. The two engines of the larger airplane, now restored and in the collection of the Experimental Aircraft Association in Oshkosh, Wisconsin, were behind the pilot and drove counter-rotating propellers via articulated drive shafts passing on either side of the pilot. That racer was nearing completion when massed Nazi troops entered Paris in June 1940, and was quickly hidden, to be recovered after the war by an auto enthusiast who wanted the engines.

Again, entries dropped out, one by one, until there were too few remaining to justify continuing with the dream of a full race.

1939

Even though the coming war was obvious to almost everyone else, the French went ahead with plans for a race on October 1. Unfortunately, their plans were superseded by the inconsiderate Germans' plans for September 1, which centered on an invasion of Poland and the resultant start of the Second World War.

Until the middle of July, however, it looked like there would not only be a race, but it could be the largest ever. There were nine entries or rumors of entry, from French manufacturers. There was a Max Holste 20 powered by a new 450 hp Chaumont Bearn vertically opposed engine, and a Payen Flechair, though it is not known which of numerous delta-winged designs was intended. Lignel, which had failed to come through with previous entries, announced it would field three Mistral 30s.

Regnier wanted to enter one airplane, powered by a 380 hp Regnier V-12. C.P.R.A. had two unspecified entries, while Bugatti wanted to race one of its two radical craft. There was even talk of entries from Great Britain and Germany — souped-up Spitfires and Messerschmitts?

As it turned out, the start of war ended not only hopes for a 1939 Coupe Deutsch Race, but the series, as well. When peace returned, Europe was in no shape to be spending money and effort on anything so frivolous as long-distance pylon racing.

The long-term impact of the Coupe Deutsch is hard to identify, except among devotees of aeronautical beauty. The Caudron racers produced greater speed for their power than anything previously seen, and later versions such as the C.560 and C.561 could well have topped the C.460's achievements. Their technological advances led to the C.714R World Speed Record contender, powered by a 900 hp Renault V-12. It was completed but never flown, being stored throughout the war in the cellars of the Renault building in downtown Paris. The C.714R has long been on display in the Musée de l'Air.

But efforts to develop the racers into light fighters failed. And no trace of their advanced ideas appeared on any other designs, even though few 21st century airplanes can match their performance on limited power. And the C.460 stands as certainly one of the high points in racing airplane design.

Chapter 17

British Racing of the 1930s

Aside from the Coupe Deutsch in France, the only regular program of closed-course competition was in Great Britain, where it was in the form of handicap racing. The centerpiece of each year's racing was the King's Cup Race, which picked up in 1930 much as it had left off at the end of the decade of the twenties.[1]

The 1930 race was one of the largest such races ever run, with 101 entries and 88 starters, most of whom completed the single lap of the 753-mile course. It was heavy with biplanes, with 46 deHavilland Moths of one or another variety, along with 11 Blackburn Bluebirds. The only racer was the little Comper Swift, a single-seat, open cockpit sportplane powered by a tiny, geared Pobjoy radial engine.

In 1931, the race was restricted to amateur pilots. Of 41 airplanes entered, 40 started and only 21 finished the 983-mile race. Again, the only real racer was a Comper Swift.

The 1932 King's Cup Race saw a big increase in racers, with 8 Comper Swifts entered, which must have been a large percentage of those produced up to this time. The race was run on two days, with a 622-mile section flown on either day.

Several elimination heats thinned out the field for the 1933 King's Cup Race from the 42-airplane entry list to the eight best, which raced for 206 miles. Among the pilots of the seven Swifts entered was future star Alex Henshaw.

The 1934 race had an entry list including seven racers: 3 Comper Swifts, 1 each of the newer Comper Kite and Comper Streak, the deHavilland Technical School's TK-1 and the prototype Percival Mew Gull. This latter was the start of the most important series of British racing airplanes other than the deHavilland Comets. Small and unusually well streamlined for 1934, it had a 200+ hp engine and top speed in the 235 mph range.

The program for 1936 had been changed completely, with a 1,300-mile race around Great Britain as the qualifying round, and a race for six laps of a 52-mile course for the treasured golden cup. As a definitive indicator of progress, 34 of the 36 entries would fly monoplanes, including two Swifts, two Miles Sparrowhawk low-wing sportsters, the Technical School's improved TK-2, two

17. British Racing of the 1930s

Miles M.5A Sparrowhawk, a handicap racer in the 1930s and 1940s (M.P. Marsh collection).

Miles M.2L Hawk Speed Six, a pre-war racer that survived to race after the war (M.P. Marsh collection).

Percival E.2 Mew Gull G-AEXF in which Alex Henshaw won the 1938 Kings Cup Race (John Garrett).

Miles Hawk Speed 6 racing developments of the Sparrowhawk, and a Mew Gull. The value, even in handicap racing, of an airplane meant for the sport, was becoming widely recognized.

In 1937, the King's Cup Race began with a 787-mile pure speed race, followed by a 656-mile finals. Almost one-third of the 31 entries flew special racers: the deH. Teck's TK-2 and TK-4, 3 mew Gulls, a Comet, a Sparrowhawk, a Speed 6 and 2 Swifts.

The 1938 King's Cup Race ran for more than 1,000 miles in the form of 20 laps of a 50.6-mile course. The percentage of racers approached 50 percent, including Swifts, the Sparrowhawk, TK-2, and Mew Gulls. But as yet there was no class racing, as these racers varied so much in horsepower, dimensions and performance.

In 1939, the King's Cup Race was scheduled for four sections, each extending for 5 laps of a 20-mile course. The event was announced for September 2, but was called off due to the increasing concern that war was getting much closer. As it turned out, Germany invaded Poland on September 1.

When the war ended, the King's Cup Race was resumed in much the same form as it had been since 1922, open to any type of airplane with a top speed of at least 100 mph. There was still no air racing elsewhere in Europe, nor would there be for another 15 years, when the American Formula One midgets inspired the construction and use of the same kinds of racers that had been in action on the western side of the Atlantic Ocean for many years.

Chapter 18

The 1935–1939 U.S. National Air Races: Dwindling Participation

1935 Cleveland National Air Races

It was called the "Benny Howard National Air Races." Neither before nor since has a major air racing program been so completely dominated by the airplanes designed and built by the same person, in this case an airline pilot with a love of speed.[1]

In the Bendix Trophy Race — 2,042 miles from Los Angeles to Cleveland — the closest long-distance race in history was won by Howard, flying his DGA-6 *Mr. Mulligan*, a white, high-wing monoplane that would later be developed into a series of fast, comfortable long-distance cruisers. Trailing Benny by a mere 24 seconds was Roscoe Turner, flying his increasingly familiar gold Wedell Williams #57. They averaged 238.70 mph and 238.52 mph, respectively, which were the second- and third-highest speeds yet recorded in such a race.

In the 550 Cu. In. Greve Trophy Race, Harold Neumann flew the Howard DGA-4 *Mike*, to an unchallenged victory by winning all three heat races, and also turning in the highest speed — 212.72 mph. Second place, on points, went to Art Chester in his *Jeep*.

For the featured 150-mile Thompson Trophy Race, Harold Neumann was at the controls of *Mr. Mulligan* and won by almost 20 seconds over Steve Wittman in his brand new *Bonzo*, a true amateur-built airplane powered by a big Curtiss V-12 engine. Neumann averaged 220.19 mph to Wittman's 218.69 mph. After retiring from competition, Neumann became an airline pilot. Wittman, on the other hand, developed the airport at Oshkosh, Wisconsin, invented and patented clever landing-gear designs, and created a string of original racers which he continued to fly into his 80s.

This was not a good year for new designs, continuing the steady erosion of that vital element in air racing.

Lee Miles flew the sole Seversky SEV-3M into 5th place in the Thompson Trophy Race at 193.59 mph; it was the only floatplane ever to race in the classic event. This was one of several prototypes built by the Russian émigré who was bent on developing a pursuit plane for the Army Air Corps.

The only other new racer at Cleveland was the Delgado *Maid*, built by a New Orleans aviation trade school and powered by a 700 hp Curtiss Conqueror V-12. It made but a single test flight before dropping out of the National Air Races. The closeness of the major races provided a distraction from the shrinking schedule of events. Aside from the Bendix, Greve and Thompson Trophy Races, there were no other cross-country races and only nine other pylon races, spread over three days.

A few months before the Cleveland Races, a committee of air racing experts, headed up by Jimmy Doolittle, sat down to take a calm, measured look at the immediate and long-range outlook for the sport. They agreed that the situation was bad and deteriorating, and that without drastic action, the National Air Races might not have more than two or three years to live. The suggestions they made were directed at what they saw as the major problems: cost, lack of safety and lack of supporting races around the country. Among their proposed solutions: a 1,000-mile race similar to France's Coupe Deutsch, a round-the-U.S. race, and events stressing range and load-carrying, as well as speed.

The only proposal that was ever enacted, and then not for 12 years, was for small, low-powered "midget" racers that could use a short course entirely in view of the crowd spectators and out of sight of the thousands of non-paying observers. Otherwise, things were left as they were.

1936 Los Angeles National Air Races

All the major races produced shocks which had nothing to do with the shift of the site from Cleveland, where major construction work was in progress, to Los Angeles.[2]

In the Bendix Trophy Race, of 2,466 miles from Bendix, N.J., the favorites all dropped out. Ben Howard in his *Mr. Mulligan* crashed in New Mexico, Joe Jacobson jumped from his Northrop Gamma when its engine exploded, and Lee Miles failed to finish in the *Q.E.D.* In their absence, an experienced team of women — Louise Thaden and Blanche Noyes in a factory-built Staggerwing Beechcraft — cruised across the finish line at the lowest winning speed in Bendix history: 165.35 mph. Not far back was another veteran racer, Laura Ingalls, in a Lockheed Orion at 157.47 mph.

When they got down to business at Mines Field, Frenchman Michel Detroyat and his Caudron C.460 took charge, winning both the Greve and Thompson races in the sleek, dark blue airplane that was able to out-run American airplanes having far more power. In the Greve Race (now with a more conventional formula of a single race) he won by more than two minutes over Harold Neumann in the Folkerts *Toots*, and set a Greve record at 247.30 mph despite having the smallest engine in the race. In the Thompson, Detroyat won at a record 264.26 mph, by almost 10 miles ahead of Earl Ortman in the Marcoux-Bromberg, which had an engine of twice the piston displacement.

Many Americans protested what they insisted must be Detroyat's government subsidization of his airplane and engine. The French denied this, and nothing has come to light to support the claim. The Americans had simply been beaten by a fine pilot flying the best engine/airplane combination the National Air Races had yet seen.

The victory by the French produced bushels of news coverage, but the fact remained that the only new airplanes at Los Angeles were the aforementioned *Toots* and the Douglas DC-2 airliner that had been flown into fourth place in the Bendix Race by George Pomeroy. Concern deepened over the outlook for air racing. Where were the clever new designs that had long fascinated the public and given the races some justification for their existence beyond entertainment and the boosting of aviation in general?

1937 Cleveland National Air Races

Back to Cleveland's new and improved airport, where the crowd was greeted by several important new airplanes which eased some of the fears that originality had vanished from the scene.[3]

Roscoe Turner, who had competed with considerable success in a Wedell Williams Racer, finally had his new machine ready: the #29 Laird-Turner LTR-14 *Meteor*, a mid-wing with a big Pratt & Whitney Twin Wasp engine rated at 1,000 hp. The detail design of such parts as air scoops and fairings was excellent, as was the speed potential. Veteran designer/builder Clayton Folkerts had his new SK-3 Jupiter *Pride of Lemont*. With a very slim fuselage, small wings and 350 hp in-line engine, it suggested an American version of the Caudron C.460; it would be flown by Rudy Kling. The third interesting newcomer was Keith Rider's R-4, similar to the Folkerts in size, shape and power.

The Bendix Race from Los Angeles saw the breaking of a record that had stood since 1932, when Frank Fuller averaged 258.24 mph to win by almost two hours over Earl Ortman in the Keith Rider R-3. In a hint of things to come, Fuller was flying a factory prototype Seversky SEV-S2, which would eventually lead to many thousands of P-47 Thunderbolt fighters. In fact, of the six finishers, only Ortman would fly a purpose-built racer.

In the 100-mile race for airplanes with limited-displacement engines, Rudy Kling and Steve Wittman (flying his re-engined *Chief Oshkosh*) put on a very exciting race, with Kling winning out by just a minute, 232.27 mph to 231.99 mph, and with Roger Don Rae 3rd in the new Rider R-4 at 231.59 mph. While not as fast as Michel Detroyat was last year, the closeness more than made up for the lack of speed.

For almost 20 laps of the 10-mile course, Kling and Ortman battled for the priceless Thompson Trophy, with the latter holding a slight lead as they bore down on the finish line. Kling, flying higher than his rival, pushed the nose of his racer down to pick up some speed, edging into the lead and winning by 0.6 seconds, 256.91 mph to 256.86 mph, in the closest finish for any major pylon race. The huge crowd roared its approval.

1938 Cleveland National Air Races

There was but one new racer at Cleveland, Art Chester's Caudron-inspired *Goon*, with a hot Menasco 6-cylinder engine and a two-position propeller like the French racer. The only other interesting development was the result of hard work by future Lockheed test pilot Tony LeVier to boost the power and reliability of the Menasco engine in the Keith Rider R-4 to previously unheard of levels in what had been re-named the Schoenfeldt *Firecracker*.[4]

The Bendix Race returned to its pattern of the early 1930s with the entry list heavy with factory-built airplanes. Not one of the six finishers flew a custom-built racer, and the first two across the finish line were in Seversky military prototypes flown by winner Jackie Cochran and runner-up Frank Fuller, of the Fuller Paint Co. family. Cochran's winning speed of 249.77 mph was only a little slower than Fuller's 1937 record.

The Americans were embarrassed by Detroyat's easy win in the 1936 Greve Trophy Race, so they went to work. In the 1938 race, winner LeVier broke the old record by 3½ mph, as he edged Art Chester by 5 seconds: 250.89 mph to 250.42 mph. The lessons had been well learned.

The bugs had been worked out of Roscoe Turner's mighty *Meteor* in time for the 300-mile Thompson Trophy Race. After more than an hour of high gs around the many pylon turns on 30 laps, Turner won by almost 1½ laps, setting the pre-war record of 283.42 mph. Earl Ortman was 2nd at 269.72 mph, which also broke Detroyat's mark. Turner became the first to win the Thompson twice.

While three significant new racers was a lot better than none, was it enough to keep the crowds coming back?

1939 Cleveland National Air Races

September 1— massed Nazi German armies crash across the Polish border to begin the Second World War.[5]

September 2 — 4,000 miles to the west, the final pre-war National Air Races open with the finish of the Bendix Trophy Race from Los Angeles, crossing an America still convinced it could remain neutral.

In the Bendix, Frank Fuller became the first pilot to win twice, as he guided

18. The 1935–1939 U.S. National Air Races

Frank Fuller's #77 Seversky SEV-S2, in which he won the 1937 and 1939 Bendix Trophy Races (John Sunyak collection).

Tony LeVier won the 1938 Greve Trophy Race in the #70 Keith Rider R-4 Schoenfeldt *Firecracker* (John Sunyak collection).

his Seversky over the finish line more than an hour ahead of Arthur Bussy in the novel Bellanca tri-motor which used two different types of engines. Fuller's speed of 282.10 mph was 14 mph faster than the 1937 record and would stand until the war had ended.

The 200-mile Greve Trophy Race was a hot battle between Art Chester and

Roscoe Turner's Pesco Special carried him to consecutive Thompson Trophy wins in 1938 and 1939 (John Sunyak collection).

Tony LeVier, both speeding much faster than the old record. Chester hung on to win at 263.39 mph, while LeVier, who averaged 272 mph for the first 10 laps, encountered engine trouble and could not finish.

The last of the "great" Thompson Trophy Races was won by Roscoe Turner, finishing more than two minutes ahead of runner-up LeVier, whose 272.54 mph was the fastest yet around the pylons by anyone but Turner. The latter became the only pilot to win the Thompson in consecutive years, and three times. Upon accepting the hefty bronze trophy, the flamboyant Turner stood on the announcers' stand resplendent in his waxed moustache and self-designed powder blue uniform, and retired from air racing.

It was the end of an era, the end of what much later would become known as the "Golden Age of Air Racing." It had been a glorious time when a couple of guys in a garage workshop could challenge not only their peers but the immutable laws of aerodynamics. Out of this came a string of amateur-built racing airplanes that could easily outrun the fastest pursuit planes the army and navy could field. More important, it gave Depression-era opportunities to talented designers and builders and pilots whose subsequent contributions to the war effort would prove priceless. And it gave tens of thousands of ordinary persons some respite from bread lines and unfulfilled dreams.

Section Three: Post–World War II

Chapter 19
The 1946–1949 Cleveland National Air Races

1946 National Air Races — August 31–September 2

Cleveland Municipal Airport, on the west side of Ohio's largest city, returned to its perch as the home of air racing on Labor Day weekend 1946. The site of so much pre-war derring-do by the likes of Jimmy Doolittle (now an army general), Roscoe Turner (now a Beechcraft dealer), Art Chester (who had built spinners for thousands of Mustang fighters) and Jackie Cochran (who had led the women of the WASPs ferrying the largest and most powerful military airplanes), once again played host to the National Air Races.[1]

And while the name was the same, and some of the old pilots were back in action, almost everything else had changed. The setting had been moved to the south side of the airport, its traditional location having been taken over by the greatly expanded laboratories of the National Advisory Committee on Aeronautics (NACA, later NASA). New grandstands were erected near a huge factory that had built wings for many hundreds of B-24 Liberator heavy bombers.

By far the most prominent changes were to be seen among the raceplanes. Gone were the colorful, custom-built Wedell Williams and Keith Riders and Lairds and Howards. In their place were war-surplus airplanes that had been stripped of much of their military gear and given a few stripes of bright paint to distinguish them from the thousands of others built in vast factories. There were twin-boomed Lockheed P-38 Lightnings, and mid-engined Bell P-39 Airacobras and P-63 Kingcobras, and P-51 Mustangs and F4U Corsairs, almost new and costing their new owners no more than $2,000, including full fuel tanks.

What brought them to Cleveland, in addition to nostalgia and tradition, were the classic trophies from Thompson Products and Bendix, along with the prospect of cheers of enormous crowds and the opportunity to show off their combat-honed skills and bravery. What brought the crowds out was the rare chance to see the famous airplanes that had played such a vital role in winning a terrible war, and see them not parked behind fences or in museums, but in action and at close range, without having to worry about dodging bullets and shrapnel.

The new breed of racing planes offered more speed and sturdier structures than anything seen previously. They were faster and they were safer and there were thousands of pilots who had learned to fly them under the most trying of conditions, and so well knew their good points and bad. Gone were the days when a pilot was lucky to have an hour's experience prior to his first race: these guys and gals were professionals. Gone also was the atmosphere of creativity and intense personal involvement that had made the pre-war races so meaningful.

The first event, as usual, was the Bendix Trophy Race, a 2,048-mile dash from Los Angeles to Cleveland which would establish the national stature of the races. A record 22 pilots started, and a record 17 finished. They flew 14 P-38s, 4 P-51s, 2 P-63s, a Douglas A-26 attack bomber and a navy Corsair. They had radios to keep track of the weather ahead, and a full panel of the latest in instruments, as well as scores of hours of bad-weather flying experience.

Not for the first time, careful planning and preparation paid off, for the winner and runner-up were both Bendix veterans. Paul Mantz, who had flown a Lockheed Orion to third place in 1939, took the trophy in an early-model Mustang whose wings had been sealed to contain enough fuel to make the entire trip without carrying drag-producing drop tanks. He climbed to the predetermined best cruising altitude and bore eastward, arriving in Cleveland after a flight lasting 4 hours, 42 minutes. His average speed of 435.501 mph broke Frank Fuller's 1939 record by almost three hours and more than 150 mph.

Less than 10 minutes behind Mantz was 1938 Bendix winner Jackie Cochran, in a similar airplane, at 421 mph. To at least temporarily settle the long-debated question about which were the fastest of the mass-produced fighters, the four Mustangs took the first four places, though the fourth was just 2½ minutes quicker than the fastest of the Lightnings. All that the spectators could see of the Bendix was the final dash across the finish line, but that was enough to set the stage for what followed.

Preliminary pylon races helped to fill out the thin schedule of competition. In the Sohio Trophy Race for those who failed to qualify for the Thompson, Dale Fulton edged pre-war veteran racer Bill Ong, both flying Mustangs, by 352.8 mph to 345.9 mph, to set a short-lived National Air Races speed record. The other race was for women pilots, who still were not permitted to race around closed courses with men. Flying North American AT-6 and SNJ advanced trainers, five of them raced for five laps around a 15-mile course, with Margaret Hurlburt winning at 200.59 mph, finishing less than one second ahead of Jane Page.

With the preliminaries neatly disposed of, it was time for the race the fans had come to see: the one for the classic Thompson Trophy. In the last Cleveland Races, seven years before, Roscoe Turner had qualified at a record 297.767 mph and then beaten Tony LeVier by more than two minutes, and a full lap, as he won at 282.54 mph. It was considered a certainty that all the records would be broken, and by large margins, thanks to the unprecedented, war-stimulated advances in engines, fuels, propellers and aerodynamics.

Alvin "Tex" Johnston, a Bell Aircraft test pilot, broke Turner's qualifying record by 111 mph (at 409 mph) in the P-39 *Cobra II*, which had been modified and prepared by Bell factory experts. His closest rival was George Welch, a North American Aviation test pilot (and an army pilot who shot down several Japanese airplanes during the 1941 attack on Pearl Harbor), who was clocked at 394.304 mph in a P-51D. Even the slowest of the dozen qualifiers—air show ace "Woody" Edmondson—was 35 mph faster than Roscoe Turner. The airplanes may not have been as colorful or individual as their pre-war counterparts, but they had at least double the power, and far more sophisticated design.

Ready to race for 10 laps of the 30-mile course on Labor Day, September 2 were five Mustangs, four Kingcobras, an Airacobra, a Lightning and a Corsair. They were lined up, side-by-side, on Cleveland's large airfield, and prepared to take off at the drop of starter Earl Steinhauer's flag. This "race horse" start was one of the most exciting—and dangerous—elements in an air race, though it had yet to lead to any harm.

The engine rpms went up, the starter's flag went down, the airplane brakes were released and 12 powerful ex-fighterplanes charged across the field, led by Johnston's *Cobra II*, which left the others in its dust. His two closest rivals—Welch and Kingcobra pilot Chuck Tucker—both retired with mechanical problems by the second lap, leaving him in a commanding position. Tex eased back on the power to preserve his engine and sped along at considerably less than his qualifying speed.

Tony LeVier, by then a veteran Lockheed test pilot, pushed his big twin hard and began to close on Johnston. The latter, realizing this, added enough power to maintain his lead, finishing at 373.908 mph, 90 mph faster than Roscoe Turner's 1938 record. LeVier, flying an airplane considered by most to be entirely too big and unwieldy for pylon racing, placed second at 370 mph. Of the 12 starters, 10 finished, with even the slowest recording more than 20 mph faster than the old record.

For all-out speed and noise, the first post-war Thompson Trophy Race was a great success. But in the hearts of so many of the spectators who remembered the glamorous old days, it was little more than a parade of factory-built airplanes. A lot of them walked out on the hour-long main event. This did not go unnoticed by the Air Foundation, which had underwritten the races and now feared for the future of the classic event if it continued to fail to meet the needs of the paying customers.

The search for a solution to this major problem centered on an idea that dated back to the mid–1930s: custom-built midget racers that would stress close competition, low cost and increased safety. The Cleveland Air Races management huddled with the revitalized Professional Race Pilots Association (PRPA), whose members went to work to bring the old idea up to date. What resulted was a radical idea that was seen as the great hope for saving the annual spectacle.

1947 National Air Races — August 30–September 1

In late December 1946, the final specifications for the new 190 Cubic Inch Class were approved by PRPA and the National Aeronautic Association (NAA), America's representative of the International Aeronautics Federation (FAI), which is the world governing body for sporting aviation. Early in 1947, the Goodyear Tire & Rubber Co. came on board as the sponsor for a series of three annual races for $25,000 each. As soon as the word spread through the American private flying community, requests began to pour in to PRPA president Art Chester for the rules and for factory-balanced 188 cu. in., four-cylinder, horizontally opposed 85 hp Continental C-85 engines offered by the manufacturer to midget raceplane builders for as little as $500.[2]

The initial response could not have been better. But there was still serious concern that the imposition of pages of minimums and maximums, of do's and don't's, would discourage those who had long seen American pylon racing as the closest thing to wide-open flying that could be found. Regardless, scores of basement and garage workshops were quickly turned into miniature airplane factories, as veterans and wide-eyed rookies, alike, began to turn dreams into airframes.

Thirteen midget racers (by now called "Goodyear Midgets") showed up at Cleveland, barely seven months after the rules had been announced. Some were well built by experienced racing people, others looked like they had been glued together at the last minute. One of them developed structural problems during qualifying tests, forcing the pilot to bail out safely, using his mandated parachute, while all the others completed tests and time trials and were ready to show if this new idea worked.

The greatest attention was directed toward the twin all-aluminum Cosmic Winds, designed and built by Lockheed people. Next in interest was the cleverly streamlined, Vee-tailed Art Chester *Swee' Pea*, with its air intake in the spinner. Receiving less attention was the dark red, square-winged *Buster*, which Steve Wittman had built from his pre-war *Chief Oshkosh*. All these airplanes were from veteran air racers, and showed it.

In line with tradition, the Bendix Race from California led off the three-day meet, attracting barely half the entrants as in 1946: six Mustangs, three Lightnings, a Corsair, an Invader and a Kingcobra. The Mustangs again dominated, taking the first six places. Paul Mantz won his second Bendix Trophy with a record 460.4 mph, while even sixth-placer Thomas Mayson finished an hour ahead of the fastest of the non–Mustang pilots. If ever the handwriting was on the wall, this was it.

19. The 1946–1949 Cleveland National Air Races

Bill Brennand's dark red #20 Wittman *Buster*, 1947 and 1949 Goodyear Race winner (Aaron King, Jr.).

Adding to the excitement was the finish of another race from California, this time by radical airplanes whose first predecessor had flown just two weeks before the last pre-war Cleveland Races. It was the Jet Division of the Bendix, with four Lockheed P-80 Shooting Stars vying for the honors. Col. Leon Gray was the only pilot to finish the race, the others having been stopped by weather or engine trouble. His speed was 507.255 mph, as he finished less than 25 minutes ahead of the winner of what was now called the "Reciprocating Division."

These were the only events of the first day, as a heavy storm washed out the rest of the program, which was then re-scheduled for Sunday, turning it into one of the busiest days in air racing history. Leading off while the crowd was still filing into the stands was the first of eight short heat races for the Goodyear midgets around the tiny 2.2-mile course. Bill Brennand won it by less than 2 seconds over Paul Penrose in Chester's *Swee' Pea*. By the end of the day there had been six races for the midgets, all of them closely contested and perfectly safe. The fact that the highest speed recorded was a mere 164 mph did little to lessen the fun.

There were three preliminary races for the Thompson-Class airplanes, each limited to a single type of airplane. Tony LeVier won the P-38s-only Sohio Trophy Race at 360.9 mph. Ken Knight won the P-63s-only Tinnerman Trophy Race at 352.2 mph. And Steve Beville won the P-51s-only Kendall Trophy Race at 384.6 mph.

The women's AT-6 race, sponsored by Cleveland's Halle Department Store, was won easily by Ruth Johnson at 223.3 mph. Two experimental AT-6s, powered by Ranger V-12 engines, failed to finish, though the one flown by Margrete McGrath had led time trials at 223 mph. Many of the airplanes displayed interesting modifications, including single-place canopies and three-bladed propellers, but attracted limited interest from the fans.

Labor Day featured championship races for the Goodyear and Thompson Trophies. In the former, Bill Brennand got off first, thanks to the pilot's 105-lb. weight, and stayed in front to win at 165.857 mph. Trailing by only two seconds was Paul Penrose in Chester's cream-and-green Vee-tail at 165.393 mph. The two factory-like Cosmic Winds were next, with Lockheed test pilot Herman "Fish" Salmon third in the future *Minnow*, and his boss, LeVier, fourth in *Little Toni*. Eight races were completed as planned, with no pilot dropping out, and only two cutting a pylon.

The Thompson Trophy Race course had been shortened to 15 miles, but with 20 laps was still a 300-mile grind. Pilots and mechanics had had a full year during which to apply the knowledge they had gained in 1946, and thus many of the racers had smoother surfaces, lower weight, hotter fuels and modified engines. But the big news was the first public appearance of Goodyear's F2G Super Corsair with its monster 28-cylinder Pratt & Whitney R-4360 Wasp Major, which put out well over 3,000 hp. Cook Cleland had manipulated three of them out of the navy, and another ex-navy pilot, Ron Puckett, had a fourth, out of just 13 built.

As shown by time trials, the over-powered Corsairs of Cleland and part-

Bob Downey's metallic green #5 Cosmic Wind *Ballerina* (Aaron King, Jr.).

19. The 1946–1949 Cleveland National Air Races

Bob Downey's chartreuse and red #16 Mercury Air *Shoestring* (Aaron King, Jr.).

Keith Sorenson's black and white #39 *Deerfly*, runner-up in the 1949 Goodyear Trophy Race (Aaron King, Jr.).

ner Dick Becker were the favorites to win, along with *Cobra II* pilot Jay Deming. They took the lead at the start, traded off positions, and settle down to the order of Cleland, Becker, and Deming, with some laps run off at over 400 mph. But this time, mechanical problems chopped away at the field, producing numerous sudden dead-stick landings and the fatal crash of Tony Janazzo in the fourth F2G. Cleland won at a record pace of 396.131 mph, Becker was second at 390.133 mph and Deming in *Cobra II* close behind at 389.837 mph. Cleland's margin of victory was a full 4½ miles, though Becker had but a ¼-mile edge over Deming, which was more exciting for the fans.

In the "J-Division" races, Col. Leon Grey repeated as the Bendix winner in a P-80 Shooting Star at 507 mph, and in the Thompson, Lieutenant Colonel Petit won a race for P-80s at 501 mph. Their speeds were of record caliber, and the crowd was treated to something new in the way of sounds, but the races looked a lot like demonstrations, even though some of the pilots had resorted to "illegal" modifications.

1948 National Air Races — September 2–4

The rapid acceptance of the highly regulated "midget" class of racers was borne out by the entry list for the second Goodyear Trophy Race: 24 airplanes (almost double that of the first), as against only 8 for the Bendix and 17 for the Thompson. The crowd was also solidly behind the experiment, having realized that close competition means more than all-out speed.[3]

Only six airplanes started the 2,000-mile dash from Los Angeles: 5 Mustangs and one rare RAF deHavilland Mosquito fighter-bomber. One of the Mustangs landed 20 miles short of the finish line, out of fuel. The others, led

#46 North American P-51C Mustang, in which Paul Mantz won the 1948 Bendix Trophy Race (Burton Kemp).

19. The 1946–1949 Cleveland National Air Races

by three-time winner Paul Mantz at 448 mph, swept the first four places. Mantz, Linton Carney, Jackie Cochran and Eddy Lunken all finished in the space of four minutes, for the closest finish on record. The Jet Bendix, for U.S. Navy FJ-1 Furys, was almost as close, with the first three separated by less than five minutes, as Ens. F.E. Brown averaged 490 mph.

In qualifications for the big-plane races, Charles Brown (*Cobra II*) at 418.3 mph and Cook Cleland (F2G) at 417.4 mph both broke the old record and became, along with F2G pilot Dick Becker and Mustang driver Anson Johnson, the favorites.

In the preliminary races, Bruce Raymond won the Tinnerman Trophy at 362 mph in the P-51D *Galloping Ghost*, which had placed well in every race entered to date. In the Sohio Trophy Race, in which the starting times were handicapped in hopes of producing a close finish, Bob Eucker won in a Kingcobra, Howard Gidovlenko was second in a Lightning and Charles Walling was third in a Mustang. The Kendall Trophy Race for AT-6s flown by women was won by Grace Harris at a record 235 mph, far ahead of "Kaddy" Landry and Dot Lemon. Most of the women had flown in the WASPs during the recent war.

The large field of Goodyear Racers was led in time trials by PRPA President Art Chester in his new *Swee' Pea II* at a record 180.000 mph, "Fish" Salmon was next in the Cosmic Wind *Minnow* at 172.745 mph, and Steve Wittman was third at 171.907 mph in his new *Bonzo*. To give the paying customers a better view, and to make it much harder for free-loaders to enjoy the races while parked in their cars in nearby farmer's fields, the course was re-located entirely

Tony LeVier #3 Lockheed P-38 Lightning, surprise runner-up in the 1946 Thompson Trophy Race (Weaver collection).

within the airport boundaries. It was shortened to two miles, yet five pilots broke the old record.

Four elimination heats and two semi-final heats narrowed the field for the 12-lap/24-mile Championships: 3 Cosmic Winds, 2 Wittmans, a Chester, a Falcon Special and two new airplanes that would soon be well known: the Pitts *Pellet*, from future aerobatic biplane guru Curtis Pitts, and the first of many Midget Mustang homebuilts, from Piper chief engineer Dave Long.

On the basis of his fastest speed in the preliminary heat races, "Fish" Salmon was the favorite, and he did not disappoint, whipping the metallic-bronze *Minnow* around at just under 170 mph. Two seconds back was Steve Wittman, two seconds behind him was Art Chester, and right behind him was 1947 winner Bill Brennand. It was another success for the midgets, as only one pilot failed to start his assigned heat race, and only two failed to finish theirs. The value of experience was in full view, as 70 percent of the prize money was won by the veteran Cosmic Wind, Wittman and Chester teams.

Despite the demonstration of close competition by the midgets, the classic Thompson Trophy Race for what later became known as the "Unlimited Class" attracted the greatest interest. Cleveland-area hero Cook Cleland was in the spotlight and expected to win, even though his qualifying speed of 417.4 mph was slightly slower than Chuck Brown's 418.3 mph in the much smaller *Cobra II*. Dick Becker was third at 405.9 mph, and Anson Johnson fourth in a Mustang at 398.6 mph. The big question was the ability of Shell's experimental 216 octane Triptane fuel to work its magic for 300 miles.

Brown was off the ground and into a solid lead before many of the others had rounded the tall Bendix pylon just to the left of the grandstands. Cleland and Becker poured it on. Brown was clocked at a heat lap record of 413.1 mph on lap 2, and then Cleland at 410.4 mph on lap 3. It looked like the most exciting race in recent Thompson history, at least until lap 3, when Becker's huge radial engine backfired and blew the top of the cowling loose, forcing him out. Two laps later, Cleland suffered the same damage and landed.

Brown appeared to have the race firmly under control, turning in the highest speeds on all but two of the first 15 laps. Then a fuselage panel near the engine, located just behind the plot, broke partially loose, allowing hot exhaust gas into the engine compartment where it heated up a fuel line and created vapor-lock. His speed dropped steadily until the engine quit with barely a lap to go and he made a dead-stick landing.

That left Anson Johnson ahead in a Mustang. He sped along to a one-lap victory at 383.8 mph, with only two others still on the course: Bruce Raymond in the amazingly reliable *Galloping Ghost* and Wilson Newhall almost four laps back in a Kingcobra. What had started out as a thrilling race finished with seven of the 10 starters parked or smashed. The start had been great, but the finish was dull.

The balance was tipping more and more toward the midgets, thanks to the inability so many of the truly fast airplanes to survive the punishment of all-out racing on a 15-mile course. When winner Johnson finished, the second-place pilot was about to start his last lap. The Thompson winner took more than three-quarters of an hour to complete the race, most of the time being out of sight of the spectators, while Salmon spent but 8½ minutes zipping around the Goodyear course in full view 100 percent of the time. It was becoming clear which race was designed for the spectators.

1949 National Air Races — September 3–5

The post-war Cleveland Races were going into their fourth year and the level of interest remained high among competitors, the press and thus the crowds. The midgets continued to whittle away at the emotional dominance of the Thompson-class airplanes, with the women's AT-6s very much in the shadows. While there was an annual multi-class racing program at Miami, Florida, each January, it was much smaller and hardly appreciated.[4]

After three straight Bendix Race victories by Paul Mantz and his Mustangs, Joe DeBona, flying actor Jimmy Stewart's similar machine, took over, winning at a record 470.1 mph. More than 10 minutes back at the finish, were Stanley Reaver and "Fish" Salmon, also in early-model Mustangs. The other three starters flew rare airplanes: a British deHavilland Mosquito, a Martin B-26 Marauder and a Republic AT-12, with the fastest of them more than an hour

Cook Cleland's #94 Goodyear F2G Super Corsair, in which he won the 1949 Thompson Trophy Race (John Sunyak collection).

back of the slowest of the Mustangs. Four years and four dominating performances by Mustangs showed the world that nothing that had been tried could hope to keep up with the best all-around fighter of World War II.

In the Jet Division, aimed more at the national press than the folks in the seats, five Republic F-84 Thunderjets were led across the finish line by Air Force Maj. Vernon Ford, at 529.6 mph.

Nineteen of the big planes qualified for the Thompson Trophy Race and its preliminary events. Fastest was Dick Becker in one of boss Cook Cleland's F2Gs, with 414.6 mph; his engine broke as he finished his qualifying lap and he flew no more. In second was Cleland at 407.2 mph. And in third, at 405.6 mph, was the airplane everyone was talking about: the dark green #7 P-51C *Beguine*, which featured radiators in modified drop-tanks on its wingtips, in place of the familiar belly scoop. The pilot chosen for it was round-the-world record holder Bill Odom, who lacked his rivals' extensive experience in single-engine fighters.

The near-stranglehold in the Goodyear Trophy Race of the "Big Three" of Wittman, Chester and the Cosmics Winds was threatened by several newcomers.

Three of the six fastest qualifiers were in new airplanes: "Kip" Mone in Art Williams' *Estrellita*, Keith Sorenson in the Mike Argander Special *Deer Fly*, and Bob Downey in #16 *Shoestring*. Top qualifier was Billie Robinson at a record 183.325 mph in LeVier's Cosmic Wind, followed by Mone at 181.6 mph, Vince

Bill Odom and his #7 North American P-51 *Beguine*. He won the 1949 Sohio Trophy Race, then crashed in the Thompson (Stephen Hudek collection).

Ast at 177.94 mph in the Cosmic Wind *Ballerina*, and Sorenson in *Deer Fly*, at 177.88 mph. This promised some very close racing and some new winners.

In the warm-up races, Bill Odom (Mustang) at 388.4 mph easily out-ran Ron Puckett (F2G) at 384.9 mph for the Sohio Trophy, though it was generally agreed that neither was giving his all. In the Tinnerman Trophy Race, Ben McKillen (F2G) was timed at 386.01 mph, to Wilson Newhall (P-51K) at 379.7 mph and Canadian J.H.G. McArthur at 359.6 mph, in a nearly stock Spitfire Mk.XIV.

The Women's Trophy Race, for less-modified trainers, was won by Grace Harris at 216.7 mph, with "Kaddy" Landry second at 214.9 mph and Helen McBride third at 210.1 mph. Only four of the five entries started, suggesting a drop in interest even among prospective competitors.

Goodyear Elimination heats were won by "Kip" Mone at 173 mph (when Robinson's Cosmic Wind lost its canopy), Keith Sorenson at 178 mph, Steve Wittman at 185 mph and Bill Brennand at 178 mph. The Consolation Race saw the first win by Warwick, NY, airport operator and Finnish immigrant Bill Falck, at 163 mph, flying his original *Rivets*, which had barely begun its long transition from ugly duckling to graceful swan.

Jay Deming's Bell P-39 *Cobra II*, third-placer in the 1947 Thompson Trophy. "Tex" Johnston had won the 1946 race in the same airplane (unknown).

The supremacy of the enormously powerful F2G Super Corsairs was on public display on Labor Day. The gull-winged ex-fighters swept the first three places in the Thompson Trophy Race, with Cook Cleland winning his second and setting a record at 397.01 mph, with a fastest lap of 406.4 mph. Ron Pucket was second at 393.5 mph, and Ben McKillen was third at 387.6 mph.

This demonstration of speed and reliability was completely overshadowed by the worst crash in National Air Races history. On lap 2, Bill Odom misjudged a turn, rolled over and dove into a house, killing a mother and her young child, as well as himself. The foolhardiness of requiring the pilots to fly over residential areas cast a pall over the conclusion of the annual event and any celebrations planned for the winners.

This marked the end of the great Cleveland National Air Races. But to lay the blame entirely on the crash would require ignoring other major factors. The main sponsors—Thompson Products, Bendix, Sohio, Tinnerman—were under increasing pressure from their boards, their advertising departments and their stockholders to re-direct their efforts toward jet airplanes and away from those with propellers. Even Goodyear refused to extend its agreement to cover more than the original three years.

In fact, plans were being made for the 1950 Cleveland Races, including the relocation of the Thompson Trophy course to more open country, when the June outbreak of fighting in Korea caused the Department of Defense to end its participation in air shows. Convinced that the stature of the National Air Races required extensive military static displays and flight demonstrations, the Air Foundation cancelled the 1950 meet and all subsequent racing activities at Cleveland Municipal Airport.

Chapter 20

The 1950–1960 Period: Midget Racing Keeps the Sport Alive

After Cleveland, Only the Midgets

When the Cleveland National Air Races vanished from the calendar, air racing people had nothing left but the Goodyear Midgets. The huge crowds went home, the flags and bunting went into storage, the press room was closed and locked. With no use in sight, the mighty Mustangs and Corsairs and Cobras and Lightnings were parked. As there was neither actual war nor a civilian warbird movement to create a demand, many of them were simply abandoned at Cleveland Airport to the rain and snow, the rust and oxidation.[1]

Only the midgets could keep American air racing alive. With more and more being built, a secondary goal of the master plan had begun to be realized: regional races. First to add its support was Continental Motors Corp., builder of the 85 hp engines that were performing so well despite being run far harder than originally intended. There had been Continental Trophy Races as part of the Miami, Florida, annual mid-winter All-American Air Maneuvers since 1948. In 1949 there was a series of small races in California, where rookies could get some low-pressure experience and veterans could try out new ideas.

When Cleveland bowed out of the picture, the National Air Races (in name, at least) moved to Detroit, Michigan, where a second series of Continental Trophy Races was held from 1950 through 1952. And while the prize money was down from Goodyear days, pilots came from as far away as Florida and California, the result being that airplanes got faster and faster. In 1952, three pilots broke the mythical "200 mph barrier" in time trials.

Then Detroit's races folded, too. The 1953 season had no real racing in the U.S., something that had never before happened when there was no war to blame. Morale among even the most enthusiastic pilots and builders sank to an all-time low, until they realized they had no choice but to face reality: no one was going to organize races for them, and so they would have to do the entire job, themselves.

The headquarters of PRPA had moved eastward, to Rochester, New York, and so that became the center of all racing activity. Pilots and mechanics searched for airports willing to let them race, and then beat the bushes for the money needed to stage races and pay the competitors a little for their efforts. It was something new to air racing, but it was either this or nothing, and "nothing" was too sad to consider.

The first serious effort produced one of the smallest NAA-sanctioned pylon races in history: a series of brief heats on July 3 and 4, 1954, at the usually quiet airport outside the small town of Dansville, New York. The Professional Race Pilots Association, PRPA, composed mainly of pilots and owners, made all the arrangements, found local sponsors, tacked up posters on telephone poles and talked the editor of the *Dansville Daily Breeze* ("Published Twice Weekly") into some free publicity.

Eleven pilots and airplanes arrived from as far away as Wisconsin and South Carolina, despite the total purse of just $4,000. Particular attention was focused on the plain yellow #111 *Cassutt Special*, the product of airline Capt. Tom Cassutt, a brilliant self-taught engineer who would eventually have a major impact on the sport of pylon racing. He failed to make the finals, as did top qualifier Bill Falck (due to the questionable call of a cut pylon), permitting Jim Miller (#14 *Little Gem*) to win at a creditable 181 mph on the 2-mile, 6-pylon oval course. More important, his margin of victory was 0.2 seconds, or about 50 feet (or three airplane-lengths), which gave the townsfolk a taste of real racing.

Following the Dansville Races, Bob Porter flew Steve Wittman's *Buster* to Washington, D.C., and presented it to the National Air (now Air & Space) Museum, where it has been on display for more than 50 years. That was the entire 1954 American air racing season. Not much, but it was something.

Nineteen-fifty-five duplicated the previous year, with the only race being at Dansville, New York. Ten pilots and airplanes qualified, led by Bill Falck in his #92 *Rivets* at 191 mph around the 2-mile course. Falck went on to win the 2-lap Trophy Dash over Steve Wittman by just $1/10$th second. The 12-lap Championship Race was yet another win for Falck, this time over Wittman, Dick Ohm in the ex-Californian *Shoestring* and Tom Cassutt, all of them faster than 180 mph.

There had been no progress, but at least the sport remained alive. The next year — 1956 — was considerably more dramatic, with three races and one remarkable survival. The first race was at Springfield, Illinois, drew 7 entrants and was swept by Falck.

The next was at Niagara Falls, New York, and drew 9, led in time trials by Bill Falck (208.8 mph), Steve Wittman (204.5 mph) and Tom Cassutt (203.2 mph). The first 10-lap heat on the 2½-mile course had barely begun when John Scoville's #50 *Stardust* began oscillating and slammed, nose-down, into the runway in front of the crowd. His airplane was destroyed and he was badly injured; it was only after he arrived at the hospital that it was discovered he was alive. After several weeks in a coma he recovered completely.

The first heat was rescheduled and saw Falck edge Cassutt by less than a second. Wittman then beat Falck in the Trophy Dash, but Falck took the Championship Race at 200.0 mph. Unlike other recent races, where attendance was sparse, this one drew an estimated 60,000 spectators.

The final race of the year was held at the airport in Oshkosh, Wisconsin, operated by Wittman since 1931, and the site since 1970 of the huge Experimental Aircraft Association (EAA) AirVenture Fly-In. The Championship Race was a tight battle between Wittman and Falck, with the former winning by just 0.3 seconds, at 196.8 mph.

There were two races in 1957: the second of a short series at Oshkosh, and the first of a longer series at Ft. Wayne, Indiana. After a few years in western New York, the center of air racing had shifted to the Midwest. At Oshkosh, the shortest course ever flown by the midgets — 1¾ miles — was ideally suited to the low weight of Wittman's yellow *Bonzo* and its better ability to make sharp turns. He won the 1-lap time trials at 193.3 mph, the fastest 10-lap heat race at 190.8 mph, and the 12-lap Championship at 192.8 mph.

The meet at Ft. Wayne — just three weeks later — attracted the largest field since the national races: 12 pilots from five states. Wittman again won time trials, at 203.1 mph, as well as the fastest heat, at 196.2 mph. But the cagey Falck held him off in the main event, 196.65 mph to 196.29 mph, with Tom Cassutt

Steve Wittman's yellow #1 Wittman "Bonzo" (author).

third at 191.42 mph. It had been probably the best season since the early 1950s, but was still a far cry from the days of the *National* Air Races. The pilots were becoming accustomed to tough times, as major improvement was not on the horizon.

The 1958 season started off with the last race of the western New York series, at Fulton. Indicative of the growing enthusiasm among the pilots was the entry list of 10, including all the regulars. Falck and Wittman tied for 1st in time trials at 202 mph, Tom Cassutt was close behind at 201 mph, as was Don Tygert in *Shoestring* at 198 mph. Falck and Wittman won semi-final races, and Falck edged Cassutt by 1½ seconds in the 12-lap finals at 196.7 mph to 196.2 mph after a nip-and-tuck race.

A few weeks later, 14 racers showed up at Ft. Wayne's Baer Field. This time, Cassutt won time trials on the 2½-mile course at 200.7 mph. His mount was the second Cassutt Racer: #11, a masterpiece of engineering that boasted, at 435 lbs., the lowest empty weight in class history. Moreover, Tom Cassutt claimed (and no one argued) that this airplane was the first prototype in aviation history to come in at 10 percent *below* design weight.

The first two 10-lap heat races saw 10- and 5-pylon cuts, respectively, and so the only pilots who didn't cut were the winners: Jim "Yogi" Williams in #39 Deerfly and Dick Ohm in #15 Ohm & Stoppelbein Special. The third heat went to Falck over Cassutt by 0.1 seconds: 194.14 mph to 194.10 mph.

The fast-learning Cassutt then won his first National Class Championship

Bill Falck's red and yellow #92 Falck "Rivets" (author).

in fine style, beating 30-year veteran Wittman by a full five seconds and averaging 196 mph.

Thirteen racers appeared at Ft. Wayne 1959 for the third race in the series. After one was grounded due to damage sustained on arrival, the others qualified, led by Jim Miller at a national record 209.56 mph. In the 3rd heat, no pilot finished. Ollie Arquilla (#30 *Miss DARA*) completed the most laps but was disqualified, leaving Kit Marsden (#76 *Belle of Bethany*) as the winner.

The Consolation Race was won easily by airline pilot John Thomson, flying Cassutt's first racer, at 184 mph, almost two laps ahead of runner-up Jimmy Leeward in the fiberglass #27 *Mr. Zip*.

In the 12-lap, 38-mile Championship Race Miller jumped to an early lead and finished 7 seconds ahead of Falck, as they averaged 199.2 mph to 196.9 mph. Miller lapped half the field and established himself as the man to beat in upcoming races.

The fourth annual Ft. Wayne Air Show & Races drew 12 entrants, with Jim Miller again winning time trials, at 207.52, and Bill Falck second at 204.06 mph. In the first 12-lap heat, Norwegian airline pilot Jan Christie lapped the field at 196 mph to become the first European to win an American race in 25 years. In the second, Jim Miller bested Falck by 207.27 mph to 204.24 mph. And in the third, Charley Bishop edged Dick Ohm by a few seconds at the finish line.

The 10-lap Consolation Race had barely begun when Bishop and Jim Rice came together near the scatter pylon and out of sight of most of the crowd. Both airplanes, badly damaged and out of control, crashed, with fatal results to two of the most popular pilots. The race continued with Dick Ohm winning at 174.4 mph, and Denny Sherman second at 173.0 mph. But the loss of the pair of experienced racers cast a dark pall over the proceedings.

The pilots, owners and crew members gathered their composure in time for the 15-lap Championship Race. It was a near-repeat of the previous year's, with Jim Miller first and Bill Falck four seconds behind. All six starters finished, and at good speed, but the accident seemed to break the sport's heart.

The loss of two pilots and airplanes, combined with the inability of PRPA to organize more than one race a year, was too much. The sport, long barely held together by the midget racers, went into hibernation. For three years — 1961, 1962 and 1963 — there was not a single class race anywhere. The enthusiasm was rapidly draining away, as was the supply of airplanes needed to fill even a modest entry list.

Something had to be done soon, or the sport that began at Reims, France, more than 50 years before, would cease to be. That "something" took shape in the mind of designer, builder, and pilot Tom Cassutt, who realized that the biggest need was more airplanes, and the most serious obstacle to a quick replenishing of the supply was the long and intimidating period needed to design and prove any new airplane.

His solution to was to make construction drawings to a modified version of his first successful racer (111m) available to the growing supply of amateur builders for the nominal price of $20. If built according to the plans, it would be the simplest high-performance airplane ever available. Once announced in EAA's *Sport Aviation* magazine, the orders poured in from not only all over the U.S. but from other countries, as well.

If anyone wanted to stage a race in the near future, there was a good chance that enough airplanes could be rounded up. If *anyone* wanted...

Section Four: The Reno Air Races Era

Chapter 21
1964: The National Air Races Return in the Desert

The First Reno Air Races

Was this somebody's idea of a joke? Big-time National Air Racing demands big-time facilities—acres of concrete runways and ramps, roomy hangars, spacious offices, towering grandstands decorated with truck loads of flags and bunting, fancy announcers' and officials' platforms, and long rows of colorful concession booths. That's the way it was at Cleveland, in the good old days that would come to be known as the "Golden Age of Air Racing."[1]

But Cleveland was a thing of the past. It was a glorious piece of history, but history, nevertheless. Cleveland was gone and would never come back, at least in a form that could continue to rival America's major sporting events like the Indianapolis 500 and the Kentucky Derby for prestige and national attention.

What was going on here, so far out in the desert? There were runways, of a sort. And rickety bleachers borrowed from a high school football field. And some simple buildings for a race headquarters. And dirt; ah, there was lots and lots of dirt.

OK, so it was being called "The National Championship Air Races." All that proved was that someone had a very active imagination. The very thought of conducting nine days of air racing for several classes in the barren high desert northeast of a little gambling town in Nevada was enough to make a true air racing fan reach for another glass of sarsaparilla.

Except that behind this bare minimum façade there lurked some serious planning. Planning that had begun a full two years before the September 1964 event was scheduled to begin.

The first clue that someone thought he could pull off the unthinkable came completely out of the blue in October 1963, in the form of a letter to the Professional Race Pilots Association (PRPA) from University of Nevada Engineering Professor Klaus Nielsen. He wanted a set of the specifications for the 190 Cu. In. Class (the Goodyear Midget Racers) so his students could design and build an airplane to be raced at Reno in 1964.

Recovering from the shock, the author, who had been the far-from-busy publicity chairman of the barely breathing PRPA, wobbled into action. He sent Professor Nielsen a copy of the rules, along with a request that he please explain what in the world he was talking about! This soon led to the first of several meetings with Bill Stead, a successful Reno cattle rancher, member of the Unlimited Hydroplane Racing Hall of Fame, and pilot of his personal Grumman F8F-2 Bearcat. Bill was the brains, the inspiration and the driving force behind a crazy scheme that he was convinced was about to make history.

Bill had long wanted to see the National Air Races, as had a lot of others. After years of waiting for those others to bring aviation's major spectator event back, he grew tired of inactivity and set out to pull it off himself. Stead was widely known and respected throughout Nevada as a businessman, and thus was able to corral the official backing of the city of Reno and the state of Nevada. Once he had those, he signed up ABC-TV's landmark weekly sports anthology, *Wide World of Sports*.

Not until his operation was on firm footing did he approach aviation people. He soon discovered that the few West Coast racepilots he was able to locate thought that what little had been left of American air racing had dried up at least 10 years before. They weren't far off the mark.

After the end of the Cleveland National Air Races and its classic Bendix and Thompson Trophy Races in 1949, all that remained of the sport was the 190 Cu. In. Class. Following the 1960 races at Ft. Wayne, Indiana, even the midgets, which had carried the ball for a decade, seemed to be finished. From 1961 through 1963, all that had survived of American air racing was the annual business meeting of PRPA, which had become a pretty depressing affair.

All the official procedures required by the National Aeronautic Association (NAA) were being followed without a hitch, suggesting that this Stead guy knew what he was doing. And so the author bravely and perhaps unselfishly volunteered to represent the sanctioning body at Reno, as no one then on the NAA staff had any first-hand experience with air racing. The 1964 National Championship Air Races were scheduled for nine days, much like the early National Air Races. They would include a Transcontinental Race, pylon races for four classes, and the first official U.S. National Aerobatics Championships, along with major competitions for hot-air balloons and sailplanes, all of it interspersed with the traditional air show acts.

And so it was that a naïve northern Virginian arrived in flamboyant Reno, ready to play some role in what he was not yet convinced would be the re-birth of his favorite sport. Greeting him at the Sky Ranch (for it was a lot more sky and ranch than airfield) was Bill Stead, who handed him a set of keys to an elderly Oldsmobile and directions to the top of Mustang Mountain, where the finish line for the transcontinental race was located and thus was about to become the focus of the first official race.

Memories of those wonderful days at the ornate, glamorous post-war

21. 1964

Cleveland Air Races came into increasingly clear focus, as the stark contrast with that bygone era was revealed. The long drive up a steep, winding dirt road, during all of which the car's fuel warning light glowed bright red, ended at the little parking lot of a Federal Aviation Administration (FAA) omni-range station. Waiting were the timers, anxious to do their part, but devoid of timing equipment and even a list of race entries and their take-off times.

This was no time to quibble about niceties. If there was no ultra-precise, sophisticated recording electronic timing gear, the author's wrist watch would have to do, as it was the only one on the mountain top that had a sweep second hand. As for the airplanes, we agreed that the only recourse was to time every thing that flew by: Mustangs, buzzards, whatever. We would write down the types, numbers and colors, and then try to match those with the airplanes that subsequently landed at the Sky Ranch. Later, we could try to figure out each pilot's time and speed, assuming someone had remembered to note just when they took off from the airport near St. Petersburg, Florida, more than 2,000 miles away.

We were lucky enough to have a radio tuned to the cross-country (X-C) race frequency. And soon the crackle of static was interrupted by the voice of Chuck Lyford, whose P-51D Mustang was bearing down on the finish line, the apparent winner. Then his voice faded away, as he dropped behind a mountain, lost his omni signal and drifted off course. In the meantime, a beautiful dark brown Mustang with a big #9 on the side, flown by somebody or other, roared past, followed a few minutes later by a white #8 Mustang, which we assumed was flown by either Chuck Lyford — or maybe another competitor, or perhaps some guy who had innocently been flying around, saw the Mustangs speeding along and decided to join in the fun. In all, six starters got through, while two others were turned back by one of those heavy thunderstorms that so often stretch across northern Florida.

After a sky blue Mustang had flown by, there came the biggest confusion of the day: three almost identically painted, red-and-white P-51Ds tore past, carrying nearly identical registrations — N651D, N351D and N551D. The latter two had race numbers that looked like 69 and 99, which added to our suspicion that we were intentionally being put to the test. Still, we got the numbers and colors down on paper, and checked them when we got back to the Sky Ranch. Eventually, we were able to produce a list of finishers in order, along with approximate times and speeds. For a remarkably unprepared timing crew, it was about all that we could expect, and so we were appropriately pleased with ourselves.

Meanwhile, back at the ranch (literally), the barren land was starting to take on something of the appearance of an air race site, though the long string of rookie problems remained about the same length. As each problem was solved, it was replaced by a new one for which no one had prepared. But it was a first-time operation, and hardly anyone could offer the benefits of experience.

The bulk of the vital officials at any air race are pylon judges and timers, with the latter requiring the most training. Bill Stead found an EAA chapter that was willing to handle the pylon judging duties, and, indeed, continued to do so for many years. While standing out all day in the middle of the sun-baked desert offers some obvious drawbacks, they were compensated with the best seats in the house. They happily supplied their own transportation, drinking water, lunches, pencils and enthusiasm.

Timers are another matter, requiring considerable experience if the races were to be recorded with any accuracy. Bill recruited a veteran crew from the American Power Boat Association, realizing that closed-course airplane and boat racing have a surprising number of previously unsuspected similarities. The author had the great pleasure of serving with these people as their spotter, much like the guy in the press box during a football game who tells the announcers who just dropped an easy pass. They handled the high-pressure assignment smoothly and cheerfully, and after just a few years of air racing practice, stopped calling the pylons "buoys," and the airplanes "boats." Well, most of the time.

The airplanes continued to gather at the Sky Ranch, and offered some stark contrasts. Of the four classes of pylon racers, only the 190 Cu. In. Class midgets had any recent history. Of the six pilots, three had raced: Steve Wittman, Bob Downey and Bob Porter. Jerry Quarton would make almost as much history as the Reno Air Races, by competing in the first plans-built Cassutt Racer. In the last Cleveland Air Races, 24 Midgets qualified.

Jerry Quarton's Cassutt Racer lllm, the first plans-built Cassutt Racer to compete (1964 Reno) (Robert Pauley).

21. 1964

The Unlimited Class (Bill Stead's coinage), with some of the same airplanes that flew in the Harold's Club Transcontinental Trophy Dash, was a descendant of the Thompson Trophy Class of 1946–49, but with all new pilots. Five of the nine would fly P-51Ds, and the others would race Grumman F8F-2 Bearcats, which were still on active duty with the U.S. Navy during the Cleveland era. Darryl Greenamyer's Bearcat and Chuck Lyford's Mustang were the only seriously modified Unlimiteds. At Cleveland in 1949, 6 airplanes raced in the Bendix and 10 others in the Thompson.

In contrast to the woefully inexperienced Unlimited pilots, Steve Wittman had been racing since 1926, and at 60, was already considered the "grand old man" of air racing. The difference was illustrated by two widely divergent approaches to long-distance navigation. The Unlimited pilots relied on the latest expensive avionics, and one could not help but wonder if some of them would be able to find their way from the hangar to the taxiway if even one device failed. Wittman, by his own admission, started out trying to use aeronautical charts "but they just got me confused, and so I stuffed them in back."

He had no radio, but had reluctantly agreed to install a compass, as per FAA regulations. "But they didn't tell me how to install it!" he gloated. The 1" Boy Scout compass was mounted vertically in the throttle knob so the needle would always point straight up! Steve covered the 1,400 miles from his home in Oshkosh, Wisconsin, to Reno over 14,000' mountains, in a single day in a 500-lb, 85-horsepower racer he had built without plans.

The Amateur-Built Biplane Class (soon to be re-named the Sport Biplane Class) was thrown together with few rules (the main one was that the airplanes had to have two wings), to satisfy a group of local EAAers who were eager to race their personal sport planes. There were Knight Twisters, EAA Biplanes, Smith Miniplanes, a Stolp Starduster and a Mong Sport. With 10 entries, this was the largest class, and it had no counterpart at Cleveland.

The fourth class was created for women, who had not been allowed to race around the pylons with men since the 1930s. Stock Piper Cherokee 180s were to be flown by pilots who had previously raced only in cross-country Powder Puff Derby events. At Cleveland in 1949, five women raced highly modified AT-6s. At both Cleveland and Reno, women flew the least interesting airplanes, and thus attracted the least attention from the fans and the press.

Limitations of the physical plant forced Bill Stead to be innovative. This produced a Bob Hoover–led flying start for the Unlimiteds. While it was not quite as exciting as Cleveland's race horse starts that sent flocks of powerful airplanes charging across the field in front of the stands, it was a lot safer. The other airplanes used "race horse" starts from the dirt strip.

An unpopular innovation was the point system which Stead borrowed from boat racing. Pilots amassed points in not only preliminary heat races, but the Championship Race, as well. This produced an Unlimited Class winner who didn't place first in the finals, and the biggest controversy of the week.

The #80 Smirnoff Bearcat, raced to victory at Reno in 1964 by Mira Slovak (Robert Pauley).

When Bob Love was called for two pylon cuts in a heat race, he lost hundreds of points and ultimately the championship, which went to recent Czech defector Mira Slovak. Love berated the rookie pylon judges and their chief loudly, until he was informed that the Chief Pylon Judge was racing and Lockheed test-flying veteran Herman "Fish" Salmon.

Ten heat races were spread over five days, leaving the racing program pretty thin. But this was multi-class racing for the first time in 15 years, and a lot of shortcomings were cheerfully overlooked. If this experiment worked, then there would be time to smooth out the rough spots.

The individual heat races were not particularly eventful, but the mere fact that they happened, and without a single mishap, was all anyone could have wished. The Unlimited Transcontinental Race was an all-Mustang parade, won by Wayne Adams at 319 mph, far slower than the Los Angeles-to-Cleveland Bendix Race record of 470 mph. The Unlimited Pylon Race went to Slovak in Bill Stead's white Smirnoff Bearcat. The 190 Cu. In. Class race was won by Bob Porter in the black-and-white *Deerfly* at 193 mph. Clyde Parsons won the biplane race in his partially fiberglass Knight Twister at 145 mph. And the Women's Stock Plane Race went to Irene Leverton, whose stock Piper Cherokee averaged a yawn-inducing 144 mph.

Chuck Lyford's P-51 *Bardahl Special*, the first highly modified Mustang of the Reno era (Jim Larsen).

There were questions about the race courses, the point system, and the crude facilities. But it was big-time air racing. And it did what Bill Stead had promised the Reno business community: turn the slowest weekend of the year into the busiest. Like Cleveland before it, the air races were not only for the fans and the competitors, but the community. A community that had long been Nevada's best known, had seen Las Vegas take its place in the spotlight, and wanted to return to its past glory.

Bill Stead, without whom there probably have been no new era of air racing, lasted less than two years before he died in the crash of a potentially winning midget racer. But he had built a foundation sturdy enough to survive him, witness the 44-year run of his National Championship Air Races. Everything that evolved from that first tentative effort owes its success to Bill's foresight.

Chapter 22

The 1960s

The first Reno National Championship Air Races completed the sport's transition from trophy-oriented classes, to those having detailed rules and regulations. The old system often produced classes created by individual race meets and duplicated nowhere else. Even the well known 550 cu. in. Greve Trophy Race was conducted only at Cleveland. Henceforth, each national or regional race meet would have several established classes available for its program. Only rarely would a pilot compete in more than one class at the same event, though some moved from class to class.

Bill Stead resurrected the old Thompson-Bendix-Sohio Trophy class flown at Cleveland in the 1940s and re-named it the Unlimited Class without making any substantive changes. The only limit, at least at first, was in restricting it to 100 percent piston-powered airplanes. A 21,000-lb. maximum weight was instituted in 1970 when a four-engined airliner appeared in a 1,000-mile race, and eventually there would be a minimum weight to keep out the new lightweight Sport Class racers, as it was feared they could have difficulty coping with the prop-wash and slipstream off larger, heavier warbirds. As for restrictions on the design and construction of the airframe, the type of engine(s), modifications to engines, type of fuel and additives and design and construction of propellers, it was left entirely up to the entrant's creativity, financing and common sense.

The types of airplanes that have been raced can be viewed as being in several different categories. The largest category is nearly-stock "warbirds," which are ex-military airplanes that have been restored and raced with no thought of winning: C-1, DC-7 and modified AT-6. The next largest is fairly stock warbirds raced for fun and competition: P-38, P-39, P-63, Yak-3 and Yak-9. More highly modified warbirds include P-51s, F8Fs, F4Us, F2G and Sea Furys. Then come full-race ex-military airplanes: P-51s, F8Fs and Yak-11s. Finally, there are custom-built pure racers: Tsunami and the Pond Racer.

While there appears to be no reasonable limit to the variety of modifications to warbirds, most of the changes fall into a few groups. The fuselage: the spinner can be made larger and/or sharper, the canopy can be made smaller and faired into the leading edge of the vertical stabilizer, and the tail cone can be extended. Engines: can be greatly boosted in horsepower or replaced with a larger and/or more reliable type. Wings: can be clipped and capped with computer-designed tips, and can be filled and smoothed.

Formula One (originally the 190 Cubic Inch Class) started out with a mixture of modified pre-war racers and original designs, with the latter prevailing after a very few years. The plans-built Cassutt Racers appeared in the 1960s, became dominant in the 1990s and eventually took over. Other types built in limited numbers from commercially available plans include the Midget Mustang, Shoestring and Owl Racer.

In the Sport Biplane Class, a wide variety of low-powered, single-seat biplanes was reduced to a few clearly faster types: the Mong Sport and the numerically superior Pitts Specials. While the majority of Pitts Special S-1S appear to be close to their original aerobatic configuration, many have engines souped-up to produce as much as 230 hp, which is acceptable by current rules.

The AT-6 (including SNJ and Harvard versions) was designed for use as a World War II advanced trainer by the U.S. Army Air Forces, U.S. Navy and most Allied nations. When it is used for this class, no substantive modifications are permitted, hence they have displayed no variety beyond pet names and variations in paint job. The speeds achieved by the fastest of them strongly suggest that they are quite different from the thousands that rolled off North American's assembly lines.

Bruce McIntyre's #17 Pitts S-1C Special, the first successful racing example of Curtiss Pitts' legendary little biplane (author).

Prototype Owl Racer #87, designed by George Owl and first raced at St. Louis in 1969 (Robert Pauley).

The most recent addition to the line-up — the Sport Class — is open to any amateur-built airplane, of which at least five examples have been built from commercial kits or are under construction, fitting the piston displacement limit of 650 cu. in., with the recent addition of the Super Sport race for those with up to 1,000 cu. in. Types include popular homebuilts such as Glasairs, Lancairs, Ventures, Swearingens and the limited-availability Sharp Nemesis NXT.

1965

It wasn't just racing fans, yearning for big-time racing after 15 years, who responded eagerly to the explosion of activity in the western desert. There suddenly was a rush of interest in organizing other races, to the end that the next year saw five events. Two were in Nevada and two in California; the fifth was in St. Petersburg, Florida, giving the far side of the country a look at the suddenly popular sport.[1]

The year's action began in late March at the St. Petersburg–Clearwater International Airport on the Gulf coast. The International Air Races (promoters apparently are not held to the same standards of accuracy as are architects and pharmacists) were advertised as a sort of "mini–Reno."

1965 Reno National Championship Air Races — September 10–12

Unlimited Class

For Reno's second season, Greenamyer clipped his wings from 35' 6" to just 29' 8" and finished them off with computer-designed concave tips. He removed most of the electrical and hydraulic systems, and replaced the original prop with a larger one from a Douglas A-1 Skyraider. Most apparent was the tiny bubble canopy made from the same mold as one of the midget racers'.

Chuck Lyford's Bardahl Special received the first nitrous-oxide injection system to be used to briefly boost the power of an Unlimited Class racer. Bob Abrams' P-51D had its wings clipped to 31' 7" and a substantial part of the ailerons removed and the tips squared off. Dick Weaver's Mustang received a highly modified Rolls Royce engine and the propeller off a Bearcat.

Any hope of a great battle between Greenamyer and Lyford at Reno ended almost before it could begin, as the Mustang's carburetor air duct collapsed just after he crossed the starting line. The Bearcat cruised to an easy win.

Two weeks later, they were at it again, at Boulder City, near Las Vegas. The meet displayed the effects of a long-dormant sport being overwhelmed by excessively rapid growth. Two similar meets were scheduled for the same weekend, only a few miles apart, and the survivor was run by infamous gambler (and air racing novice) Jimmy "The Greek" Snyder. The airport was barely sufficient for pylon racing, having vital power lines from Hoover Dam to Los Angeles crossing the Unlimited course at racing altitude!

Things started out spectacularly, with Greenamyer finally breaking Chuck Brown's 1948 qualifying record in *Cobra II* with a run at 423.4 mph, followed closely by Lyford at 418.1 mph. Hard work and good flying were starting to pay off. Sadly, the newly revitalized sport experienced its first competition fatality, when Bob Abrams pulled out of a heat race with engine trouble and crashed as he was lining up for an emergency landing.

In the Finals of the Las Vegas National Air Races, the two dominant forces fought it out until the Bearcat dropped out with mechanical troubles, allowing Lyford to win at the excellent speed of 391.6 mph.

190 Cubic Inch Class

Time trials for the race at Tampa–St. Petersburg, Florida, were won by Bob Downey at 197.2 mph, followed by Bob Porter at 187.6 mph and Bill Falck at 184.4 mph. Their speeds were obviously not representative of the potential of their airplanes. Two heat races around the 2½-mile course were won by Downey

Downey-Miller #14 *Ole Tiger*, built in 1949 and still racing in 1981 (Jim Larsen).

at 185.4 mph and Porter at 181.1 mph. But as only five airplanes were on hand, everyone qualified for the finals.

Martin jumped into a quick lead, only to be passed by Downey on lap 1. Falck, his airplane the heaviest of the bunch, got off to his usual slow start but steadily gained speed and position, taking over the lead on lap 8. Downey hung on, never more than a couple of hundred feet back. On the final run to the finish line, the high flying Falck went into a shallow dive, picked up speed and erased Downey's brief lead. The stopwatches showed them with identical times, but the retired, veteran race pilots serving as finish line judges agreed that Falck had won by no more than three feet.

Two months later, the scene shifted to California's Antelope Valley, near Edwards Air Force Base (AFB). More racers showed up despite concern over the promoters, whose advance claims were rarely borne out. There was disagreement over the length of the midgets' race course, but the heats and finals went off with minimal fuss. Bob Downey won in Miller's *Little Gem*, future aerobatic star and college professor Art Scholl was 2nd in the former Kistler Special, and Bud Jury was 3rd in what had been Garland Pack's *Grey Ghost*. Speeds were in the 190 mph range.

Reno's second National Championship Air Races more nearly justified the name than had its first. Twice as many midgets were on hand, one result being a qualifying record for the new era, of 205.48 mph by Bill Falck in his #92 *Rivets*. He and Bob Porter, now in #39 *Deerfly*, shared victories in the four heat races.

In the 12-lap Finals around the 2½-mile course at the Sky Ranch, Falck quickly worked his way to the lead, but then was passed by Porter when he could not coax full power from his 85 hp engine. Porter went on to a solid victory at a Reno record 202.14 mph. Falck was 2nd and Bob Downey was 3rd in *Little Gem*.

A mere two weeks passed before the season's fourth race was run at Boulder City, not far from Las Vegas, and by infamous gambler Jimmy "The Greek" Snyder, whose knowledge of the sport was rarely evident. The physical plant was barely acceptable, especially the battered main runway. But the pilots were so eager to race after so many years of inactivity, that a long list of shortcomings was overlooked. When the speed of some of the qualifiers turned out to be obviously wrong, the length of the course was re-calculated on the basis of an estimate of one airplane's probable speed!

Nevertheless, the racing went on with few problems. Falck and John Paul Jones (#16 Shoestring) shared the honors in the four heat races. In the Consolation Race, Mike Dewey, in the former Foss Special, took the lead just before the finish line, relegating Bill Stead to 2nd in his first try at air racing. The Finals saw Falck and Porter in a close battle as the finish neared, when Porter edged ahead to win by 0.4 seconds.

The fifth and final race of the season lasted almost two years! It was part of a very professional operation at Palm Springs, California, called the International Aeroclassic. Planned as a combination multi-sport extravaganza and a mini–Paris Air Show, pressure from commercial exhibitors forced the elimination of all competition but the midgets. Rain, during what was supposed to be the driest week of the year, turned it into a financial disaster.

Racing started off with a flourish, as John Paul Jones finally broke Jim Miller's 1960 national 1-lap record with a dash at 210.28 mph. Falck, Porter and Downey also topped 200 mph, as did the winners of four of the five preliminary heats. The Finals saw a close race between eventual winner Jones (202.17 mph) and Porter (201.64 mph), and by Falck (3rd at 1912.56 mph) over Wittman (4th at 191 35 mph), both of whom were nursing sick engines.

Immediately after the race, a protest over mandated engine inspections locked up the prize money. Even though the inspections had been properly waived just prior to racing, it wasn't until 1967 that the winners were recognized and the purse distributed by the court.

Sport Biplane Class

This class continued to live up to its billing as a true "sport" class, with a rule book requiring only that airplanes must be amateur-built single-seat

Clay Lacy's P-51, in a striking shade of purple that belied its considerable speed (Jim Larsen).

biplanes. Nothing was specified about the size of wings or engines or anything else. As long as the pilots and owners understood this, and didn't set out to find loop-holes which would give them unsporting advantages, all would be well. But the history of sporting motor-races strongly suggests that the desire to win will quickly become the controlling factor.

Entrants flew standard EAA homebuilt types of airplanes—Mong Sports, Smith Miniplanes, Stolp Stardusters, EAA Biplanes and Knight Twisters—all of which could be built from purchased construction drawings. But there was nothing prohibiting major modifications, such as clipping wings and installing the largest possible souped-up engine.

In 1965, Bill Boland flew his personal Mong Sport to 1st in time trials at 152.80 mph and then to 1st in the 6-lap Finals at 148.68 mph. In second place was 1964 winner Clyde Parsons, in his Knight Twister, at 146.06 mph. The next fastest—Fred Rechenmacher—was a lap and a half behind at the finish line. Most important, everyone had a good time, which was the main reason they were racing.

1966 Reno National Championship Air Races — September 23–25

After two years of fighting the dust and dirt at the Sky Ranch, Stead Air Force Base was deactivated and became available for racing. Any feelings of nostalgia for the site of the re-birth of National Air Racing were lost in the multiple joys of moving a few miles to long concrete runways, vast paved ramps, more than enough permanent hangers and plenty of office space. Here was the physical plant that could accommodate any reasonable amount of growth.[2]

Unlimited Class

Airframe and engine modifications continued. Greenamyer's Bearcat had its vertical tail shortened one foot, and gap seals were applied to the control surfaces. It was Chuck Lyford's Mustang *Challenger* that got the lion's share of the re-work. The wingspan was reduced from 37'0" to 30'7", with exotically shaped tips attached. The horizontal tail span was reduced by 15." The engine received the kind of modification to increase horsepower and keep it from

Greenamyer's Bearcat, at an early stage in its modification program, as witness the tiny canopy (Jim Larsen).

blowing up that had been developed in unlimited hydroplane racing. The result was that an engine which originally could produce 1,800–2,000 hp was able to churn out more than 3,000 hp.

Other Mustangs and Bearcats began showing up with clipped wings, lower-drag canopies and boosted engines, though none yet which combined all these into a single airplane that could rival the Greenamyer and Lyford machines.

An important new type appeared at Reno: the British-built Hawker Sea Fury, great-grandchild of the Hurricane of Battle of Britain fame, and the last piston-engined fighter to be produced in quantity. It was powered by a 2,350 cu. in. sleeve-valve, 18-cylinder Bristol Centaurus radial engine, rated at 2,000 hp with its 5-bladed, reverse-turning Rotol propeller, and without modifications. It was owned by Mike Carroll, who was responsible for its clipped wings, tiny bubble canopy and the hot rod-style flaming paint job, and it would be flown by Lyle Shelton.

Lyford blew his engine during time trials, yet still managed to clock 390.1 mph. With the pressure off, Greenamyer turned 410.0 mph. The Finals was almost a repeat, as Lyford burned up another engine, allowing Greenamyer to ease off slightly, still averaging 396.1 mph and almost breaking Cook Cleland's 1940s record.

190 Cubic Inch Class

Florida hosted the first race of the year and its second in a row. It was also the scene of a tragedy when Bill Stead, who brought air racing back from the grave, crashed into Tampa Bay during practice due to a mechanical failure and was killed. It would be a while before it could be seen if the Reno Races could continue without him.

To demonstrate the sport's vitality, Bill Falck promptly broke the qualifying record with a 212.77 mph lap. The next fastest was Bob Downey, 17 mph slower, and then rookie Nick Jones who, at 192.72 mph, was the fastest-ever new pilot in a new airplane, a Cassutt Racer that was about to become the first of its line to show true competitive potential.

The Finals, for 12 laps, saw Steve Wittman jump off to a good lead that was first overcome by slower starters Downey and then Falck. The latter moved into the lead on lap four and continued to pour it on, rather than settling back and allowing the race to "look good." Falck eventually won by almost a half lap over Wittman.

The second California National Air Races provided plenty of action. Newcomer Hal Lund broke an aileron and barely got the airplane down in one piece. Also in his first race, Ray Cote (new owner of *Shoestring*) hit a power line which put a large gash in his wing. Then promoter Butterfield tried to qualify the Cosmic Wind *Little Toni*, experienced an engine failure and landed so hard that he folded the landing gear. And this was before any actual racing had begun.

Not surprising for a Butterfield operated race, the rookie timers weren't up to the challenge and so all the numbers for time trials had to be thrown out. They learned, however, and things gradually approached normal. In the Final Race, Nick Jones took the early lead, with Art Scholl, Bob Downey and Ray Cote next in line. On the first lap, Downey passed Scholl. On lap two, both Downey and Cote passed Jones. On lap four, Cote passed Downey and Scholl passed Jones. The order stayed that way to the finish. But then an illegal part was found in Cote's engine, he was dropped to last and so Downey became the winner.

On Labor Day weekend — the traditional time for the old National Air Races — a three-class race was held at Frederick, MD, north of Washington, D.C. Wittman tied with the quick-learning Jones for 1st in time trials at 194.78 mph; Falck was 3rd at 193.38 mph. In the Finals, with a battle for first between Falck and Downey expected, the race was progressing routinely until the end of lap 10. Jones and Jerry Quarton came together in a hail of parts and pieces, Quarton crashing directly in front of the grandstands and Jones staggering away toward a cornfield.

When it was all over, the large crowd was in mourning because of what had obviously happened. Then Nick Jones returned from the hospital with nothing worse than a bandage across the bridge of his nose — and the shocking news that Jerry had suffered no serious injuries beyond a couple of cracked ribs. While it was one of the worst *looking* accidents in air racing history, it was also one of the least injurious. While the crowd was still in shock, Bill Falck had won the race by one second over Bob Downey.

Reno's third annual races was something of an anti-climax after all the unplanned action earlier in the season. While it would be the first since the death of its founder, its move to spacious, well equipped and just deactivated Stead Air Force Base, north of Reno, would set the stage for steady growth.

Only a dozen midget racers gathered at the new site, and two of those would be declared unfit for racing; those that were ready to race were, for the most part, veterans of past races. Time trials, while not record-setting, were led by Ray Cote at 204.55 mph, Bill Falck at 200 mph and Steve Wittman at 195 mph.

Those three dominated the 12-lap Finals, with Wittman jumping into an immediate lead and holding it until lap eight, when he was forced to slow slightly for traffic and let Falck, flying high above the pack as usual, pass Cote and then Wittman, to win by 300 yards, 193.10 mph to 191.90 mph.

Following the race, the process was begun for the first major rules change in the class' 30-year history. With 85 hp Continental engines out of production and increasingly difficult to find, the displacement limit was increased from 190 to 201 cubic inches, making the more readily available 100 hp Continental O-200 engine eligible. The change would take place at the beginning of 1968.

Sport Biplane Class

Fifteen qualified, more than double any previous race, yet speeds remained about the same, strongly suggesting no one had yet gone the hot-rod route. Bruce McIntyre, in one of the very popular Pitts Specials, won time trials at 151.26 mph, while last year's champion, Bill Boland, averaged 151.01 mph, just $1/10$th of a second slower. In the Championship Race, Dr. Chuck Wickliffe, flying the one-of-a-kind Clark Dollar Special, won at a tame 147.72 mph, rookie Sid White was second in his orange Starduster at 144.72 mph, and McIntyre was a half second back at 144.67 mph. The class was still composed of a bunch of guys flying their personal airplanes, out for a lark.

1967 Reno National Championships

The traditional opening of Reno's National Championship Air Races was the transcontinental race, as it had been the Bendix Trophy Race, years before. This year, for the very first time, the winner did not fly a P-51 Mustang but a Hawker Sea Fury, flown to a 418 mph average by Mike Carroll, over five Mustangs. He had pushed the big Bristol engine hard for four hours.[3]

Among the Unlimited pylon racers there were two Vought F4U Corsairs and another Sea Fury. Time trials were only slightly more informative than usual, with Greenamyer first at 408.8 mph, Lyford 2nd at 400.3 mph, and Ed Weiner 3rd in his second Mustang, at 399.8 mph.

In the 80-mile Finals Race, Lyford pulled up and out, trailing smoke, before crossing the starting line, his engine once again having failed catastrophically. Lacking serious competition, Greenamyer nevertheless averaged 392.6 mph. Weiner was far back in 2nd at 373.7 mph, while Clay Lacy edged Chuck Hall, both in Mustangs, by just 0.3 seconds: 363.2 mph to 363.1 mph. Reno had already hung on longer than its marginally financed rival at Lancaster, Calif., and was well on its way to establishing the Nevada gambling town as the world center of pylon racing.

190 Cubic Inch Class

This was the year air racing would return to its ancestral home over Labor Day weekend, September 2–4: Cleveland. Not as a civic effort; not as the most important race of the year; not even at the big airport on the west side; but it would return after an 18-year absence. The new site—Burke Lakefront Airport—offered unlimited visibility and transportation access for the crowd. The top qualifiers were Falck, Downey and Wittman, all of whom had raced here in the 1940s; Wittman had raced here in the 1920s and 1930s, as well. They shared victories in the preliminary heat races.

In the Finals around a course that was half over land and half over Lake Erie, it was a classic performance by Willie Falck. Handicapped by the heaviest airplane in the class, Falck needed several laps to build up speed and then to catch those who initially had pulled away from him. He passed Wittman and took over 2nd place on lap 5 and set out after Downey, narrowing his lead on each succeeding lap. Using his greater altitude to his advantage, he finally pushed the nose down and dove past Downey to the roars of the crowd and almost audible groan of the Whittier, California, paint store owner as Falck won.

This was the end of the line for Don Butterfield as an air race promoter, as he would never again be involved in the sport. He had left bad feelings wherever he operated, along with a long list of unpaid bills. While he had added color and excitement to races from coast to coast, few would miss him.

Sport Biplane Class

The class continued its rapid growth, fueled by the booming amateur-construction hobby that has resulted in hundreds of new homebuilt airplanes being added to the U.S. Civil Register each year. As yet, expensive modifications and larger engines had not entered the scene to price victory out of the range of the true amateur. This year, 19 airplanes qualified, making the class turnout the largest at Reno.

Tops in time trials was Bill Boland in his clean Mong Sport at 153.58 mph, followed by rookie Clem Fischer, flying another Mong, at 149.50 mph and then Sid White at 148.76 mph. The Finals saw an unusually close race, with lots of passing, as Boland edged White for 1st by 1.3 seconds: 151.64 mph to 151.31 mph. McIntyre was 0.1 second back at 151.29 mph. While the little biplanes were the slowest airplanes to be raced in the U.S., they produced closer competition than the much faster planes.

1968 — Reno National Championship Air Races, September 20–22

The line-up for Reno's fifth annual meet was similar to the previous one, except that Chuck Hall's #5 Mustang was getting the full treatment: wings clipped, exotically tipped, filled and smoothed, and a water-alcohol injection system for his Packard-built Rolls Royce engine. With all this, it was expected to perform with the best.[4]

In the Final race, Greenamyer held back to keep the race from being dull, then picked up his speed on the last lap to pass Clay Lacy and win at 388.75 mph to 388.12 mph, after which Lacy was dropped to 3rd due to an uncharacteristic pylon cut. Chuck Hall, at 386.85 mph, was then elevated to 2nd.

Formula One

The changeover from the 190 Cu. In. Class was complete, even though a lot of airplanes would be equipped with the basic C-85 engine which had its pistons, connecting rods, and so on upgraded to O-200 standards. The expected increase in speed was about 10 mph, though improved availability was the true justification for the new engines.

To guarantee new speed records for his Maryland National Air Races at Frederick, rookie promoter John Tegler laid out the longest course yet used for the midgets: a 3½-mile oval. Bill Falck obliged with a run at 224.87 mph, adding 12 mph to the old mark. The long-standing 200 mph "barrier" was forgotten

In the 35-mile Final Race, Falck got off to his usual slow start, but had worked his way up to 2nd place by the end of lap two. He then set out after Bob Downey while flying high and a bit wide to make certain he didn't cut any pylons. As the pair roared down the homestretch, Falck eased by from overhead and finished with a lead of several airplane-lengths: 218.18 mph to 217.99 mph, both far faster than the old record.

From there it was back to Cleveland, where promoter Don Butterfield had been replaced by local people. The Finals was almost a carbon copy of previous ones, with Falck nipping Downey at the last moment as he averaged 215.25 mph on the shorter course.

Falck's eight-race winning streak — a record in itself — was on the line at Reno, where his airplane's excessive weight was a serious handicap due to the altitude and resultant thin air. Of equal concern to Falck was Ray Cote's unique knowledge of his engine, which had been produced by his employer; no one else had access to the blueprints which are necessary to extract maximum horsepower.

The 12-lap Final Race started out with Cote in the lead and Falck last. While Falck methodically passed four of the others, Cote had too much of a lead and finished the race well ahead. His 214.61 mph was a Reno record, thanks to a combination of sophisticated streamlining and a little more power than all the rest.

Sport Biplane Class

It was inevitable: the urge to not merely compete but to win took over. Bill Boland and rookie Dallas Christian spent the months since the last Reno Races re-working their Mong Sports into more powerful, better streamlined racers. Boland's #3 and Christian's #99 (now called the *Mongster*) introduced real racing to what had been a fun class. Dallas added almost 20 mph to the old qualifying record, with a run at 171.43 mph, while Boland was clocked at 169.81 mph. No one else was within 13 mph.

In the 10-lap Finals, Christian got off in 4th place and worked his way into the lead on lap 6, crossing the finish line with a lead of more than a half mile over Boland by averaging 175.13 mph and adding more than 23 mph to Boland's old record. The class had come of age.

AT-6 Class

This new class was the result of pressure from a group of men who owned World War II era advanced trainers built by North American Aviation, Inc. They appealed first to the Reno Air Races management and then to the spectators because of their exciting noise and close races. Because of the lack of technical innovation and creativity evident in these ostensibly stock airplanes, they will not be covered in any detail here. While their speeds have gradually risen past the 235 mph mark, the reasons for this remain murky, as they probably have involved modifications which bend, if not break, some class rules.

1969 — Reno National Championship Air Races, September 19–21

The year started off with yet another attempt by Darryl Greenamyer to break the World Speed Record for piston-engined airplanes, which had stood at 469 mph since 1939. Then, Fritz Wendel set it in a barely flyable prototype Messerschmitt 209V in an attempt to intimidate those Germany was preparing to attack by claiming it was no more than a slightly modified production Me.109 fighter. On August 16, Greenamyer finally had everything ready, and set an official 3-km. record at 482.46 mph.[5]

The improvement program for Chuck Hall's #5 was about complete, with a low-drag canopy faired into a low turtledeck, a pointed spinner and lightweight pistons. But most of the attention was focused on Lyle Shelton's previously stock Bearcat, which now sported a big Wright R-3350 Cyclone 18 engine with a spinner and cut-down propeller from a DC-7 airliner. This was the first time a larger engine had been installed in a fighter purely for racing, though the idea had been under consideration for its obvious speed advantage since the 1940s.

Also of more than passing interest was the return of the P-51D #77 *Galloping Ghost*, which had placed no lower than fourth in all four post-war Thompson Trophy Races. As #69, it was flown by owner Dr. Cliff Cummins.

Greenamyer, on the strength of his new straight-line speed record, was even more of a favorite than usual. In the Finals, he set a record for a complete heat race at 412.63 mph, easily topping Cook Cleland's old mark of 397 mph, set 20 years before. With Chuck Lyford retired, no one was in position to make a serious run for the lead, leaving the increasingly knowledgeable Reno fans thirsting for some real competition.

Formula One

The season opened February 14–16 at Ft. Lauderdale, Fla. New airplanes included Henry Watts' high-wing *Midget Monocoupe* (which was rejected for racing due to questionable flying characteristics) and Nick Jones' new #7 Cassutt Racer which replaced the one in which he had survived two crashes. Bill Falck blew open the record book with a qualifying lap at 231.26 mph, which would still have been good enough to qualify for the Gold Race at Reno in 2008!

The line-up for the Finals included the fastest from preliminary heats, but they never got to show their stuff. The schedule ran late, allowing dark storm clouds to gather and reduce visibility to less than the safety requirement. Places and prizes were awarded on the basis for prior heat finishes.

St. Louis, Mo., August 9–10, was a new venue and offered a large population center from which to draw. Moreover, the races were run by the County Police Welfare Fund, guaranteeing lots of free help and free publicity. A new design would get its trial run: the Owl Racer, designed by leading aeronautical engineer George Owl and containing a number of interesting innovations. Also present was Ray Cote in a rare venture eastward; it would be interesting to see if his *Shoestring* would give him as much of an advantage over Falck near sea level as it had at 5,000 feet in the Sierra Nevada Mountains north of Reno.

Cote won time trials at 227.85 mph to Falck's 227.37 mph. In the Finals, Cote was away at the drop of the flag and had a huge lead by the time he crossed the starting line, thanks to a lower-pitch propeller which gives an effect similar to a lower gear in a car. Falck, seeing the blatant challenge, abandoned his usual position well above the fray where passing was easy, and blasted around the course at pylon-top height. First-time race goers and veteran racepilots, alike, marveled at this new view of Falck. On lap eight, with Cote momentarily slowed by traffic, Falck blew right past him. Seeing he had the situation under control, Falck eased off and won by a full second, though it could have been much more.

Sport Biplane Class

Men and women had not been permitted to race against each other around the pylons since the 1930s. That changed in 1969, when a threat of legal action by air show pilot Betty Skelton forced the Professional Race Pilots Association to change its rules. The first to take advantage of this was Stock Plane racer Dot Etheridge, who flew a modified Pitts Special in Heat 2 on August 9, 1969. She would be followed by others in desegregating every class where a woman wanted to race.

The fast got faster at a greater rate than did the slower. Dallas Christian raised his qualifying record by another 7 mph, to 178.51 mph, while Bill Boland, his Mong now sporting an original set of plywood-covered laminar flow wings, improved to 174.19 mph. The next fastest was almost 20 mph back, most of them content to fly standard sport biplanes which lacked advanced streamlining and then-legal souped-up engines.

Boland jumped into an early lead in the Championship Race, only to be passed just after the halfway point by Christian, who held it to the finish. He won by less than two seconds and broke the Reno record by 9 mph, as he averaged 184.02 mph. Boland, 2nd, averaged 183.49 mph. Dave Forbes, in a cleaned-up Miniplane, was a lap and a half back.

Chapter 23

The 1970s

1970 Reno National Championship Air Races — September 18–20

The sport saw two of its most interesting experiments in memory, while Reno produced another disappointing Unlimited Finals.[1]

With a record number and variety of Unlimiteds at Reno, ready to race, the main threats fizzled quickly. Greenamyer was unable to fully retract his landing gear, while Shelton dropped out early. Clay Lacy (#64 purple Mustang) won at just 387.3 mph after successfully appealing a pylon cut call.

Not long afterward, a field of 20 Unlimiteds showed up at Mojave, California, for a 1,000-mile race! There would be 66 laps of a 15-mile course, and pit stops. There were Mustangs, Bearcats and Sea Furys; Lightnings, Corsairs and an Invader — and one Douglas DC-7B airliner, which could easily go the distance non-stop. The winner, despite having to make a stop, was Sherman Cooper in the Sea Fury introduced by Mike Carroll, averaging an impressive 344 mph for almost three hours and finishing five laps ahead of runner-up Cliff Cummins. Only the dedicated warbird fan could be expected to concentrate his full attention for a three-hour parade, and so the future of this idea was unclear.

Formula One

April was a historic month for American air racing, with events at Ft. Lauderdale, Fla., on the 16th through the 19th, and on the Isle of Man, off the southwest coast of Scotland, on the 24th and 25th. The latter was conducted entirely by the British, but according to the American F/1 rules, and brought class racing to the eastern side of the Atlantic Ocean for the first time. This will be covered in detail in Chapter 27.

The south Florida race attracted entries from as far away as California, including Joan Alford, the first woman to compete in the class. Bill Falck, at 229.61 mph, was easily the fastest in qualifications, and proceeded to win both of his races by suspiciously narrow margins. In the 10-lap, 32-mile Finals, he

23. The 1970s

This #11 Owl Racer *Fang*, whose bright purple-and-blue was surprisingly hard to see against Reno's mountainous background (Al Chute).

edged Steve Wittman by 1 second, though Falck was well under his qualifying speed. His methodical program of working on one portion of his racer during each long, inactive winter at his small airport near Warwick, NY, was continuing to pay off for the Finnish émigré.

At Reno, the turn-out of F/1s finally matched that of the best year of the Goodyear Races at Cleveland, with 25 airplanes, six of which were new. Falck tied his qualifying record with 231.26 mph, well ahead of Ray Cote at 224.53 mph. Any hope that the Championship Race would be another exciting tussle between Cote and Falck faded when the latter's engine failed to develop its full power. Cote won by more than a half mile, 220.07 mph to 215.96 mph.

Sport Biplane Class

Souped-up engines were ruled impermissible, as of January 1, thus bringing the class into accord with the other class of custom-built airplanes, Formula One. Henceforth, only 4-cylinder, horizontally opposed, air-cooled Lycoming O-290 engines could be used. The modification of standard types of airframes was still permitted, as was the construction of original-design airplanes. Speeds dropped, but only slightly, as the streamlining of airplanes has a much greater impact on racing speeds than does the increasing of horsepower.

Bill Boland led time trials at 181.82 mph, with Dallas Christian second at 177.92 mph, and Roy Berry, flying Bill Warwick's one-of-a-kind negative-stagger #97 *Hot Canary*, at 171.70 mph. Boland won the Lucky Lager Championship Race at 177.45 mph, Christian was 2nd at 168.49 mph, and Dave Forbes was 3rd at 163.67 mph.

1971

The overall picture for the Unlimited Class was changing. There would be two long-distance pylon races and the usual series of short heat races at Reno. If the former could continue to draw crowds, would Reno be under pressure to modify its format?[2]

The first of the season's long races was July 18 at San Diego, Calif., and extended for 100 laps of a 10-mile course. The field was barely half the size of the first, but included enough genuinely fast airplanes to make it interesting. Sherman Cooper won again, though this time, Frank Sanders was a close second in another Sea Fury. Their larger engines needn't be pushed as hard, hence stood a better chance of lasting until the finish.

As if to tell the world that much shorter, all-in-view races were superior, the leading lights of the class put on the best Unlimited race yet, at Reno, September 24–26. The action began during qualifying time trials with Gunther Balz turning in the second-fastest speed ever: 419.5 mph. Close behind were Lyle Shelton at 418.0 mph, Howie Keefe (#11 *Miss America*) at 412.6 mph, and Greenamyer at 406 mph. Some of the fastest speeds ever clocked during heat races made it clear that the crowd was in for real excitement as the finalists lined up abreast of starter Bob Hoover in his yellow Mustang pace-plane.

Mike Loening jumped into a surprise lead in his #2 Mustang with an unofficial 415 mph on his first lap, but was forced to drop out on the next lap with a damaged engine. Greenamyer upped the speed and took the lead, bringing along Shelton in his Bearcat and Cooper in the first Sea Fury to be pushed hard. Lap after lap, they charged on, demanding their engines go to and beyond their limits. On lap 10, Keefe's engine was giving out and so he pulled up and landed. The others pushed and pushed.

As the flagman finally swung his flag downward, it was Greenamyer, Shelton, Cooper and Balz, all finishing within a space of less than five seconds. The winner averaged a record 413.99 mph, Shelton also topped the record at 413.07 mph, while Cooper at 412.58 mph and Balz at 412.10 mph completed the fastest and closest race in Unlimited Class history. That all of their engines were able to produce full power for more than 14 minutes of full-throttle racing was a tribute to their crews of mechanics. The last race of an unusually busy season was a 1,000-km. grind at Mojave. While shorter than the first long-distance pylon races, it offered most of the same advantages and disadvantages. The increasingly competitive Howie Keefe led the field of 14 for the first 23 (of 41) laps, when he had to make the required pit-stop. Frank Sanders, thanks to a rapid turn-around, took over the lead. Keefe, unbeknown to the crowd, was out of serious contention, as he had been penalized two laps for cutting two pylons. Sanders, in the #0 Sea Fury, won at 346.55 mph, a permanent record for this style of race, as no more were to be held. An interesting idea, it didn't offer enough to draw the large crowds and generous sponsors needed to keep it alive.

Formula One

The first highlight of the season was the so-called Formula One World Championships at Cleveland which drew 25 entries including the first Cassutt Racer with a longer, tapered wing, designed to work better in Reno's thin air. With no other classes on the schedule, it was up to the midgets, which had three races each day. The large crowd was fully primed for a battle between Falck and USAF Col. Bob Moeller (#81 *BooRay*). Falck again worked his magic with a come-from-behind victory by two seconds, 213.02 mph to 212.22 mph.

Reno drew 27 entries, including six new ones representing five different designs. Top qualifier was Bill Falck with a record-setting 232.58 mph. The winner of the Silver Race (1st consolation heat) was Judy Wagner, the first woman to win an F/1 heat race.

The 12-lap Gold Race again demonstrated the value of longer wings and lower weight, as Ray Cote beat Falck easily. *Rivets'* higher weight held it back at the start, and its shorter-span wing was less able to cope with the thin air when turning. While much about Rivets had been modified, there was no way the heavier basic structure of *Rivets* could be lightened.

Sport Biplane Class

The value in streamlining the airframes of standard types of sport biplanes had not escaped the more enthusiastic competitors, and so newly modified machines were appearing in increasing numbers. The top six in qualifying all flew these special airplanes, with Bill Boland winning at 180.00 mph. Jim Hall was next in the new gull-top-winged #76 *Jonathan Livingston Seagull* at 177.92 mph. And in third was Paul Deschamps, flying Lee Mahoney's sleek, all-metal #89 *Sorceress*, with its gull lower wing and lack of interplane struts, at 177.05 mph. The old shapes and the old speeds were a thing of the past.

This #92 Falck *Rivets*, from an "ugly duckling" in 1948, it became the dominant midget racer of the late 1960s (Robert Pauley).

In the Finals, Boland continued his string of victories, this time clocking 181.67 mph, and finishing almost a mile ahead of Deschamps at 175.29 mph and Christian at 173.84 mph. It was clear that if you wanted to stand any chance of making the Finals, let alone winning, you had a lot of work ahead of you.

1972

There was but a single Unlimited race this year, at Reno, September 15–17, which drew only 16 entrants. There were no significant new ones, nor any that had received more than modest incremental improvements. Try as they will, race organizers cannot guarantee interesting new airplanes. The top qualifier was NASA test pilot Richard Laidley, in the #1 Bearcat, replacing Darryl Greenamyer, who had been suspended because he was forced to fly so low due to the airplane's lack of downward visibility that the officials objected. His insistence that he had to do this to keep the other airplanes in sight carried no weight.[3]

The Finals was an all-out race between Laidley and Gunther Balz, with the latter in a Mustang which finally beat the 6-time champion Bearcat, with a record 416.16 mph. Laidley was promptly disqualified for low flying, allowing Shelton to claim 2nd place at 404.70 mph.

Formula One

"Transpo 72" at Dulles International Airport, outside Washington, D.C., offered static displays and exhibits comparable to the Paris Air Show, plus a major flying program which brought huge crowds out to see, among other things, F/1 air racing. While the event was a big success, its future was dimmed by the rapid growth of airline traffic. Bob Downey (#14 *Ole Tiger*) and Bill Falck both exceeded 230 mph in time trials, but a mid-air collision took the life of one rookie pilot and would probably have eliminated racing from future "Transpos," had there been any.

The Reno F/1 races saw the beginnings of internal strife among groups of pilots, with two being disqualified for illegal engines and a third voluntarily dropping out before his airplane could be inspected. The Championship Race was delayed by Bob Hoover's impromptu extension of his air show act, leaving racing engines running and over-heating. Cote won easily at 223.95 mph, while Bill Falck dropped out when his too-hot engine began to lose power.

Sport Biplane Class

Fully half the qualifiers flew airplanes specially designed or at least specially modified for racing. Tops in time trials was Don Beck, in the #89 *Sorceress*, at 190.48 mph, adding 6 mph to the old record. Second was Bill Boland at 187.15 mph, and third was Jim Hall at 185.25 mph.

All went well until the Final Race when, on the backstretch, Tommy Thomas, flying his new #7 *Miss Q*, which had a Cassutt Formula One fuselage married to a new set of wings, suddenly nosed down and crashed, apparently after its pilot had suffered a stroke. Don Beck went on to win at a record 189.72 mph, followed by Jim Hall at 180.38 mph.

1973 Reno National Championship Air Races, September 14–16

Long, hard work by engineers, engine builders and mechanics to strengthen engines was starting to pay dividends. Radials and V-12s, which had been briefly producing enormous power before expelling vital parts through jagged new holes in their crankcases, were now holding together. Bob Love's new #97 Mustang *Oogahonk Special* had gotten one of these special V-12s, along with an extensive program of cleaning-up and lightening. This paid off with a qualifying record of 423.0 mph. A potential new winner had appeared out of nowhere, at least until Lyle Shelton was clocked at 426.6 mph, for another national record.[4]

Action continued through the usually tame preliminary heats, with Shelton winning one at 406 mph, followed by Love winning the other at a heat-race record 410.8 mph. This set up a Finals having as much pre-race excitement as had been seen in a long time. Love and Shelton traded the lead for the first two laps, when Love's engine began to go sour. Shelton continued to go all-out, winning by two miles at an all-time record of 428.16 mph. Cliff Cummins was far back in 2nd place with 417.08 mph, which would have won any previous race.

Formula One

Another attempt was made to return air racing to south Florida, January 19–21, with the Great Miami Air Race, but weaknesses in the planning and organization were obvious. It was another "Falck-fest," as he tied his national qualifying record and then won both his heat races with dramatic dives to the finish line. In the Finals, he went all out, beating Bob Downey by a mile, 224.53 mph to 217.74 mph.

Reno started out its 10th consecutive race with Bill Falck's latest qualifying record: 235.29 mph, followed closely by Bob Moeller at 234.27 mph and Ray Cote at 228.33 mph. In both heat races, the first two finishers topped 220 mph, with John Paul Jones (#21 *Stinger*) setting a heat record at 229.46 mph. A fast Finals was all but assured.

Bob Moeller was off first, followed by DeLuca, Jones and Cote. The last-named methodically passed the others, winning at a record 231.26 mph. Jones was clocked at 229.54 mph, Moeller at 225.38 mph and Falck at 224.16 mph. Concern was being expressed openly about the legality of the airplanes flown by Cote and Moeller, but there was no proof of rule breaking.

Sport Biplane Class

The gap between sporty biplanes and racing biplanes widened with the arrival of the second all-metal racer. #1 *Sundancer*, to be flown by veteran Sid White, used the fuselage and tail from a Midget Mustang homebuilt monoplane, with the addition of a top wing. That it was an effective combination was borne out in time trials, when White broke Don Beck's old record with a run at 194.25 mph. The other metal biplane—*Sorceress*—was second at 184.30 mph, 3 seconds per lap slower. The entry list of just 9 airplanes was the shortest in years.

White continued his dash to the fore with a Finals win at a record 194.95 mph, even faster than he qualified. Beck was 2nd, a mile and a quarter back, at 184.62 mph, just ³⁄₁₀ths of a second ahead of Dave Forbes, at 184.50 mph.

1974

The 11th Reno National Championship Air Races, September 13–15, picked up where the 10th had left off, with Lyle Shelton setting yet another qualifying

Gary Levitz's P-38L *Lightning* was nearly stock and raced for the nostalgia of it (Tom Forrest).

speed record, this time at 432.25 mph, followed by Cliff Cummins at 420.28 mph. Once again, the stage was set for a great Championship Race. Lyle charged into a lead and held it to the finish, averaging just under 430 mph, which would have been a record, except that he was severely penalized for failing to climb to the agreed-upon safety altitude during two separate emergencies. Bob Love staggered across the finish line with a dying engine, then was disqualified for not crossing the line in the approved manner. His 430+ mph speed would have been a record.[5]

The winner, by default, was Ken Burnstine, who turned just 382.5 mph in #33, a good, but nearly stock Mustang, like the only other three finishers.

This year's October 13-15 races at Mojave, Calif., followed the conventional format, starting with an Unlimited race of 8 laps around the 8½-mile course. While it was as slow as the Reno race, winner Roy MClain, in the slick #5 Mustang recently acquired from Chuck Hall, edged Lyle Shelton by 382.21 mph to 381.72 mph. Most of the 11 starters either cut pylons or dropped out.

Formula One

A regional race at Evansville, Indiana, June 29-30, turned out to offer more than the usual. Goodyear veteran Jim Miller introduced the first radical design in almost 25 years, with his *Texas Gem* fiberglass pusher. And airline pilot Charlie Chambers became the first African-American to race an airplane in any class. In addition, local conditions precluded the usual race-horse start, and so a flying start was used — and successfully — for the first time with airplanes not equipped with radios. Bill Falck won the race at 214 mph on a short course. It would not be his last experience with air starts.

At Reno, Ray Cote (#16 *Shoestring*) smashed the old qualifying record by almost 5 mph. The 8-lap Championship Race turned out to be a surprisingly easy win for Cote, as he won by almost a mile. His 235.42 mph was a new record for a Championship Race, exceeding his own two-year old mark, and also beating John Paul Jones' record for any heat race, set two days earlier. Bob Moeller (#81 *BooRay*) was second at 226.24 mph and Vince DeLuca was third at 222.68 mph. The next four — John Paul Jones, Nick Jones, Bill Falck and Jim Stevenson (#11 Owl *Fang*) — crossed the finish line in the space of less than two seconds, giving the fans the excitement they no doubt would have preferred to see at the front of the pack.

Sport Biplane Class

Sid White added another 4 mph to his qualifying record in the still-new *Sundancer* which almost broke the 200 mph barrier with a 198.53 mph lap. Don Beck in *Sorceress* was close behind in the other all-metal special at 195.65 mph. White then won his heat race at 196.01 mph, and had an easy time of it in the Championship, beating Don Beck by almost a mile, 198.17 mph (a new record) to 191.53 mph.

1975

The June 21–22 races at Mojave seemed to be moving in the direction of stability, drawing increasingly large crowds, though not yet threatening Reno's dominant position. This year's races revealed the #5 P-51D flown by McClain, now called the Red Baron RB-51 and powered by a Rolls Royce Griffon, larger and more powerful than the usual Merlin, and attached to a pair of three-bladed, contra-rotating propellers. The not-yet proven engine installation was good enough for 3rd in time trials at 401.5 mph, well behind Greenamyer at 418.5 mph and Shelton at 407 mph. In the Championship Race, Cummins led Shelton at the finish by 0.4 seconds, as they were timed at 422.00 mph and 421.69 mph, respectively.[6]

At Reno, September 12–14, Greenamyer continued the string of records with a qualifying lap at 435.56 mph, with Shelton second at 423.53 mph. This strongly suggested an exciting Championship Race, which unfortunately did not materialize. Greenamyer couldn't start because of mechanical problems.

Cummins dropped out on lap 2, and Burnstine on lap 7. But Shelton and Cummins blasted on, the former winning at a record pace, 429.92 mph, and Roy McClain almost as fast, at 427.31 mph. The gap between the truly dedicated competitors and the also-rans continued to widen.

Formula One

Regional races were conducted at Miramar, Calif., where Cote won over 16 qualifiers, and at Flora, Ill. (July 19–20), where Marion Baker (#20 *Aquarius*) edged Bob Moeller and seven others.

At Reno, dark clouds and rain put a damper on the proceedings, but the races went off about as scheduled. Cote was top qualifier at a Reno record 241.61 mph and then won his heat race at 228.94 mph. He and Vince DeLuca flew almost as one until the backstretch of the last lap of the Finals, when Cote sprinted ahead in a burst of speed and won by 150 yards, at 227.46 mph.

Sport Biplane Class

The discrepancy in speeds between sport and racing biplanes widened, with the result that the class was effectively dividing itself into two divisions. The standard EAA sport planes were completely out of contention, as the very nature of the class and its appeal had changed. Sid White demonstrated this conclusively by adding more than 6 mph to the old record and becoming the first biplane racer to exceed 200 mph, with a lap at 204.93 mph, edging up on the Formula Ones.

This #0 Hawker Sea Fury, was raced by Ormond Hatden-Baillie, an RAF pilot serving with the Canadian Air Force (Al Chute).

White then set a heat record in winning 1-A at 202.62 mph, but ceded the winner's trophy to Don Beck, who won at 198.99 mph to White's 196.401 mph. As they crossed the finish line they were closing in on the 3rd placer and would have lapped him, had the race been much longer.

1976

The fourth annual California National Air Races at Mojave (June 18–20) started out badly, when Ken Burnstine, who had just arrived and was orbiting above the field prior to landing, suddenly spun into the desert floor. No cause was ever determined, though it was widely known that he was scheduled to testify in a major drug smuggling case the following week. This left "Mac" McClain in the RB-51 to lead at 416.27 mph. In the Championship Race, McClain won at 406.72 mph, almost a lap ahead of runner-up Gary Levitz in his #81 Mustang.[7]

Emotions were unusually high for time trials at Reno (September 10–12). Shelton's damaged *Rare Bear* was not fully repaired, and Cummins had made a forced landing on the way to Reno. McClain set a national record at 436.09 mph, which was promptly broken by John Crocker (flying the ex-Burnstine #34 *Miss Foxy Lady*, which had been turned into #6 *Somethin' Else*) with a lap at 436.63 mph. That, in turn, was beaten by Don Whittington in his #09 *Precious Metal* at 438.81 mph.

The all-Mustang Championship Race started off with a sky-full of V-12s screaming their way toward the mountains beyond the far side of the race course, John Crocker leading McClain and Whittington. On lap three Whittington broke a connecting rod and was out. A lap later, McClain's supercharger gears failed and he, too, was forced to pull up and out. John Crocker's apparent victory faded when he was disqualified for flying over the safety line. "Lefty" Gardner was declared the winner, despite his 379.61 speed which was only marginally faster than the winning speeds for the two consolation races. The fans could be excused for their feelings of disappointment.

Formula One

The season started out at Sturgis, Ky., May 22–23, with a regional race that attracted a dozen entries. In the Consolation Race, veteran Jack Lowers (#76 Paul Musso's *Spirit of '76*) was leading going into a turn when he and rookie John Rowe collided, both crashing fatally. The Final Race was a hot battle between top qualifiers Nick Jones and Bob Moeller until Jones' engine blew up on lap nine, Moeller then cruising to an easy win.

More internal problems arose during a regional race at Mojave, Calif., (June 18–20) when apparent winner Ray Cote and 3rd-placer Glen Tuttle were disqualified after failing the post-race engine inspections. Cote received a one-year suspension from racing, which served to deepen the already serious disagreements over the manner in which rules and inspections were being enforced.

At Reno, Judy Wagner made history by becoming the first woman to win time trials, with a lap at 231.76 mph, but only after a faster qualifier — Fred Wofford, in #9 *Proud Bird*— withdrew rather than submitting to a technical inspection resulting from a formal protest of his engine's legality.

Any chance of Wagner being the first woman to win a Championship at Reno ended when a sparkplug worked loose on lap five, allowing Vince DeLuca to take the lead and win at 228.75 mph. Bill Falck was back in 3rd place at 221.65 mph in what was looking increasingly like the twilight of his long career.

Sport Biplane Class

The pair of metal biplanes extended their lead over every other airplane, with Don Beck setting records in time trials (208.90 mph), and in a heat race (203.135 mph) before winning the Finals at his third record of the year, 202.15 mph. Logan Hines, taking over for Sid White in *Sundancer* was 2nd each time, with a best speed of 200.37 mph in qualifying.

1977

The number of wrecked engines and dreams at Reno in 1976 (September 10–12) produced some uncharacteristic but timely caution. "Klay" Klabo's 402.74 mph qualifying lap was the only one over 400 mph, as pilots took it easy until the Championship Race, when the bulk of the prize money and prestige would be distributed. There was only one really impressive speed turned in during preliminary heats, and that was Darryl Greenamyer's 420.25 mph in the #5 Red Baron RB-51.[8]

Darryl, along with Don Whittington (#39 Precious Metal) and Cliff Cummins (#69 *Jeannie*) were the obvious favorites on the basis of past performance, and they did not disappoint. From the airborne starter's radioed, "Gentlemen, you have a race!" to the final checkered flag, it was Greenamyer at his best, the result being a national record 430.70 mph. But close behind was Whittington at 425.70 mph, and even closer to him, Cummins at 424.36 mph. It clearly paid off for the 2nd- and 3rd-placers to have held back until the Championship Race.

Formula One

Thirty years after Bill Falck had begun his air racing career at Cleveland in the first Goodyear Trophy Race, he ended it at Cleveland. During an airstart required by the FAA but opposed by the pilots, he was forming up with the pace plane over Lakefront Airport when he suddenly heeled over and dove into the water at the edge of Lake Erie. Just why a pilot with his skill and his intimate knowledge of his airplane did this is still the subject of debates and arguments. The September 3–5 race was won by Bob Moeller at 224.06 mph, but it was a hollow victory in view of the loss of one of the class' most outstanding competitors. Falck had been a symbol of the midget class, being the designer, builder, owner, pilot and crew chief of *Rivets*. His long domination of the class had not been sullied by a single suggestion of rules bending.

At Reno, the long-smoldering conflict over engine rules broke into the open, with those supporting a much more liberal set of specifications winning out over those who favored sticking to the class' original philosophy. Henceforth, the rules would allow the souping-up of engines, which more and more competitors had been doing in secret. Formula One thus became IXL, the International Experimental Limited Class. A partial boycott by F/1 loyalists produced the smallest turn-out in many years.

Ray Cote broke the Reno qualifying record with a lap at 240.00 mph, then failed to finish the Finals when he broke a connecting rod in his engine. The Gold Championship Race went to John Parker (#93 *Top Turkey*) at 226.12 mph.

Sport Biplane Class

For several, years the Reno Air Races management had viewed the Sport Biplane Class as of little over-all importance and of little interest to the crowd. In 1977 they decided to drop the class, not bringing it back onto the schedule until 1980.

1978

Just Reno, again. The rival race meets had failed to hang on, leaving the sole venue that could now call on a decade and a half of experience. Twenty-four airplanes showed up for the September 15–17 event, 21 qualified, and the three at the top were the same that had been there for several years: #5 RB-51 (with young Steve Hinton replacing Greenamyer in the cockpit), #69 *Jeannie*, now with extensive airframe and engine modifications and Cliff Cummins still the pilot, and #39 *Precious Metal* (Whittington). Their qualifying speeds were encouraging: 427.15 mph, 400.67 mph, and 400.20 mph, respectively.[9]

Weather was the big winner, as low temperatures, high winds and even snow flurries wiped out Championship races for some of the classes of lighter weight airplanes, and shortened the Unlimited Championship Race to just five laps. With Cummins out as the result of engine damage in a previous heat, it was Hinton and Whittington, wingtip-to-wingtip for the entire race. Hinton finally won out at 415.46 mph to 414.77 mph, Whittington trailing by less than a second at the flag.

Formula One

The sport was extended to Mexicali, Mexico (January 6–8) with a race using a modified handicap system which made the finishes closer, but not confusing. In the eight-lap Final Race, Bill Skliar was the winner, even though Downey's speed was the highest.

At Cleveland, September 2–4, time trials was won by Bob Moeller (#81 *BooRay*) at 234.27 mph, with Don Beck (#18 Cassutt *Gnat*) second at 231.26 mph. The Finals, for the Hansen Trophy, went to veteran Bob Downey in the new #28 Williams *Falcon* at 225.89 mph, well ahead of Beck at 222.68 mph.

Reno experienced some of the worst weather in its 15 years of air racing. While time trials and two heat races went off as planned, both the Consolation and Championship Races had to be cancelled due to high winds. The purses were split evenly among those who raced in the faster and slower heats.

1979

The season started out at Homestead in south Florida, February 27–March 1, where the Whittington-produced International Air Races was the first Unlimiteds-only event held. It attracted 28 airplanes—mostly Mustangs—and most of the top competitors. Time trials on the short 7-mile course were won by Steve Hinton in the RB-51 at 395 mph. In the Mustangs-only Championship Race, Hinton prevailed at 384.79 mph.[10]

This #5 Red Baron RB-51 had been a stock Mustang before installation of a big Rolls Royce Griffon engine and contra-rotating propellers (Roger Huntington collection).

Prior to the races at Reno, Hinton broke Greenamyer's 10 year-old World Speed Record with an average of four runs at 499.06 mph. At Reno (September 14–16), he qualified at a record 441.90 mph, but it never got into the record book, as "Mac" McClain topped it in the much-improved #69 *Jeannie* with a run at 446.93 mph. Teams' knowledge of what it takes to develop horsepower without unnecessarily risking an engine's reliability was paying big dividends.

For the 98-mile Championship Race, the three top qualifiers were the obvious favorites. While they were forming up for the air start, McClain declared an emergency, *Jeannie*'s engine having shown signs of developing problems, so he pulled out and landed. Crocker led Hinton for most of the race, starting to ease up as the latter's engine began encountering troubles. Crocker won at 422.3 mph, as mechanical matters became serious for the RB-51.

In rapid progression, a bearing failed, the supercharger gears burned out, an oil pump broke and the drive shaft froze up. Despite the obvious signs that his engine's life was down to a few seconds, Hinton pressed on. He finished 2nd at 415.97 mph as the engine quit, and he bellied into a field strewn with boulders. There was little of the airplane remaining intact but the cockpit and the pilot, who survived serious injuries to continue a great flying career. John Crocker won at 422.30 mph, and John Putnam was 3rd at 399.91 mph.

Formula One

The second Reno races under the IXL banner saw few competitors from east of the Mississippi River. Top qualifier, with an IXL record, was Ray Cote at 246.01 mph. Close behind was John Parker at 241.61 mph. Third was Fred Wofford, in #9 *Proud Bird*, who then crashed fatally near the scatter pylon during the start of Heat 1A. In the Championship Race, John Parker set an IXL record at 240.09 mph for a complete race heat, with Ray Cote 2nd at 236.01 mph. That was the only American midget race of the year.

Chapter 24

The 1980s

1980

The Unlimited Class race at Reno (September 12–14) would be one fans would talk about for many years to come, and all because of the miraculous recovery of *Jeannie*. On its final pre-race test flight immediately prior to flying to Reno for time trials, its engine stopped, the ensuing forced landing doing extensive damage to the airplane. Rather than throw up their hands in frustration, the crew set out to re-build the airplane, which required round-the-clock work. With but *one minute* remaining before the deadline for arrivals, McClain and *Jeannie* appeared in the sky above the old Stead AFB, looking somewhat the worse for wear, but ready to race.[1]

Mustangs dominated time trials, Whittington leading at a modest 421.6 mph; *Jeannie* was 6th at 396 mph. As the time for the Championship Race approached, John Crocker and Lyle Shelton were parked, engine failures having been too damaging for on-the-field repairs. In the main race, McClain led from the start and was followed closely by Crocker, as the others tried but failed to keep pace. At the finish, it was McClain and *Jeannie* in first place at the record speed of 433.01 mph, with Crocker clocking the 4th fastest heat race ever, at 429.78 mph. The miraculous recovery had been completed, and the uninhibited celebration by the winning crew was fully justified.

Formula One

The season lasted barely two weeks, starting with Cleveland (August 30-September 1) and ending with Reno. At Cleveland, Bob Anspach, flying the #93 Shoestring *Pole Cat*, set a qualifying record for the 3.3-mile land-and-lake course of 235.25 mph, then won the feature race at 233.88 mph, just ahead of Chuck Andrews at 232.80 mph in Paul Musso's #68 Cassutt/Owl *Real Sporty*. Bill Falck's nephew, John "Dusty" Dowd, placed 3rd at 224.47 mph in #5 Cassutt *Illusion*.

At Reno, Ray Cote set an IXL qualifying record of 254.06 mph, a speed that would not be equaled by a true Formula One until the appearance of an

Grumman F8F-2 Bearcat *Rare Bear*, winner at Reno in three decades (author).

ultra-high-tech midget racer in the 1990s. In the Championship Race, after an unusual amount of passing, John Parker prevailed, winning at an IXL record 249.07 mph, with Cote in 2nd at 242.96 mph.

Sport Biplane Class

After a three-year hiatus, the biplanes returned to Reno. Several competitors used the time wisely, with the result that the old qualifying record was shattered twice. Pat Hines, flying the #1 *Sundancer*, was timed at 218.57 mph, while Don Beck in the #89 *Sorceress* was close behind at 215.01 mph. In addition, a near-clone of *Sundancer*, the #22 *Cobra*, was flown by Al Kramer to third at 204.65 mph.

Pat Hines had an easy win in the Championship Race, adding 4 mph to Don Beck's record with an average of 206.62 mph. Almost a full lap back was Al Kramer, at 177.05 mph, followed closely by Don Fairbanks in his #5 Knight Twister Imperial *White Knight* at 176.38 mph. Don Beck actually finished first, but was placed last after being penalized for "illegal passing," a term usually applied when a pass is made to the inside, or left, of the airplane being passed.

1981

Jeannie was in the spotlight at Reno (September 15–20), even though her new pilot, military and test pilot Skip Holm, was a bit of a mystery when he replaced McClain, who was seriously ill. Holm came through with a record time trials run at 450.09 mph. Don Whittington was close, at 442.2 mph, followed by John Crocker at 430.9 mph. Heat races were more exciting than usual, Shelton winning one at 416.7 mph, and Holm the other at 427.8 mph. In the latter, Shelton's *Rare Bear* suffered a burned piston and failed to finish.[2]

In the 8-lap, 74-mile Championship Race, Holm led all the way and won with a near-record 431.3 mph. John Crocker was two miles back at 419.37 mph after Whittington dropped out with a rough-running engine.

Ray Cote's 244.72 mph winning speed in time trials was overshadowed by the loss of Goodyear Race veteran Bob Downey in a still-unexplained crash during on-course practice, after which Bob Moeller retired from racing. In the Championship Race, Ray Cote captured his ninth win at Reno in Formula One, IXL or its latest name, IFM, for International Formula Midgets. He turned 232.13 mph to Judy Wagner's 221.87 mph and soon retired the original *Shoestring* to a museum.

Sport Biplane Class

Yet another pure racer appeared, this time the radical tandem-winged design by Burt Rutan called the #3 Amsoil-Rutan Racer and flown by Danny Mortensen. It was qualified at 212.25 mph, second only to Pat Hines and the *Sundancer*, who set yet another record, at 220.13 mph. Hines repeated as Champion, clocking a record 209.44 mph. Mortensen appeared to have finished 2nd, but was penalized back to 3rd for pylon cuts. This elevated Al Kramer to 2nd, at 187.13 mph.

1982

There were two new airplanes in the spotlight at Reno (September 14–19), one of them the reincarnation of an old type — the Goodyear-built Vought F2G Super Corsair. Cook Cleland & Co. dominated the classic Thompson Trophy Race with a trio of them. Like the prototype, it had been built by installing a huge Pratt & Whitney Wasp Major engine in a standard Corsair, and would be raced by Steve Hinton. The other was #4 *Dago Red*, the next step forward in the streamlining, lightening and increasing the power of a Mustang; Ron Hevle was the pilot.[3]

Victory in time trials went to Hevle and #4 P-51 *Dago Red* with the fourth fastest lap in history: 440.57 mph. John Crocker was 2nd at 434 mph, as Mustangs made up most of the entry list. In the Championship Race, Hevle took the lead as the airplanes were released, and held it to the end, averaging a tame 405.09 mph and winning by more than three miles, as no one was pressing him.

Formula One

The turnout for Reno was markedly improved, as the influence of the IXL/IFM crowd faded. Top qualifier at "only" 230.85 mph was Ralph Wise in the #7 Owl Racer, with Phil Fogg in the #1 Owl Racer 2nd at 228.68 mph. Farther down the list was Mercury astronaut Donald "Deke" Slayton, who had just bought the Art Williams #21 *Stinger*.

The Championship Race was run in damp, gloomy conditions (regardless of Chamber of Commerce claims), with Jon Sharp winning in #43 *Aero Magic* at 224.52 mph, Fogg was 2nd at 223.90 mph, and Dowd was 3rd at 222.87 mph. The lower speeds resulted from the return to stock engines and the accompanying closer competition.

Biplane Classes

After so many years of what amounted to two races in one — the built-for-racing specials easily outdistancing the true sport biplanes by so much as to make them appear foolish — the class was divided into two divisions: the Racing Biplane and the Sport Biplane.

Skip Holm's #18 *Tsunami*, the first, and so far the only, custom-built Unlimited racer to be competitive (author).

24. The 1980s

In the former, Pat Hines set another qualifying record with 223.88 mph, and then won the five-plane Championships at 209.44 mph, also a record. In the latter, Don Fairbanks qualified at 185.98 mph and then won at 172.73 mph; eight airplanes competed. The new arrangement was certainly more realistic and no doubt also more satisfying.

1983

It was inevitable that someone would improve the clean but large and heavy Sea Fury airframe with a much larger engine. The replacement of the original 18-cylinder Bristol Centaurus with a 28-cylinder Pratt & Whitney R-4360 boosted the power of the new Sea Fury Mk.T.11 two-seat fighter-trainer from 2,300 hp to almost 4,000 hp. The result was #8 *Dreadnought*, to be flown by General Dynamics Corp. test pilot Neil Anderson, to the end that he qualified first at 446.39 mph. Close on his tail were Rick Brickert (#4 *Dago Red*) at 439.2 mph, Hevle (#7 *Strega*) at 436.0 mph, Don Whittington (*Precious Metal*) at 434.9 mph and Lyle Shelton at 432.0 mph.[4]

Hard racing continued right into the preliminary heats, the second seeing Anderson setting a heat-race record of 435.6 mph, with Brickert 2nd at 433.9 mph, and Shelton 3rd at 432.3 mph. So far, engines were holding up surprisingly well.

But not in the Championship Race. Anderson and Shelton moved into a quick lead, only to see Hevle and Brickert pass the *Rare Bear*. Still on their way to the starting line, Hevle's oil line broke, sending him out. A variety of minor problems were adding up to more serious problems for Shelton, who eased back on the power. On lap six, Brickert's propeller spinner cracked, setting up a major vibration and, not knowing the full extent of the problem, he retired from the fray. On lap eight, Whittington went to full power in hopes of catching Anderson, his engine backfired and something broke, ending his day. Anderson cruised along, winning at a comfortable 425.24 mph. With 2½ times the piston displacement of the Mustangs, he had no need to over-stress his engine. But it doesn't always work out that way.

Formula One

European F/1 racing, unknown to most American racing fans, finally emerged into the open at Reno, as British Champion Steve Thompson made the 6,000-mile trip from The Old World and placed 7th in time trials at 226.96 mph in his #71 Cassutt *The Empire Strikes Back*. Well ahead was Chuck Wentworth in #69 *Flexi Flyer*, a lightweight Cassutt with a tapered composite wing, at 239.23 mph.

The 10-lap, 31-mile Championship Race was an easy win for Wentworth at 239.02 mph, but Thompson worked his way up to 2nd at the finish; he averaged 224.85 mph and demonstrated that the Europeans were now fully competitive.

Biplane Classes

The Racing Biplanes continued to display speed, with Hines leading qualifying with 220.92 mph, but when Mortensen crashed while avoiding an accident during a heat race (with extensive damage to the airplane but not to its pilot) only three were left for the Championship Race. Pat Hines won with still another record: with 217.60 mph; he had but two competitors on the 3.11-mile course.

Don Fairbanks again won the Sport Biplane qualifications with 185.58 mph, ahead of 11 others. He had a much closer Championship Race, finishing two seconds ahead of Mic Williams in Bill Boland's old #3 Mong Sport: 179.59 mph to 178.51 mph.

The lack of competition among the Racing Biplanes spelled the end of the division and left the remaining pure racing two-wingers with nowhere to race, as they would not be accepted in the Sport Biplane Class. Several of them went into museums.

1984

The steadily growing Unlimited Class entry list at Reno (September 10–16) topped 30 for the first time, with just over half being Mustangs. The most talked-about was the most thoroughly modified Mustang yet: #84 *Stiletto*, which had all the usual changes plus the relocation of its belly scoop and radiator into the wings. Time trials suggested high speeds and very close competition: Neil Anderson repeated, at 442.75 mph, Crocker was 2nd at 442.57 mph, Hevle was 3rd at 440.98 mph. If these speeds were representative of their true capabilities over a multi-lap race, some exciting racing was in the offing.[5]

In Heat #6, Anderson was 1st at 429.9 mph, Holm (*Stiletto*) was 2nd at 425.9 mph, and Brickert was 3rd (*Dago Red*) at 425.7 mph. In the 9th, Brickert won at a heat race record 439.83 mph, Hinton was 2nd at 422.7 mph and Holm was 3rd at 422.5 mph. Again, engines were pushed hard, yet held together.

The Championship Race (now re-named the Gold Race) included 8 Mustangs and a Super Corsair; for the first time, all of them were extensively modified. Three of the hot Mustangs—flown by Hevle, Brickert and Destefani—dropped out with debilitating engine damage. The rest survived, with Holm winning at 437.6 mph, a mile ahead of Crocker and four miles ahead of Hinton. If not for the glorious sounds of powerful engines echoing off the nearby mountains, it would have been a rather dull race.

Formula One

Two former champions and one future champion dominated time trials, with Ray Cote, now flying the ex-Judy Wagner #44 Shoestring, first at 238.57 mph, Jon Sharp 2nd at 228.49 mph and Jim Miller in his prototype pusher at 228.30 mph. Cote stayed at the fore, winning the Championship Race at 236.07 mph to 235.34 mph for Tom Aslett in what had been Chuck Wentworth's #69, and Sharp 3rd at 233.81 mph.

Sport Biplane Class

Relieved of the distractions of the exceedingly fast racing biplanes, the remaining airplanes returned the class to its roots as the playground of personal planes. Competition blossomed, with Don Fairbanks setting a record in time trials at 192.37 mph, Don Beck 2nd in his #00 Mong Sport at 192.041 mph, and Dan Mortensen 3rd in another Mong, the #91 *Amsoil Dealer Special*, at 190.34 mph. In the Championship Race, Beck out-ran Fairbanks by 189.97 mph to 185.35 mph.

Jim Miller's #14 Miller *Pushy Cat*, the design that first showed that a radical race could succeed (Al Wimer).

1985

Thirty-two pilots qualified for the Unlimited races at Reno (September 9–14), more than for any previous race. While the slowest — a World War II B-

25 bomber — was barely 1 mph quicker than the fastest little Formula One racer, the top three whipped around the 9.222-mile course at almost identical speeds. Anderson at 443.13 mph, Holm at 442.48 mph, and Brickert at 442.01 mph, as 11 of them topped the 400 mph mark. In the fastest of the heat races, Anderson won at 436.95 mph, to runner-up Hinton's 433.84 mph.[6]

The Gold Race line-up consisted of 6 Mustangs, a Sea Fury and a Super Corsair. Two of the Mustangs failed to start as they were nursing damage suffered earlier; three others dropped out with engine problems. Hinton won in the Super Corsair at 438.19 mph, Anderson had looked like the winner in Dreadnought at 440.8 mph, but was penalized for cutting inside a pylon and dropped to 2nd. In third was Brickert in *Dago Red* at 426.85 mph. It was a well fought race, even if almost half the starters failed to complete the eight laps. One wonders how they might have fared in one of the 300-mile Thompson Trophy Races.

Formula One

Time trials were again led by Ray Cote (241.09 mph) and Jon Sharp (237.66 mph), with Kirk Hanna 3rd at 236.20 mph in #7 Owl Racer. The Bronze Race (2nd Consolation) was won by Sharp, competing because he had failed to start his second preliminary heat; his speed of 230.51 mph exceed that of the Gold Race winner. The latter was again won by Ray Cote, at 229.09 mph, with Aslett 2nd at 226.35 mph and Miller 3rd in the pusher at 220.70 mph, as he steadily moved his radical-design machine toward the fore.

Sport Biplane Class

The speeds of the sporty biplanes continued to creep up toward the level of the now-banned racing biplanes. Don Beck added a fraction of a mile-per-hour to the qualifying record, winning at 193.20 mph, with Don Fairbanks but 0.4 seconds slower, at 191.88 mph. In the Championship Race, Beck broke his own year-old record in winning at 195.62 mph, 2½ miles ahead of runner-up Fairbanks, who could manage only 177.67 mph.

1986

The long-rumored appearance of a truly original-design Unlimited at Reno (September 8–14) was finally realized. The idea had first been broached in 1964, when Reno founder Bill Stead asked veteran designer/builder Steve Wittman for suggestions for improving Bill's Bearcat. Steve responded with thoughts about building a racer from scratch, with one of the popular V-12 engines, that could easily whip the Mustangs. The idea died with Bill in 1966. Now, a team of aeronautical engineers and craftsmen had created what looked like a Mustang meant for racing right from the start, rather than for combat. *Tsunami* was smaller, lighter and more streamlined, and thus should have greater potential.[7]

While the first truly homebuilt Unlimited since Art Chester's *Goon* in 1938 was getting the lion's share of the attention, there were 15 Mustangs, 7 Sea Furys and an assortment of other types in the pit area. Fastest in qualifying for the fourth straight year was #8 *Dreadnought*, now flown by Rick Brickert, who set a national one-lap record of 452.7 mph. Skip Holm was 2nd at 437 mph in *Stiletto*, and Hinton was third in *Tsunami* at 435 mph.

In the Championship Race, Steve Hinton pulled out with a minor engine problem shortly after the airplanes were released to head downhill toward the race course. Holm and Brickert fought for the lead for more than four laps until Holm was forced out by an oil leak. Brickert charged on as if he had another airplane hot on his tail, eventually crossing the finish line with a mile lead over the other Sea Fury, flown by Lloyd Hamilton. They averaged 434.49 mph to 429.37 mph in the first one-two finish for the big British fighters.

Formula One

Speeds continued their slow rise as the replacement of standard Cassutt ("barn-door") wings with longer tapered wings built from advance composite materials increased. Jon Sharp won his second time trials at 240.83 mph to 236.00 mph for Alan Preston in the *Shoestring* that had been Judy Wagner's. Sharp then won the Finals at 229.61 mph, almost a full mile ahead of Bob Drew (#2 Friberg Special) at 222.41 mph and Jim Miller at 221.39 mph.

Sport Biplane Class

In an attempt to expand the dwindling entry lists, the leaders of the class voted to increase the allowable engine size to 361 cubic inches. This would bring into compliance the scores of aerobatic Pitts Specials powered by the highly reliable 180 hp Lycoming O-360 which some had boosted to as much as 230 hp. As pilots who are serious about aerobatics are considered among the best, it was reasonably assumed there would be no down-side to this move. In 1986, the 15-plane entry list included 10 Pitts Specials.

Tops in time trials was Alan Preston, new pilot of the #00 Mong Sport, with a record 198.62 mph, 5 mph faster than the previous year. In the Gold Championship Race, Preston won at 192.67 mph as he lapped all the other airplanes in the race.

1987

At Reno (September 14–20) in just its second outing, the one-of-a-kind *Tsunami* began to display the wisdom of its designers. After Bill "Tiger" Destefani set a qualifying record in his #7 *Strega* at 466.67 mph, Steve Hinton also exceeded the old mark, with 464.65 mph. But it was to be Destefani's year at Reno. In his first heat race, he broke the old record for a full race, with 441.50 mph, barely ahead of Rick Brickert (#8 Sea Fury) at 441.29 mph and Steve Hinton at 439.80 mph. In his second, he increased that to 445.32 mph, and still his engine continued to develop full power. Brickert was second at 444.92 mph, while Hinton was unable to finish in the still-teething *Tsunami*. Yet another Sea Fury appeared on the ramp—#88 *Blind Man's Bluff*—this one set up to burn pure alcohol, but this proved problematic and it reverted to gasoline.[8]

In the Championship Race, Brickert took the lead and held it for six laps as both he and Destefani were topping 450 mph. On lap 7, Destefani jumped into the lead with a lap unofficially timed at 465 mph. The winner averaged 452.56 mph, not only his third heat race record of the week, but a full 14 mph over the old Championship record. There had never been such a performance: qualifying and three races at record speed and yet not an engine was damaged.

Formula One

This would be the first year that metal propellers were banned, as a safety measure; there had been too many instances when they had broken at high rpm, creating violent imbalance and sometimes shaking an engine completely off the airplane. The turn-out of midget racers appeared to be stabilizing in the low-20s, with a steady increase in the percentage of pilots flying personally customized versions of the Cassutt Racer. Alan Preston took the top spot in time trials with a lap at 241.19 mph, with only Jon Sharp close, at 237.25 mph. In the Championship Race, it looked like a solid win for Jim Miller in his pusher, until Preston began to gain in the late laps. Miller crossed the finish line barely hanging on to first place at just over 233 mph, but was then penalized back to 3rd for having cut the scatter pylon at the start of the race.

Sport Biplane Class

Back on top after more than a decade was the one-time Bill Boland #3 Mong, now highly modified and called #31 *Long Gone Mong* by its new owner/pilot Tom Aberle. The combination won time trials at a record 199.82 mph, with Fairbanks in 2nd at 190.93 mph and Dave Morss 3rd in the #91 Mong *Pacific Flyer* at 184.87 mph. The entry list had grown to a welcome 22 airplanes.

In the 8-lap Gold Championship Race, Aberle had no serious competition, winning by 2½ miles over Fairbanks, 196.47 mph to 179.28 mph

Sanders brothers' Hawker Sea Fury *Dreadnought,* the last type of piston-engined fighter to be produced; this one was the first to race with a much larger engine (unknown).

1988

Two years of major increases in speed records and in the spirit of competition led to a big jump in the size of the field of competitors: among the 38 Unlimiteds at Reno (September 12–18) were 10 different types of airplanes. Attracting much of the pre-race attention were two highly modified Russian Yak-11 advanced trainers having huge American engines, and John Dilley's P-51 *Vendetta,* which had the wing and horizontal tail from a Learjet. None of these was ready to pose a serious challenge to the highly developed Mustangs, Bearcats and Sea Furys, but they pointed the way to the future.[9]

The willingness of pilots to push airplanes to their limits in time trials continued, with Lyle Shelton, in the much-improved *Rare Bear,* blasting around the course at 474.62 mph and adding another 8 mph to the record. A mere half second behind was Steve Hinton and *Tsunami,* at 470.90 mph. Rick Brickert (*Dreadnought*) was 3rd at 458.92 mph, and Jimmy Leeward (flying the former *Jeannie/Galloping Ghost*) was 4th at 457.08 mph. The pressure to go all-out was not subsiding. Heat race speeds showed some tendency on the part of pilots to preserve valuable engines, at least until Heat 3-A, when Steve Hinton showed what Tsunami could do, adding almost 10 mph to the heat race record, as he averaged 462.22 mph. Brickert tried to keep up, recording a speed of 457.01 mph, the second-fastest in any race.

In the eagerly awaited Championship Race, the effects of so much punishment inflicted on metal parts began to be realized, as Don Whittington's *Precious Metal*, now powered by a Griffon engine turning contra-rotating propellers, lost a large quantity of oil, forcing him to make a belly landing in a field. Shelton took the initial lead and steadily pulled ahead until he finished the race with a lead over Brickert of more than 7 seconds, which works out to almost a mile.

Formula One

Alan Preston, flying the #44 Shoestring, set a new Formula One (not IXL/IFM) record at 246.228 mph, almost 2 seconds/lap quicker than Jim Miller, Jon Sharp and Ray Cote who had almost identical times. In the Gold Championship Race, Preston prevailed with another record — 240.75 mph — beating Sharp by more than a half mile. Miller failed to finish, while Cote had been relegated to the Silver Race, which he won decisively.

Sport Biplane Class

The entry list was up to 25, with 70 percent being Pitts Specials, most of them also flown in aerobatics. But it was the highly modified Mong Sports that ruled, with Tom Aberle being the class' first to exceed 200 mph, with a qualifying lap at 207.72 mph. Alan Preston was 2nd at 197.81 mph, and Dave Morss 3rd at 190.41 mph, all in Mongs.

In heat races, it was all Preston, as he topped 200 mph in 1-A with an average of 202.00 mph, and then took the Gold Championship at a record 205.92 mph. The banning of Racing Biplanes seemed to have motivated builders to push the limits of streamlining.

1989

A month before the Reno Air Races, Lyle Shelton made a long-rumored run at Steve Hinton's 10 year-old World Speed Record for piston-engined airplanes, as Las Vegas, NM. He was not satisfied with a series of runs averaging 516 mph, which would have broken the record, feeling the mighty *Rare Bear* had still more speed. A second set of official FAI runs worked out to 528.33 mph and he was understandably pleased.[10]

Shelton, the odds-on favorite, led time trials with a near-record 467.38 mph, Hinton was 2nd in *Tsunami* at 462.02 mph, and Brickert 3rd in *Dread-*

nought at 456.58 mph. Down in 14th was the #101 Yak-11 *Perestroika* of Bob Yancey, which had undergone more changes than any previous Unlimited: wings metalized, 800 hp Russian engine replaced by a 2,000 hp American one, a huge propeller, bulbous spinner and bubble canopy. More than any of the other Unlimiteds, it looked like a true racing plane, both on the ground and in the air. He built up his heat race speeds from 395 mph to 397 mph to 407 mph.

The most exciting heat race was 3A, when Shelton pushed his airplane as hard as ever, crossing the finish line with a long lead over runner-up Destefani, but losing almost all of it to a penalty for having cut a pylon. The official results showed Shelton at 445.81 mph and Destefani at 444.37 mph. In the Championship, no one was able to sustain a challenge to Shelton, the result being an easy win by more than three miles, the average being 450.91 mph. Yancey, in *Perestroika*, placed 4th at 406 mph.

Formula One

Time trials produced yet more record performances, with Jon Sharp fastest at 242.55 mph in the #96 Boyd *Blue Streak*, Ray Cote was 0.05 seconds — the blink of an eye — slower, at 242.29 mph in the #4 Owl *Alley Cat*. The Gold Championship Race was hard fought by Cote and Miller, whose radical racer continued to improve and had carried him to a first heat race record of 243.54 mph. Cote prevailed in the race that matters, 231.25 mph to 229.95 mph, while Sharp dropped out on the first lap, and 4th qualifier Jim Bumford (#55 *Bummer's Bullet*) was penalized for "low and erratic flying."

Sport Biplane Class

The Pitts Special, long America's choice for both air show and competition aerobatics, was about to stake its claim in pylon racing. While Tom Aberle retained his hold on qualifying with a run at 206.99 mph, the next two pilots flew "Pa" Pitts' famous flyer. Sam Maxwell was 2nd at 186.26 mph in a two-aileron, flat-wing S-1C that had been raced by a variety of pilots since 1974. In 3rd was Mike Penketh at 178.96 mph in the #1, a four-aileron, round-wing type S-1S.

Chapter 25

The 1990s

1990

Dissatisfaction rumbled through the Unlimited Class, having built up for years of pilots feeling the Reno Air Race Association (RARA) had not properly expressed its appreciation for the time, hard work and money expended by what almost everyone agreed was the flagship class. In an effort to create rival events that, in turn, might encourage RARA to become more responsive, races were run at Sherman, Texas, and Denver, Colorado, but they both had major shortcomings. A drive to convince pilots and owners that a boycott of Reno might display their importance had little impact even though several of the top Unlimited pilots stayed home.

For the first time, four pilots exceeded 465 mph in time trials at Reno (September 14–20), and only Destefani flew a factory-built airplane which used its original engine. In the Championship Race, Skip Holm and *Tsunami* led into the latter part of the second lap, when Lyle Shelton surged past him and clipped off laps close to 470 mph, which meant at least 500 mph on the straightaways. Shelton held on to win at 468.61 mph, beating Destefani's old record by 16 mph.[1]

History was made when Erin Rheinschild won the Bronze (second consolation) Heat to become the first woman to win any Unlimited Class Race. Her husband, Bill, then won the Silver Race.

Formula One

The long awaited debut of Jon Sharp's very high-tech *Nemesis* was delayed a year, but that didn't spoil the fun. Jim Bumford set yet another qualifying mark, with a lap at 244.08 mph. Jim Miller was close behind at 241.55 mph, as was Hep Porter, the latest pilot of #44 Shoestring, at 241.19 mph. The Gold Championship Race was the scene of major air racing history, as Miller pulled off the first win by a radical-design airplane since the sport was born 80 years before. His margin of ½ second may not have been comfortable, but it was more than sufficient, as he averaged 237.41 mph to Porter's 237.08 mph.

Sharp #3 *Nemesis*, proof that high-tech techniques can produce a consistent winner (author).

Sport Biplane Class

The "take-over" by aerobatic Pitts Specials was almost complete, as they made up 80 percent of the 21-plane field, and almost all of them were the S-1S version which is better for aerobatics, but somewhat slower than the earlier S-1C. Top qualifier was, of course, flying a Mong Sport, Dan Mortensen's #91, at 188.07 mph. In the Gold Championship Race, Dan prevailed, winning by ¾ mile, at 192.28 mph.

1991

The future arrived at Reno (September 9–15) in the form of the Pond Racer, a radical-design airframe powered by a pair of auto racing engines. It was the creation of Burt Rutan, who continued to demonstrate that airplanes with carefully thought-out novel shapes can produce superior performance. This one had twin booms like a P-38 Lightning, and a central pilot's pod extending from the trailing edge of the wing to the horizontal tail. The Pond Racer wasn't much larger than a Formula One, but had two engines that were supposed to develop 1,000-hp, each, and was built almost entirely of high-tech composite materials. It would be flown by veteran Rick Brickert and watched carefully by everyone, but it dropped out of each of its heat races with engine problems that were becoming endemic. The owner, industrialist Robert Pond, is said to have spent $3.5 million on it.[2]

Time trials produced another record: 475.899 mph by Shelton in his #77 *Rare Bear*, with Holm in *Tsunami* 2nd at 456.91 mph, while down in 7th was Bob Yancey in the increasingly fast Yak-11 *Perestroika*. The 1991 Gold Championship Race is still referred to by many as the greatest pylon race of all time. The trio charged off, pushing hard all the way as if engine failure was of no concern. All three broke the old record, to the utter delight of the crowd. Shelton won at 481.618 mph, adding 13 mph to the old mark. Destefani was 2nd at 478.68 mph, and Holm was third in the custom-built racer at 478.14 mph, just a half second back. Contrary to history and to expectations, all three engines held together long enough to see the checkered flag. A few days later, *Tsunami* was destroyed in a landing accident on its way home, killing owner John Sandberg.

Formula One

A bright spotlight was on Jon Sharp's exotic-but-conventional #3 *Nemesis*, with which he was about to become the first person in the class' history to take advantage of his unique access to expensive advanced technology, as a Lockheed engineer, to defeat the "backyard mechanics." It was they who had created and maintained the midgets as the home of everyman's racing. Until the introduction of this superb machine, the emphasis had been on creativity and craftsmanship; now some of it would be shifted to the availability of the kind of information that can only come from terribly expensive wind tunnels and very large computers.

While veteran racepilot Sharp qualified 4th at 236.65 mph, he won the Gold Championship Race at a record 245.26 mph, something that had never before been done with a brand new airplane. The outlook for the small team that had more ideas than dollars was about to take a nose dive. Lost in all the fuss was Jim Miller's 242.21 mph runner-up performance in the Gold Race.

Sport Biplane Class

The Reno Air Races took a major step in the direction of becoming an international event with the appearance of Takehisa "Ken" Ueno, of Tokyo, Japan. Flying what had been Dan Mortensen's #91 Mong Sport, now #31 *Samurai*, he led 24 pilots in time trials at 193.27 mph, and then won the Gold Championship Race at 195.27 mph. He thus became the first pilot from outside the U.S. to win a major air racing event since 1936, when Michel Detroyat of France won the Thompson Trophy Race at Los Angeles. One-third of a lap back in 2nd place was aerobatic pilot Norman Way in his #27 Pitts Special S-1S *Magic*, at 183.84 mph.

1992

Thirty-one Unlimited racers crowded the Reno pit area during September 14–20 with a wide variety of types, but not a new machine of interest. Top speed in qualifying was Lyle Shelton's record-breaking 482.89 mph in *Rare Bear*. The nearest anyone else could come was 4½ seconds slower by Destefani at 452.13 mph. The fastest of nine preliminary heat races was #3A, won by Destefani at 453.49 mph to Shelton's 449.98 mph.[3]

The Championship Race was highly competitive until halfway through the 8 laps, when Shelton pulled out, letting Destefani win at 450.84 mph. Brian Sanders, co-owner of #8 *Dreadnought*, was 2nd at 442.50 mph, and Bob Yancey was 3rd in Yak-11 *Perestroika* at 433.56 mph, a personal best.

Formula One

Surprisingly, the new qualifying record was set not by Jon Sharp but by Jim Bumford, at 252.79 mph. While his airplane—#55 *Bummer's Bullet*—lacked some of the design advantages of Sharp's, it was built almost entirely of composite materials and had a wing of unusually high aspect ratio (long and thin), which was efficient, but was so thin near the tips that it tended to flap a bit in propwash and rough air. Sharp was 2nd at 249.74 mph, which would have been a national record if not for Bumford, and Miller was 3rd at 242.13 mph.

Sharp flew one of his heat races at 243.67 mph and then won the Gold Championship Race at 238.18 mph. Hep Porter was 2nd at 232.31 mph, Miller 3rd at 231.01 mph. Bumford dropped to 4th as he was at a disadvantage when following other planes and fighting their propwash.

Sport Biplane Class

It was never expected when the class rules were changed to permit larger engines that one result would be a *reduction* in the variety of airplanes. But the use of aerobatic airplanes by aerobatic pilots was so successful that, in 1992, they made up more than 80 percent of the entrants. Only at the very top of the list was there no great impact of this change, as Jim Smith won time trials in the #88 Mong Sport at 203.68 mph. In 2nd was former U.S. Aerobatic Team member Patti Johnson-Nelson in the old Boland Mong, at 195.91 mph, but right behind her was Earl Allen in the #69 Pitts Special at 195.22 mph.

Positions were changed in the 6-lap Gold Championship, won by Smith at 193.89 mph, with Allen 2nd at 192.10 mph and in 3rd, Johnson-Nelson at 191.90 mph in what had been re-named *Twerpster*.

1993

Of the 29 airplanes at Reno (September 13–19), 17 were P-51 Mustangs, 6 were Hawker Sea Furys, 2 were Yakovlev Yak-11s, and there was one each F2G Super Corsair, F8F Bearcat, P-38 Lightning and Pond Racer. Rick Brickert was testing the exotic Pond Racer when yet another engine fire precipitated a rapid descent, which turned into a crash landing and a fire that destroyed the airplane and killed Brickert. Two of the great hopes for the future of Unlimited Class racing—*Tsunami* and the Pond Racer—were now gone, and it wasn't clear when any other custom-built racers might take their places, as individuals willing to risk millions on such a project were rare.[4]

Time trials was uneventful, Destefani being fastest at 452.94 mph, and no one else clocking as fast as 440 mph. He and Sanders put on an exciting Heat 2A, with the former winning at 440.18 mph to 439.85 mph. In the Championship Gold Race on Sunday, it was Destefani at 455.38 mph to Sanders' 450.62 mph and Yancey's 439.54 mph.

Formula One

The era of total domination by Jon Sharp began with his qualifying record of 254.22 mph, followed by a heat win at 255.26 mph and a Gold Championship win at 246.85 mph. But unlike Bill Falck in the days he was unbeatable, Sharp

World Jet #39 *Precious Metal* P-51, a Mustang with a big engine and contra-rotating propellers (John Garrett).

made no effort to make his races look close for the enjoyment of the spectators. He won by 6 mph, 13 mph and 13 mph, and in the process redirected attention to the more entertaining battles back in the pack. When finals' runner-up Alberto Rossi (Cassutt Racer #63 *Chico Puro*) edged Jim Miller by a half second, it was truly enjoyable competition, even though Rossi was subsequently fined for low flying.

Sport Biplane Class

In just her second year of air racing, Patti Johnson took charge, winning time trials at 211.77 mph, two seconds/lap faster than any of the other 25 pilots. Ron Cox was second in his new original design, which conformed with the class rules, at 204.20 mph. Patti then won the Gold Championship Race just as decisively at 208.47 mph to Cox' 202.49 mph, leading him across the finish line by a half mile.

1994

A potential rival to Reno appeared at the deactivated Williams AFB, outside Phoenix, Arizona, March 15–20, where a new organization staged an outstanding first-time operation, but spent so much money in the process that it was unable to follow this with a second major event the next year. While the racing portion of the program went off with no obvious snags, an in-flight fire put paid to the F2G Super Corsair; pilot Kevin Eldridge jumped to safety, but was injured as his empty airplane dove straight into the ground.[5]

Destefani led time trials at 465.75 mph, followed by David Price in #4 *Dago Red* Mustang at 450.47 mph. In the Championship Race, John Penney replaced Lyle Shelton as pilot, winning at 434.16 mph despite being penalized for cutting a pylon. Brian Sanders was 2nd in *Dreadnought*, while Destefani dropped out on the first lap.

At Reno (September 12–18), the field had shrunk a bit to 26, of which 23 qualified. Tops was Penney in *Rare Bear* at 471.33 mph, 2nd was Price at 458.57 mph and 3rd Destefani at 453.69 mph, suggesting a fast Championship Race. Before time trials had been completed, Bill Speer's P-51 developed a serious oil leak which coated his windshield and obliterated his forward visibility. The resulting handicapped landing was entirely too fast, the airplane was destroyed and its pilot lost.[6]

A new scheme for the Unlimited Championship Race was an experiment. The three fastest would go at it in the "Super Gold Race," and the regular Gold Race would be for the next fastest group. Unfortunately, running just three airplanes around a 9-mile course was a mistake, as too much time elapsed between passes by the grandstands. The winner of the "Super" race was Penney at 424.41 mph, while in second was Brian Sanders (#8 *Dreadnought*) at 416.63 mph. In the Gold Championship Race, Alan Preston (#11 *Miss America*) won at 413.77 mph and David Price was second at 413.12 mph. Hardly anyone found the experiment satisfying, and it was quietly shelved.

Formula One

Jon Sharp continued to reign supreme, winning one-lap time trials by almost 200 yards, two of his heats by almost a mile and the Gold Championship Race by more than a mile. The least knowledgeable spectator could not have missed his superiority, based on unmatched aerodynamic design, unsurpassed power and excellent flying skill. But when he crossed the final finish line, only one airplane was within two miles of his streaking racer, and the fans could hardly have been thrilled.

Sport Biplane Class

For the first time, a woman was dominating a major class: Patti Johnson barely missed breaking her own qualifying record with a lap at 211.29 mph, as 22 of the record 27 entrants flew Pitts Specials. In her first heat race, she broke the heat record she had set in 1993, with 214.99 mph. In the Gold Championship

#97 Pitts S-1C Special, by far the most popular type to race in the Sport Biplane Class (John Garrett).

Race she probably would have won again, but she dropped out on lap 4 with engine trouble, Earl Allen winning at 203.31 mph in his Pitts *Legal Eagle*.

1995

The fastest qualifier at Reno (September 11–17) was #77 *Rare Bear*, John Penney pushing it to yet another record: 489.802 mph, 7 mph faster than Shelton's 1992 mark in the same airplane. David Price in #4 *Dago Red* was more than 30 mph slower, at 458.18 mph while Destefani led him by 1.6 seconds, 464 mph to 462 mph in Heat 3A to warm up the crowd.[7]

The pair went at it again in the Gold Championship Race, with the same outcome, their speeds being 467.03 mph to 465.16 mph. Destefani crossed the finish line with a lead of just two seconds. Price was just a few seconds behind him, but was then penalized 16 seconds for having cut inside a pylon.

Formula One

Jon Sharp continued to display his and his airplane's superiority, winning time trials at 253.48 mph to 233.84 mph for Kathy Gray in the former Boyd *Blue Streak*. His lead was equal to 400 yards *per lap*. In Sharp's two heat races, he put 1½ miles between himself and the runner-up, and in the Gold Championship Race, the gap was stretched to 1¾ miles back to Bruce Bohannon in another Miller Pusher, at 232.40 mph. The impact of his seeming invincibility was a drop in the number of entries and in the level of competition in general.

Sport Biplane Class

Patti Johnson continued her reign, with a qualifying run 5 mph faster than her old record: 217.23 mph. Earl Allen was 2nd at 207.07 mph. The slowest of the biplanes—mainly the purely standard ones—had all but disappeared from Reno, as the number of competitive airplanes increased. Only one of the 20 qualifiers was below 160 mph. Moreover, the sport/racing biplanes had improved their reliability to the point that not one dropped out of any of the six races. In the Gold Championships, Johnson won with ease, beating Allen by 10 seconds, equal to about a half mile: 202.13 mph to 196.11 mph. Johnson's speed would have been 210 mph had she not cut a pylon and been penalized 12 seconds.

1996

John Penney and David Price both broke the national one-lap record in time trials at Reno (September 9–15), Penney becoming the new holder with

491.266 mph; Price was just 0.06 seconds back, at 490.816 mph. Destefani was in 3rd with 465.52 mph. The trio went all-out in Heat 2A, tearing around the course for 6 laps at 479.93 mph (Price), 477.63 mph (Destefani) and 473.16 mph (Penney).[8]

The 8-lap, 73-mile Championship Race looked like a solid win for Price, who averaged 476.8 mph to lead Destefani by 7 seconds, equal to a mile and a half. But he was called for cutting the #6 pylon on lap 5, which brought a 16-second penalty and a revised speed of 460.56 mph to Destefani's winning 467.95 mph. The others were far back at the finish.

Formula One

Jon Sharp's repeated demonstrations of the potential of the Formula One specifications motivated others to higher speeds, especially Jim Miller's 254.63 mph in placing second to Sharp's record-setting 258.27 mph in time trials. While Cassutts provided more than half the 23 qualifiers, only two of them got into the top 10. Heat races and the Gold Championship Race again saw easy wins for Sharp, though he set no records. Miller failed to start his second heat race and found himself relegated to the Bronze Race, which he was unable to finish.

Sport Biplane Class

It was becoming predictable: Johnson, Allen and Smith leading the way. Patti qualified first at 216.43 mph, Allen 2nd at 205.58 mph, and Smith 3rd at 204.34 mph. In the 6-lap Gold Championship Race, Patti set a finals record at 212.81 mph, Allen was 2nd at 204.85 mph, and Smith was 3rd at 201.18 mph.

1997

At Reno, September 8–14, it looked like a Mustang, but in reality was more of a home-built. Gary Levitz #38 P-51R "Miss Ashley II" had a newly built Mustang-like fuselage and vertical tail combined with the wing and horizontal tail from a Learjet executive jet. The engine was a Rolls Royce Griffon V-12 turning a contra-rotating propeller. In its first time on a race course, Levitz was clearly going easy and so qualified 10th at 392.38 mph, while Bill Destefani was clocked at 464.25 mph and Lyle Shelton was 2nd at 461.51 mph, both in well-proven airplanes.[9]

The fastest of the heat races was #2A, in which Destefani averaged 458.82 mph to Shelton's 455.40 mph. He won the 8-lap Gold Championship Race at 453.13 mph. Shelton placed 2nd at 438 mph, but was dropped to 3rd for cutting a pylon and was given an official speed of 423.81 mph. Brian Sanders (#8

Dreadnought) was moved up to 2nd, having averaged 441.47 mph. Gary Levitz was 4th in the pseudo-Mustang at 414.33 mph, as he became more familiar with the new airplane and gradually increased the power.

Formula One

Again, Jon Sharp won time trials with ease — 254.22 mph to 245.63 mph for Randy Howell in #96, now called the Grove *Madder Maxx*. Dan Gilbert was 4th in #39 *Shadow*, a "*Nemesis* clone." In the Gold Race, Sharp had an easy time beating Howell by a mile, 245.04 mph to 234.56 mph.

Sport Biplane Class

In the absence of Patti Johnson and her #40 Mong Sport, runner-up Earl Allen took over, winning time trials at 204.01 mph, with Norman Way (#27 Pitts Special *Magic*) 2nd at 199.82 mph, and Jim Smith yet again 3rd, at 196.22 mph. When the Championship Race was cancelled due to high winds, the results of Heat 1-A were declared that of the finals, with the result that Allen was the winner at 198.74 mph, Smith was 2nd at 194.21 mph, and Way was 3rd at 191.39 mph. Wind was becoming a serious problem for the lightweight classes — Formula One and the Biplanes — and the solution, running their races as early as 8 A.M., was less than ideal, as few spectators were in their seats.

1998

In the absence of long-time top qualifiers Destefani and Shelton, a newcomer assumed the top of the mountain at Reno, September 14–20. The increasingly modified *Voodoo*, flown by former motocross champion Bob Hannah, was timed at 452.55 mph. Not far back was Bruce Lockwood in *Dago Red* at 443.93 mph. Gary Levitz, in his #38 *Miss Ashley II*, was 3rd at 437.38 mph.[10]

In the Gold Championship Race, Bruce Lockwood survived a close encounter with the propwash off *Dreadnought* that flipped him and almost inverted him. He then passed Dennis Sanders and stayed clear, winning at 450.60 mph, far below the maximum achieved in this airplane in the past. Sanders was 2nd at 445.31 mph, and Bill Rheinschild (#45 *Risky Business*) was 3rd at 420.57 mph. Bob Hannah's airplane suffered elevator control damage in a heat race and competed no more. Compared with recent races, it was something of an anticlimax.

Formula One

Despite propeller experimentation and an engine not performing up to expectations, Jon Sharp's *Nemesis* was fast enough to set a qualifying record at

260.07 mph, win both heats and then the Gold Championship Race, though not by the usual margins. Ray Cote, in the #4 Owl Racer, was 2nd at 241.90 mph, and Gary Hubler in the modified-beyond-recognition Cassutt #95 *Mariah*, was 3rd at 240.45 mph.

Sport Biplane Class

Jim Smith, in his #88 Mong Sport *Glass Slipper*, flew his qualifying lap around the 6-pylon, 3.11-mile course almost a half second quicker than 1997 leader Earl Allen, averaging 203.56 mph to 201.98 mph. In the Gold Championship Race, Smith finished more than four seconds in the lead, as he averaged 201.70 mph to Allen's 199.11 mph. While the speeds had dropped since Patti Johnson had retired, the competition had grown closer and the fans more excited.

Sport Class

Yet another class composed of available airplanes was introduced at Reno, but this time it was an immediate success. The kit-built airplanes had been designed to provide comfortable long-distance cruising at high speed, but turned out to be much faster than expected. Of the 13 qualifiers, 5 flew Glasairs, 5 flew Lancairs, 2 flew Questair Ventures and 1 flew a Swearingen SX300. Top qualifier was Formula One veteran and free-lance test pilot Dave Morss, who coaxed 301.69 mph out of his prototype, pressurized Lancair IV, with Rittner Will 2nd in a Venture at 292.45 mph, and Lee Behel 3rd in the other Venture at 286.70 mph.

In the first heat race, Morss extended his engine to win at 314.29 mph, with Behel 2nd at 302.33 mph. In the Gold Championship Race, Morss won easily at 306.16 mph to Behel's 297.20 mph. The class offered greater speed than expected, but the airplanes looked a lot alike, even to their color schemes. The availability of scores of these airplanes in regular use pointed to a good future for the class.

1999

Speeds began to pick up, though no records were endangered at Reno, September 14–20. The only new type to be seen was a World War II Soviet Yak-9 fighter, newly built in a Russian factory with an American Allison V-12 engine, entered by Dave Morss as #28 *Rush-n-Roulette*. He qualified 28th and last at 320 mph. In first place in time trials was Bill Destefani at 479.62 mph in *Strega*. Lockwood was close behind in *Dago Red* at 479.24 mph. In a heat race, Gary Levitz's *Miss Ashley II* experienced the catastrophic failure of its tail structure and crashed. This was the first fatal accident in actual Unlimited Class racing (excluding qualifying and practice flights) in 36 years of racing at Reno.[11]

In the Gold Championship Race, Destefani pulled out on the next-to-last lap, leaving Lockwood to cruise to victory at 471.33 mph, almost a half lap ahead of Brian Sanders in the reliable *Dreadnought*, at 441.22 mph.

Formula One

Once again, Jon Sharp broke his old qualifying record, this time upping it to 263.19 mph, a full 11 mph faster than his nearest rival, Ray Cote. In the 10-lap Gold Championship Race, Sharp's speed was 20 mph slower than in qualifying, yet he had no trouble beating Cote, by 243.51 mph to 239.60 mph. After winning, Jon Sharp retired from Formula One racing after nine consecutive victories in order to concentrate on developing a new airplane for the Sport class.

Sport Biplane Class

Jim Smith again took the honors in qualifying with a lap at 204.05 mph. Second was Tom Aberle in #21 Pitts Special "Class Action" at 198.55 mph and Stephen Brown in his #00 "Tonopah Low at 194.58 mph. Down in 14th place was David Rose in #3 *Rags*, which had been Bill Boland's Mong in the early days at Reno before it had been modified about as much as any racer in any class. In the Gold Championship, Rose showed what he and *Rags* could do, by winning at 210.12 mph, almost 14 seconds ahead of Jim Smith, and even more ahead of Tom Aberle.

Sport Class

In just the second year of competition, this class began to reveal the route to victory. Of four Lancairs entered, three flew their way into the Gold Race, but of seven Glassairs entered, not one was able to do so. Dave Morss stayed on top, winning time trials with a record 335.29 mph, followed by David Anders in #25 Venture *Eggstra Special* at 311.62 mph. The Gold Championship, for 6 laps around the next-to-longest course, went to Morss with another record, 319.67 mph. Anders was 2nd at 302.78 mph.

Chapter 26
The 2000s

2000

There were more Hawker Sea Furys (including one land-based Fury) racing at Reno (September 11–17) than P-51 Mustangs. And for the first time since the type first became available for purchase as military surplus, there wasn't a single Grumman Bearcat among the qualifiers. The versatile Skip Holm qualified both first and last: a near-record 489.68 mph in #4 Mustang *Dago Red*, and 297.05 mph in #28 T-28 trainer at 297.05 mph. No other pilot was within 50 mph of Holm at the top. In the Gold Championship Race, Holm easily outran AT-6 Class veteran Tom Dwelle in the #10 Sea Fury *Critical Mass*, which was now fueled with gasoline rather than alcohol. Their speeds of 462.01 mph and 434.96 mph meant that Holm had half an 8-mile lap lead at the finish.[1]

Hoover #11 "Endeavor" (John Garrett).

Formula One

Ray Cote (#4 Owl Racer *Alley Cat*) was back on top after an absence of more than 10 years. His 249.84 mph qualifying lap was just enough ahead of David Hoover in the #96 Grove GR-7, at 248.68 mph. In third was Scotty Crandlemire in #12 Cassutt *Outrageous* at 244.40 mph. In the Gold Championship Race, Cote was pressed by Gary Hubler in #95 Cassut *Mariah* but won by 245.91 mph to 242.97 mph.

Sport Biplane Class

1999 Gold winner David Rose won time trials at 209.64 mph, Tom Aberle was 2nd at 206.97 mph, and Stephen Brown was 3rd at 206.25 mph. In the Gold Championship Race on Sunday, David Rose won at 209.43 mph and Tom Aberle was 2nd at 206.73 mph, both at speeds almost identical to those at which they qualified. Stephen Brown, in 3rd, averaged 200.81 mph.

Sport Class

Like the Unlimited Class in its early days, this one was already developing fan enthusiasm for specific pilots and types of airplanes. Dave Morss and his factory-prepared Lancair IV was one combination, even though they lost the time trials leadership to dentist David Anders, who was timed at a near-record 331.90 mph in his dicey little Questaire Venture. Morse was just over a second slower, at 325.34 mph. In the Gold Championship Race, Morss prevailed at 328.05 mph, much faster than his old record. Lou Meyer was 2nd in his #4 Thunder Mustang, a scaled-down P-51 with an automotive V-8 engine, at 312.94 mph.

2001

Monday, September 10, the first day of qualifying, went off as scheduled, with 14 Unlimiteds completing time trials, led by Skip Holm at 458.88 mph in #4 *Dago Red*. A dozen Formula Ones were led by Ray Cote at 243.59 mph. A pair of AT-6 Class airplanes saw Fred Telling ahead at just 207.72 mph. In the Sport Biplane Class, 9 racers were led by Stephen Brown at 208.39 mph and three Sport Class airplanes qualified, with Lee Behel first at 309.01 mph.

Before time trials could be resumed early on Tuesday, all non-military aircraft in the U.S. were grounded, following the airborne terrorist attacks on New York and Washington. The racing airplanes were parked and their pilots and crews milled about, wondering what it all meant and what was going to happen next. It soon became obvious that the emergency would not end quickly, and so everyone was sent home. The 2001 National Championship Air Races were cancelled.

2002

As if to tell the world that air racing was back at Reno, September 9–15, Skip Holm whipped once around the course to set the first new qualifying record in six years: 497.79 mph in the #4 P-51 *Dago Red*. Bill Destefani was almost as fast in his #7 *Strega*, at 486.80 mph. Mike Brown placed 3rd in the highly modified Sea Fury #232 *September Fury*, at 468.27 mph.[2]

In the Gold Championship Race, Skip Holm won for the 4th time, at a near-record 466.84 mph, to 455.97 mph for Michael Brown. Destefani failed to complete the first lap.

Formula One

Gary Hubler (#95 *Mariah*) qualified at a Sharp-like 258.52 mph which would turn out to be the fastest ever recorded at Reno using the traditional system of measurement. Well back was Charlie Greer's 243.39 mph in the #69, now called *Miss B Haven*, and Hep Porter in the #4 Owl Racer which had previously been raced by Ray Cote. The order remained the same in the Gold Championship Race, with speeds of 249.56 mph, 244.22 mph and 240.694 mph.

Sport Biplane Class

David Rose's modifications to Bill Boland's Mong stretched the rules to their limit, appearing to be an original-design racer that wasn't exactly a biplane, but rather a sesquiplane, with its lower wing much smaller than the upper. But it was accepted, and he promptly broke the old *Racing Biplane* record of 223.88 mph set by Pat Hines in 1982. No one else was within 16 mph. In the Gold Championship Race, Rose won at another record, 224.20 mph, leading by a spectator-numbing half lap in front of Norman Way at 207.17 mph.

Sport Class

There were new names at the top of the list of 21 qualifiers. Unlimited Class legend Darryl Greenamyer was first, adding 15 mph to Morss' old record with a run at 347.77 mph in a modified Lancair IV. Second was Michael Lacey in the #71 Venture *Fool's Gold* he had been racing, at 331.87 mph, and in 3rd, John Parker in #351 Thunder Mustang *Blue Bijou* at 331.68 mph. The 6-lap Gold Championship Race was the class' closest yet, with Greenamyer winning

Tom Aberle's #62 modified Mong Sport Phantom, the first Sport Biplane to outrun the Formula Ones (John Garrett).

out at a record-breaking 328.97 mph to Parker's 327.67 mph and Dave Morss' 307.70 mph.

2003

Pilots arriving for this year's Reno races (September 9–15) were greeted with the Reno Air Racing Association's decision to change the way race courses were measured. While the new system was based on a more realistic, mathematically derived optimum route around the turns, this had the unfortunate drawback of making it impossible to compare speeds from all other previous races going back to 1909, which was via straight lines from pylon to pylon. The new way also happened to increase the chances of records being broken.[3]

The fastest Unlimited Class qualifier was John Penney, returning after a short absence, in #77 *Rare Bear*, with the second-best-ever speed of 495.04 mph. Right on his tail was record-holder Skip Holm in *Dago Red* at 492.72 mph. Of interest, at least for their novelty, were two World War II U.S. Navy Grumman carrier-based fighters: Mike Brown's twin-engined #1 F7F Tigercat *Big Bossman*, and Tom Camp's #2 F4F Wildcat *Bisquit*.

The goal of a 500 mph lap was achieved in Heat 2A, when Holm flew six laps at an average speed of 507.105 mph, with two laps unofficially clocked at 512 mph. John Penney was a strong 2nd at 492.94 mph, no doubt emboldened by Holm's flying. Any possible arguments about course length measurement vanished when it was determined that Holm would also have topped 500 mph by the traditional way of measuring.

The two went at it again in the Gold Championship Race, with Holm winning out at 487.94 mph to Penney's 483.94 mph. At least two teams had learned how to continue to keep engines from blowing up while producing far more power than their designers ever had in mind. Of the eight airplanes to finish the race, only Holm's was driven by a V-12 engine. Five of the others were Sea Furys, one was a Bearcat and one was a highly modified Yak-11.

Formula One

Gary Hubler won time trials again, with a time of 44.11 seconds for his lap, which was .67 slower than in 2002. But his speed was 260.15 mph, more than 1 mph *faster* than the previous year. In second was Charlie Greer at 44.31 seconds for 258.97 mph. Henceforth it would be more meaningful to compare times than speeds, though confusion continued. But as always, it was the order-of-finish that really mattered.

Gary Hubler won his second Formula One Gold Race, at 253.82 mph, with Hep Porter 2nd in the Owl Racer at 249.48 mph, and Birch Entriken 3rd in a hot taper-wing Cassutt #50 *Scarlet Screamer* at 240.69 mph.

#57 Goodyear F2G Super Corsair, raced by Ben McKillen in 1949, and by Bob Odegaard in 2006 (John Garrett).

Sport Biplane Class

Two airplanes shared the spotlight. David Rose's sesquiplane now had two relatively equal wings that were long and slender and designed to cut through Reno's thin air with minimal loss of speed. Tom Aberle's #62 *Phantom* was a drastically modified Mong, with extensive use of carbon-fiber. Rough air during their qualifying runs kept both airplane's speeds down to 221.29 mph and 219.72 mph, respectively.

Aberle won Heat 1-A at 220.62, mph, then retired, as his exotic composite propeller was starting to fail under racing conditions. Rose won the Gold Championship Race at 219.18 mph, a mile ahead of Norman Way. To all intents and purposes, the "Racing Biplane" class was being re-invented within the Sport Biplane Class rules, thanks to a lot of originality.

Sport Class

It was the year of the new factory-prepared Lancair Legacy: four were entered and three of their pilots took the top spots in time trials. Greenamyer barely missed breaking his own record, with 347.62 mph, Lee Behel was 2nd in #5 at 307.82 mph, and Rick Vandam was 3rd in #68 at 302.53 mph. Greenamyer had blown his engine in his third heat race, but all-night repair work had it back in working order, though it was uncertain if it would produce its rumored 600 hp in the Gold Championship Race. He managed his power carefully, using no more than necessary to hold onto the lead. On lap 4, Vandam slipped past, but Greenamyer added power, re-passed him and finished first at 324.50 mph to Vandam's 323.04 mph. No one else was close.

2004

The never-ending duels continued at Reno, September: Holm versus Penney, Mustang versus Bearcat, Vee versus radial engine, army versus navy origins. Time trials settled nothing, even though both pilots went all-out and their mounts performed to the limit. Holm averaged 490.82 mph to Penney's 490.03 mph, with just 0.1 seconds between them. Mike Brown, in his slick *September Fury*, was almost 25 mph back.[4]

Both Holm and Penney exceeded 470 mph in their fastest heat races, setting the stage for yet another edge-of-the-seat Gold Championship Race. After 8 laps, Holm crossed the line in 8:34.26 for 474.91 mph, to Penney's 8:35.45. But when Holm was penalized 16 seconds for having cut a pylon, dropping him to 2nd place at 456.83 mph, Penney was declared the winner at 469.96 mph. Of course, what the crowd saw was Holm's 1-second victory after almost 70 miles of howling engines and screaming propeller tips.

Formula One

Gary Hubler continued to lead the pack, qualifying first at 255.58 mph, with Scotty Crandlemire 2nd in #12 *Outrageous* at 250.28 mph, both of them in highly modified Cassutts, with Jason Somes (#4 Owl Racer) in 3rd place with a speed of 233.41 mph.

Sport Biplane Class

The weather was better for time trials and so Tom Aberle used it wisely to boost the qualifying record to 241.05 mph, which would have placed him 4th among the supposedly faster Formula Ones. David Rose was 2nd at 228.83 mph. In the Gold Championship Race, Aberle showed his tail feathers to the field in winning by 1½ miles over Rose, as they were clocked at 237.93 mph and 219.40 mph. While a biplane's extra wing and wing struts tend it slow it down, the class' engine specifications permitted much more extensive modifying, hence as much as twice the power.

Sport Class

After a long gestation period, Jon Sharp's logical development of his unbeatable Nemesis Formula One finally appeared among the Sport Class airplanes. While at first glance the appearance was similar to the midget, the new NXT was larger, had more power and a retractable landing gear. In its first outing, he qualified 3rd at 324.76 mph, well behind John Parker at 349.51 mph and Greenamyer at 343.66 mph. While landing after time trials, the NXT's landing gear collapsed, doing too much damage to permit on-the-field repairs.

Greenamyer took advantage of the situation and won at 333.18 mph. Barely two seconds behind him was John Parker at 332.13 mph. Lee Behel was almost 25 mph back in 3rd place.

2005

Penney picked up where he had left off at Reno, September 12–18, winning time trials at 470.8 mph, to Brian Sanders' (#8 Sea Fury *Dreadnought*) at 452.5 mph. In the Gold Championship Race, Penney cruised to victory at 466.30 mph, 2½ miles ahead of Brian Sanders at 448.83 mph, and more than a half lap ahead of 3rd place Stuart Dawson in #105 Sea Fury *Spirit of Texas* at 430.38 mph. All three flew radial-engined, ex-navy airplanes.[5]

Formula One

A new name appeared at the top of the list: Gary Hubler, flying #95 *Mariah*, a Cassutt Racer that bore no external similarity to the original design. That his modifications were well thought out was displayed in time trials, when he finished 1st at class record 257.10 mph, with Dave Hoover 2nd in his #11 *Endeavor* at 249.82 mph, and Charlie Greer 3rd in #69 at 249.10 mph. In their

Jon Sharp's #3 "Nemesis NXT," the first Sport Class racer to exceed 400 mph (John Garrett).

first heat race, Hubler and Hoover were never far apart, with Hubler winning by ½ second: 254.73 mph to 254.42 mph. In the Gold Championship Race, Hubler made it clear who was the best, winning at 252.30 mph to Hoover's 250.70 mph. Using the traditional system for measuring course length would reduce their speeds by only a few mph.

Sport Biplane Class

More changes: Jeffrey Lo, owner/pilot of #13, a highly modified Pitts Special *Miss Gianna*, set a qualifying record at 237.05 mph, not far ahead of Andy Buehler, flying #62 "Phantom" for Tom Aberle, who was 2nd at 232.71 mph, while Norman Way was 3rd at 216.69 mph. In the Gold Championship Race, Lo encountered severe turbulence, cut a pylon and was penalized out of a close finish with winner Buehler at 230.83 mph.

Sport Class

John Parker—#351 Thunder Mustang—added 17 mph to the qualifying record with 361.92 mph. Greenamyer was 2nd at 358.44 mph, and Kevin Eldridge was 3rd in the second Nemesis NXT at 336.35 mph. Jon Sharp, 4th at 323.38 mph, was not yet living up to expectations. Greenamyer then set a heat race record at 359.69 mph, alerting everyone to the coming close battle in the Gold Championship Race. After 6 laps of all-out racing, he won the Gold at a record 364.95 mph, to Parker's 356.74 mph and Eldridge's 343.13 mph. The Sport Class airplanes were now flying in the speed range of the Unlimited Bronze (2nd consolation) Race, and both Greenamyer and Parker displayed enough speed to win it.

2006

For the first time in two decades, an airplane other than *Rare Bear*, *Strega* and *Dago Red* would dominate at Reno, September 10–16, a much-needed indication that competition, without which no sport can long survive, was improving. Moreover, only 4 of the top 14 qualifiers flew American-built airplanes; 9 of them flew Hawker Sea Furys, long recognized as the most durable, and now being very effectively race-modified. First in time trials was Mike Brown, flying his *September Fury* at 478.51 mph, Ron Bucarelli took over Shelton's *Rare Bear* and averaged 455.77 mph.[6]

Jimmy Leeward dropped out even before the airplanes joined up prior to the start, while Destefani was unable to complete lap 5 before engine trouble spelled the end of his race.

Brown bettered his qualifying speed in winning the Gold Championship

Race at 481.62 mph. More than a half minute behind was Matt Jackson in *Dreadnought* at 453.56.

Formula One

Gary Hubler became only the third Formula One pilot, after Ray Cote and Jon Sharp, to win five consecutive National Championships, and did it in record-setting form. He added 11 mph to the old qualifying mark with 257.27 mph, and 7 mph to the Finals record with 257.01 mp h. Second in both categories was David Hoover, and third was Charlie Greer. Even after adjusting to the traditional system of measuring, his speeds were the equal of anything achieved by the all-conquering Sharp. Anders Trygg, from Sweden, became the first European pilot to compete at Reno since 1983, placing his #22 Cassutt *Dancing Queen* 19th among 22 qualifiers and then 6th in the Bronze Championship Race at 189.99 mph.

Sport Biplane Class

Tom Aberle was just as dominant as Hubler, adding 12 mph to the qualifying record with a run at 249.19 mph, and 14 mph to the old heat race record by averaging 251.96 mph. His qualifying speed would have placed him 2nd in Formula One, while his winning speed would also have placed him 2nd in Formula One. Clearly, the limit to which a small biplane can be streamlined had not been reached.

Sport Class

Darryl Greenamyer had retired from his second class, and this left his airplane to Rod von Grote, who placed 1st in qualifying at 354.74 mph. A tenth of a second slower was John Parker at 353.64 mph, with Jon Sharp 3rd at 351.67 mph. Three pilots whipping around the course within 0.3 seconds difference hinted at excitement to come. John Parker, in his third preliminary heat race, added to the anticipation by breaking the old record with an average of 370.05 mph., 4 mph ahead of von Grote.

In the Gold Championship Race. Von Grote broke the finals record with 369.38 mph, but was penalized back to 2nd place at 358.56 mph. This elevated Jon Sharp into his first Sport Class win in his NXT, at 360.39 mph. John Parker was 3rd at 350.34 mph.

2007

The trend toward foreign-built airplanes continued at Reno, September 10–16, with 9 of the 11 fastest qualifiers flying machines built in either Great

Britain or Czechoslovakia. In first for the second year running, the fastest qualifier was Mike Brown, at 472.85 mph, with John Penney 2nd in *Rare Bear* at 452.28 mph and Matt Jackson 3rd at 451.39 mph. While most of the other classes were experiencing serious accidents, the Unlimiteds soldiered on.[7]

The only heat race which saw pilots really push the limits was #3A on Saturday. Mike Brown and Bill Destefani went at it for two laps, at which time the latter began streaming white smoke and wisely pulled out. Brown kept up the speed despite the lack of serious pressure, averaging 470.06 mph for the six laps.

In the Gold Championship Race, John Penney took the lead in *Rare Bear*, which was finally developing the power it had lacked all week. He was followed by Brown and by Matt Jackson in *Dreadnought* until the last lap, when Brown pulled out. Penney sped on, finishing at 478.39 mph, and Sherman Smoot (#84 *Czech Mate*) was elevated to 2nd place when Jackson was disqualified for violating the safety deadline. After the race, Penney's throttle couldn't be pulled back to reduce speed prior to landing. He eventually made an excellent deadstick landing.

Formula One

While the Swedish Cassutt had been sold to an American, there were two Cassutts from Canada, as interest north of the border was clearly building. Gary Hubler set another qualifying record with 258.28 mph and a heat race record at 259.87 mph, but in the next heat race collided with Jason Somes in #4 *Alley Cat* and died, while Somes survived serious injuries; blame was placed on the novel starting direction with which hardly anyone had experience. In the Championship Race, David Hoover won at 245.87 mph.

Sport Biplane Class

The worst year in Reno history started off even before the first heat race, when Steve Dari, former Formula One pilot who had bought David Rose's winning #3 *Peregrine*, caught fire while taking off for a practice flight and crashed fatally. Tom Aberle repeated as time trials winner, though at a sub-record 251.60 mph. Jeffrey Lo was 2nd at 234.95 mph. In the Gold Championship Race, Aberle was well on his way to winning when a burned piston forced him out, allowing Cris Ferguson to win at 233.47 mph in the #13 *Miss Gianna*, usually raced by Jeffrey Lo.

Sport Class

Hard work during the past few off-seasons paid off for Jon Sharp, as he set a qualifying record of 386.90 mph, breaking the old mark by a shocking 25 mph. In 2nd, also flying a Sharp NXT, was Unlimited racer Kevin Eldridge at 378.29

26. The 2000s

Darryl Greenamyer's #33 Lancair dominated the early years of the Sport Class (Al Wimer).

mph, more than 20 mph faster than anyone else. Sharp and Eldridge flew two heat races almost as fast, proving their time trials speeds were not flukes.

For this year the class had been divided into two sections: Sport and Supersport, the latter for engines up to 1,000 cu. in. and permitting nitrous-oxide and other injectable substances. No racers with larger engines were ready for this year, so the fastest went into the Supersport Gold, while the Gold Championship Race was for the next fastest group, previously relegated to the Silver Race. In the Supersport Gold, Sharp won with yet another record — 385.65 mph, which would have been fast enough to place 2nd in the Unlimited Bronze Race, 5th in the Unlimited Silver or 7th in the Unlimited Gold. Barely noticed was the 383.13 mph turned in by Eldridge for 2nd place.

2008

Bill Destefani came out of retirement to equal Darryl Greernamyer's record of seven wins, at Reno, September 8–14. Dan Martin, in P-51 #4 *Dago Red* took time trials at 474.14 mph to Michael Brown's 473.48 mph and Destefani's 472.79 mph. Among the top dozen qualifiers, only two flew Mustangs, while six flew Sea Furys, 2 flew Yak-11s and two flew Bearcats. In the Gold Championship Race, Destefani won comfortably by 1¼ miles, averaging 483.06 mph to Martin's 474.31 mph. John Penney, in the venerable *Rare Bear*, dropped out on lap 4.[8]

Formula One

It was a year for unfamiliar names in familiar airplanes. Leading time trials was Steve Senegal in what had been David Hoover's #11 *Endeavor* at 251.83 mph. In 2nd was Doug Bodine in the #92 Cassutt *Yellow Peril* formerly flown by Hong Kong–based airline pilot Eric Mattheson, at 242.99 mph, and 3rd was "Smokey" Young in the old Judy Wagner *Shoestring* at 242.79 mph. In the Gold Championship Race, Senegal came through with his first win, at 246.12 mph. In 2nd was Gary Davis, new owner of the #50 *Scarlet Screamer*, at 239.33 mph, and then Bodine in #92 at 239.04 mph, just ½ second back.

Sport Biplane Class

Only three of the 17 qualifiers flew anything but a Pitts Special, as the reliable, easy-to-fly and exceptionally maneuverable aerobatic airplane had proven its worth. Tom Aberle again led the way in his Mong Sport at 249.387 mph, coming close to beating all the Formula Ones. He then broke his own Championship record by the slimmest of margins, averaging 251.98 mph, which would have won in F/1 and lapping everyone but runner-up Norman Way, who averaged 213.16 mph.

Sport Class

Jon Sharp continued with his attack on the record book, becoming the first person in history to officially exceed 400 mph in a privately built airplane. His 409.30 mph qualifying lap would have ranked him 11th of the 24 Unlimited Class racers this year. Any thought of his entering the Unlimited Class was halted, however, when members of the Unlimited Class voted to ban all airplanes under 4,000 lbs. Mike Dacey was 2nd in time trials with 375.33 mph in his #71 *Venture*, while Giboney was 3rd in the #75 Thunder Mustang *Rapid Travel* at 350.26 mph. Sharp then set a record in Heat 1-A at 393.22 mph.

The Supersport Gold Championship Race was an easy win for Sharp, as he set a finals record at 392.25 mph, winning by 2½ miles over Dacey, who averaged 368.39 mph.

Chapter 27
Formula One Invades Europe

Until 1970, all-out racing for distinct classes of airplanes which had been developed expressly for speed competition was a uniquely American activity. England had long had its handicap races, and there were rallies and speed/efficiency competitions in many countries. But exciting wingtip-to-wingtip, full-throttle races around short pylon courses could be found only in the states between the Atlantic and Pacific Oceans.[1]

Then the winds of change began to blow eastward, gently at first and then more briskly. In 1961 the Cosmic Wind *Ballerina* was imported into England and then purchased by the Tiger Club, which enabled it to be seen by tens of thousands at air shows and handicap races, and test-flown by some of Britain's best, who raved about sprightliness of the "little Spitfire."

In 1964, Rollason Aircraft Ltd. conducted a "Midget Racer Design Competition" which attracted a fascinating variety of designs for a sport-racer to be operated by flying clubs, and was won by the all-wood, low-wing Beta. First prize was a prototype airplane to be built by Rollasons, and which was raced initially in handicap events. By late 1968, veteran handicap racer Tom Storey had begun to build a set of three Cassutt Racers from purchased plans, and Rollasons was building more Betas. As soon as there were more than a couple of midgets flying, there was probably no way to keep them from racing.

And so, at Jurby, a deactivated World War II training field on the scenic little Isle of Man, in the middle of the Irish Sea, the inevitable finally happened. On the weekend of April 24–27, 1970, five midget racers lined up on the World War II runway, awaiting the starter's flag. But that was about all that resembled other midget races. From the impossibly green grass on the surrounding low hills to the dilapidated old RAF control tower, it was as different from Reno and Cleveland and Miami as it could have been.

But once the flag went down, the engines began to wind up beyond their government-certified limit and the little machines quickly accelerated into the air, the way *real* racing planes are meant to do. Moreover, every decibel produced sounded just like their cousins had long been doing in Ohio and Nevada and Florida.

Unlike handicap races with their gentlemanly individual starts, this race

Vincent Martinez's #46 Cassutt, modified with a composite wing (owner/pilot).

was drama from the green flag to the checkered flag, a few laps later. When Fred Marsh sped across the finish line in his #56 Beta *Forerunner* at 174.36 mph, a mere four-tenths of a second in front of the fast-closing Michael Jones in #74 Beta *Blue Chip*, few in the large crowd could have failed to realize that a new era had begun before their eyes.

Before the 1970 season had ended, there had been five Formula One races in Great Britain, at such quaintly named venues as Tollerton, Halfpenny Green, Shobdon and Teeside. The speed had passed the 180 mph mark, but more important, many tens of thousands of aviation enthusiasts and just plain blokes had seen what happens when you send true racers off to battle on an aerial race track. Using the little-known NAA point system, frozen meatpie entrepreneur Fred Marsh was 1970 National Champion. And the British racing scene had seen its biggest change since before the First World War.

Under the Formula Air Racing Association (FARA) the sport thrived, with four or five races each year and a growing body of knowledgeable fans. It was in 1976 that the sport spread to France, where, at the famed Paul Ricard auto racing circuit at Le Castellet in the extreme southeast of the country, there were 8 British racers, 1 French and 1 American ready to race in the French Grand Prix. The experience of Kentucky state senator and World War II fighter pilot

27. The Formula One Invades Europe

William Lobet, many-time French champion, in his own-built Cassutt Racer (owner/pilot).

Bill Sullivan proved too much for the Europeans, as he set European records for time trials (225.79 mph) and the Championship Race (210.45 mph).

Yearly champions came and went. In 1972, with six races, it was Ian McCowen, in the original LeVier #3 Cosmic Wind *Little Toni*, recently imported. In 1973, it was Tom Storey, flying the #1 Cassutt, now with a tapered wing. In 1974, Bill Walker won four of the five races in the #5 Cosmic Wind *Ballerina Mk.II*, built from the remains of the original Goodyear racer. In 1975, Storey returned to win the Championship. In 1976, Fred Marsh had two 1sts and a 2nd, and in 1977 he won all four races in *Ballerina Mk.II*. In 1978, Mick Crossley won the first race of the season in the new #22 Cassutt *Bananas*, while John Mirley won three 1sts and a 2nd in *Ballerina Mk.II*. For 1979, Mirley was the winner, though by just a slight margin.

In the decades of the 1970s and 1980s—the highpoint of Formula One racing—there were, on average, eight races a year, more than half of them in Europe, with Denmark and Belgium joining in the fun. In the 1990s, F/1 racing spiraled downward, with the last race in England being in 1994, and no more than 2 races in Europe for any year after 1990. In England, the men who had been pouring so much effort into organizing races seem to have run out of gas, as their hard work had not produced anything lasting.

Rollason Beta, a British design, was prominent in the first years of Formula One racing in Great Britain (M.P. Marsh).

The French marched on, but in the absence of British participation, could not field enough airplanes for good competition. In 1998, the combined British and French Grands Prix were held in England, with few spectators in evidence. Still, there were signs of a healthy revival in France in the early 2000s, but accidents in racing demonstrations seriously injured Xavier Beck and killed Pierre Yout, both having been very active organizers, as well as competitors.

Chapter 28

Short-Lived and Minor Classes

Some experiments work, while others don't. Some air racing classes go on and on, while others fade quickly, their shortcomings usually evident to all. It is in the nature of the game that new ideas must be tried. Otherwise, men would still be racing wobbly Bleriots and Antoinettes, powered by highly unreliable 30 hp Anzanis and 50 hp V-8s.

When Bill Stead created his National Championship Air Races at Reno in 1964, much of the program was experimental, as there was little that remained of 1940's and 1950's racing. His most successful new idea was the Sport Biplane Class, a result of pleading by a group of amateur sport pilots who wanted to

Brian Dempsey won several Formula V National titles in his Monnett Sonerai *Miss Annapolis* (author).

race the low-powered single-seaters they had built at home and were flying routinely, for fun. It worked, and with gradual modifications to its increasingly comprehensive set of rules, continues to this day. Over the years, five more new classes were tried and, for various reasons, three of them failed to become permanent elements on the racing calendar.

Ladies' Stock Plane Class, 1964–1969

A second Stead invention — the Ladies' Stock Plane Class — would never have come about had not the NAA rules prohibited women from racing around the pylons with men. It was a holdover from the 1930s, when a well known woman racepilot was killed in a racing crash which, in turn, led to fear of further negative publicity if another woman was involved in a fatal accident. Bill found some stock 180 hp Piper Cherokees, and a group of women who had been flying in cross-country rally-like races who agreed to fly them.

The 1964 inaugural race at Reno was closely contested, thanks to the identical airplanes, but they were no faster than the little open-cockpit biplanes, they were relatively quiet, and they offered no opportunity for technical innovation. For 1965, the rules were opened up to permit any type of four-seat, piston-engined factory-stock personal plane, regardless of engine size. This added variety, which quickly led to greater speed, but retained their ostensibly stock look, if not always condition.

Cherokees were replaced by Comanches and Bonanzas and Mooneys and Meyers 200s. The racing was close and it was hard, with more than one stock airplane being stressed beyond not only its design limitations but sometimes even its ultimate-g limitations. By all rights, there should have been a few structural failures and serious accidents, but lady luck kept smiling.

Judy Wagner dominated the Ladies Stock Plane Class in this and other Beech Bonanzas (author).

The dominating force was the tall, glamorous Judy Wagner and a series of well prepared Beech Bonanzas with which she won more races than any other two pilots, and almost always held the major speed records. Still, the races were competitive and therefore well received by promoters.

In 1968, air show pilot/auto racer Betty Skelton threatened legal action to get all the pylon racing classes opened to women, as other sports, including thoroughbred horse racing, had seen a precedent established. The attorney for the Professional Race Pilots Association decided that opposition to this move would be futile, and so the classes quickly opened up. There was one Stock Plane class race at Cleveland in which both men and women flew, and that was the end of the class, as its reason to exist had evaporated. Some of women switched to other classes, but most returned to cross-country racing and rallying.

Formula V, 1977–1997

The idea was first proposed during a planning session for what was to have been a professionally produced major air racing program at Palm Springs, California, in 1965: the AeroClassic. The rules for what was initially called the 95 Cu. In. Class were very much like those of the highly successful Formula One rules, with their concern for low cost, close competition and safety. The new class would be limited to 1,600 cc. Volkswagen auto engines, with other specifications modified accordingly.

The AeroClassic came and went without a single VW-powered racer in sight, thanks to a basic paradox of the sport. Few people will build racers for a new class until at least one race is firmly scheduled and sponsored (which the Palm Springs event could not promise). But no race organizer was about to put prize money in escrow until he was assured that there were enough airplanes for good competition. There could be no chickens without a few eggs, but how do you get those first eggs without chickens?

The first sanctioned race for what had become Formula V wasn't held until 1977, when several of them raced around the pylons at Sturgis, Kentucky, with 73-year-old Steve Wittman winning in his prototype V-Witt. Under the energetic and creative leadership of Jim Vliet, the class grew and prospered, racing mainly where there were no other classes in action. It seemed to offer something that air racing needed: a class that for minimum cost to the participants and race organizers would produce close, exciting races. While it grew to the point that as many as 10 airplanes raced together, it never appealed to Reno and other major multi-class operations. Apparently the visual similarity to Formula One, combined with less noise and speed, permanently limited it to the status of a supporting event.

The loss in action of two successive class presidents was too much. Several pilots retired, leaving too few teams to populate a good race. Jim Vliet eventually ran out of enthusiasm, leaving what remained of the class without the kind of leadership it desperately needed. The last sanctioned race was held in 1997, and while there have been sporadic attempts to organize more meets, nothing happened. An effort to stir up some interest by builder Ed Fisher in the early-2000s was met with silence.

T-28 Class, 1996–1998

This idea followed the pattern of creating a new class from a large supply of existing airplanes. It had worked well with the Sport Biplane Class in 1964, and with the AT-6 Class in 1968. The Reno Air Racing Association felt there were enough surplus North American T-28 Trojan piston-engined trainers being flown by private owners in 1996 to justify creating a class. The airplanes' similarity in speed was expected to produce close races and thus fan interest.

The first race saw but five entries, only two of which completed time trials. The three 5-lap heat races were increasingly close at the finish, but this did not fool many spectators. In the third heat, the first four planes finished in the space of 1 second, in a demonstration of close formation flying and carefully (but rather amateurishly) staged races. Almost as troublesome was the inabil-

A typical North American T-28 Nomad military trainer that raced in the short-lived T-28 Class (author).

ity of the announcers, let alone the fans, to tell one airplane from another. All were painted in authentic military colors and markings, with squadron numbers and letters cluttering up the sides, making it difficult to distinguish race numbers while the airplanes were speeding past at 250 mph.

A second try in 1998 produced more of the same confusion and transparent "competition." The fans yawned and the Reno management made the only possible move, dropping the class after just two tries. With little competition and no technical variety among the airplanes, there was simply nothing to hold it together.

Summary and Outlook

Where We've Come From

In 1909, prior to the Great Week of the Champagne, there had been no closed-course air racing anywhere in the world. Even when it burst into existence at Reims before a huge gathering of spectators, it remained a solitary event. Then, gradually, the idea began to catch on. The James Gordon Bennett Trophy Race gained stature as the premier award. Handicap pylon racing became a weekly entertainment in England. The sight of several airplanes battling it out in full view (most of the time) of the paying crowd became an accepted part of life for the increasingly large community of aviation enthusiasts.

After the First World War, air racing was divided into closed-course and cross-country competitions, and into prestigious international races such as those for the Schneider Cup, and a continuation of English handicap races, and the American National Air Races which stressed short races mainly for military airplanes flown by military pilots.

The big change came at Cleveland in 1929, when a custom-built racer beat the best airplanes the American military had to offer. This ignited a rush to design and build original racers in what later became known as The Golden Age of Air Racing, with the likes of Jimmy Doolittle and Roscoe Turner flying airplanes such as the GeeBees and Wedell Williams Specials.

After a long pause for World War II, American racing came back with stock and then modified ex-military fighters: Mustangs, Corsairs, Cobras. Their sameness motivated those running the sport to create the Goodyear midget class and a return to individuality, originality and affordability.

The long drought after the end of the classic Cleveland National Air Races was relieved by a completely new group of people in a completely different part of the world: Reno, Nevada, which has now played host to the multi-class National Championship Air Races for more than 40 years.

Where We Are

As these words are written in late 2008, there is but one racing meet in the world that can be depended on: Reno. Formula One air racing had a good run in England, but hasn't been seen there since the mid-1990s. It was very active also in France, but began experiencing organizational problems in the mid-2000s and is not in good health.

Depending so completely on one race a year, no matter how large and how successful it may be, is hardly conducive to stability. If, for any reason, the Reno Air Races would be cancelled, the air racing community would be left with nothing to do save moan wistfully about the good ol' days. And hope that another Bill Stead might some day come galloping out of the west to work another miracle.

Where We May Be Going

There are new kinds of air racing appearing. The Red Bull series involves high-powered aerobatic airplanes flown singly around a slalom course over the water the while performing mild aerobatic maneuvers. Is this racing, or is it aerobatics? Its supporters say it is both, while the dedicated fans of the traditional style of pylon racing turn up their noses or turn their backs.

Not so the hundreds of thousands who watch these races—at no charge in most cases—and who know little or nothing about the Reno way of flying together around an aerial oval "race track" at very high speed.

One variation on this is the brainchild of the Rocket Racing League, which continues to advertise its high-tech ideas. While the small, rocket-powered homebuilts will race one-at-a-time through a course which is projected on each airplane's windshield, the details of the action is to be communicated to the audience via special hand-held devices. This is seen as a way to combine air racing and the intense enthusiasm for electronic devices of the younger generation. As yet, all that has been seen are demonstrations of the airplanes.

Is air racing as we know it out of date? Are propeller-driven airplanes a symbol of the long-distant past? Are young people turned off by anything suggesting antiquity? Reno continues to draw large crowds, considering its remote location. One-off multi-class races held near population centers have shown considerable potential before succumbing to financial woes. Auto racing continues to experience very good health and has not yet seen the need to go high-tech.

There are currently six classes in action. The unlimited class is considered the star of the sport, thanks in great part to the marvelous speed and sounds of its airplanes. Its impending demise due to the steady erosion of airplanes has been predicted for at least 25 years, and yet the entry lists at Reno have not shrunk as expected. Not even the failure of custom-built Unlimiteds has had any great impact on the situation.

Formula One, which carried the sport on its own for many years, is as competitive as ever, now that Jon Sharp has switched to the Sport Class. As a supporting class, the Sport Biplanes continue to provide some of the closest and most exciting races while retaining their air of nostalgia. The AT-6 Class has never offered visual creativity, but still is able to contribute close and noisy races. The new Jet Class is the fastest of the lot, but rarely has produced close races and has the same need for long courses as the Unlimiteds, and that has reduced its visibility from the grandstands. That leaves the still growing Sport Class which gives the fans variety and originality, though not as much as with the true "home-built" classes. The rapid increase in the speed of the fastest suggests it may well be there when the Unlimiteds eventually fade due to cost and the inevitable losses resulting from crashes and the re-converting of racers back into authentic warbirds whose resale value is considerably greater. There is little doubt that if additional facilities can be found, along with the needed financing and manpower required for major, multi-class races, that there will be sufficient airplanes to fill the entry lists.

Historically, the only racing series that have achieved long-term success have been those that were non-profit, civic efforts. Profit-making races have not been able to hang on long enough to start showing a profit so they can eventually become fully self-sustaining. One of the main reasons for the initial financial losses experienced by new racing meets is the lack of public and press familiarity with the sport. Let's face it: if the only football game of the year was the Super Bowl, there wouldn't be enough people with sufficient interest to fill even an average high school stadium.

If air racing is to become generally successful, there must be an annual series of local and regional races—comparable to baseball's minor leagues—that would give people in all parts of the country an opportunity to become familiar with the people and airplanes and the way the sport operates. Moreover, this would enable more pilots, officials, organizers and the local press to hone their skills.

As these words were written, there was no reason for optimism.

Chapter Notes

Chapter 1
1. Coverage in *Flight* magazine: Aug. 28, 1909, pg. 521.
2. *Flight* magazine: Aug. 28, 1909, p. 521.
3. *Flight* magazine: Aug. 28, 1909, p. 521.
4. *Flight* magazine: Aug. 28, 1909, p. 521.
5. Owen Lieberg, *The First Air Race* (New York: Doubleday, 1974), pp. 34–35.
6. From here through end of chapter: coverage in *Flight* magazine, Aug. 28, Sept. 4, and Sept. 11.

Chapter 2
1. Various issues of *Flight* magazine for 1911.

Chapter 3
1. Most of the information in this chapter comes from Peter Lewis' *British Racing and Record-Breaking Aircraft* (Putnam, 1970).

Chapter 4
1. *Aero*, a weekly magazine, for Oct. 29 and November 5, 1910; *Aircraft*, a monthly magazine, for December, 1910, and *Scientific American* for Nov. 5, 1910.
2. *The Aeroplane*, a British weekly, for July 6, 1911; and *l'Aerophile*.
3. *Aero and Hydro*, an American weekly, for Sept. 14, 1912.
4. *The New York Herald, Paris Edition*, for Sept. 30, 1913; *Flight* for Oct. 4, 1913.

Chapter 5
1. Elison Hawks, *British Seaplanes Triumph in the International Schneider Trophy Contests* (Real Photographs Co., Ltd., 1945); and Thomas G. Foxworth, *The Speed Seekers* (Doubleday, 1975).

Chapter 6
1. Thomas G. Foxworth, *The Speed Seekers* (Doubleday).

Chapter 7
1. Thomas G. Foxworth, *The Speed Seekers* (Doubleday, 1975); Peter Lewis, *British Racing and Record-Breaking Aircraft* (Putnam, 1970).

Chapter 8
1. Thomas G. Foxworth, *The Speed Seekers* (Doubleday, 1975); Reed Kinert, *Racing Planes and Air Races*, Volumes I and II (Aero Publishers, 1969).

Chapter 9
1. Peter Lewis, *British Racing and Record-Breaking Aircraft* (Putnam, 1970); "The King's Cup Race," *Flight* magazine for Sept. 5, 1935, pp. 238–246.

Chapter 10
1. Lesley Forden, *Glory Gamblers: The Story of the Dole Race* (Alameda, Calif.: Nottingham Press, 1986); "The Dole Pacific Race," *Aero Digest* magazine, September 1927.

Chapter 11
1. Gary Williams, *Air Racing Results 1909 to 1939* (Scottsdale, Ariz.).
2. W.H. Schmid, and Truman Weaver, *The Golden Age of Air Racing, Volume I* (EAA Aviation Foundation, 1983); Thomas G. Foxworth, *The Speed Seekers* (Doubleday).

Chapter 12

1. John T. Nevill, "The 1929 National Air Races," *Western Flying* magazine, Sept. 7, 1929; Fred F. Marshall, "The 1929 National Air Races and Aeronautical Exposition," *Aerial Age* magazine, September 1929; official race results, as prepared on the field and distributed to the working press.

Chapter 13

1. 1925 and 1926 races covered in Thomas G. Foxworth's *The Speed Seekers* (New York: Doubleday, 1975).
2. All races covered in Reed Kinert's *Racing Planes and Air Races, Volumes I and II* (Fallbrook, Calif.: Aero Publishers, 1969), and Elison Hawks' *British Seaplanes Triumph in the International Schneider Trophy Contests* (Southport, U.K.: Real Photographs, 1945).

Chapter 14

1. Clifford Henderson, *The Value of National Air Races, Aero Digest*, July 1930; complete tabulated race results, as prepared on the field.
2. "Setting the Stage for the 1931 Races," *Aviation* magazine, September 1931; complete race results; Z.D. Granville, "GeeBee Super Sportster," *Aero Digest*, October 1931.
3. Clifford W. Henderson, "Warming Up for Cleveland," *Aero Digest*, August 1932; Donald J. Seiler, "The 1932 Thompson Trophy Race," *Air Classics*, August 1972; official race results.
4. "Los Angeles Scene of 1933 Nationals," *Aero Digest*, June 1933; official race results.
5. *Aviation* magazine, October 1934; official race results.

Chapter 15

1. British weekly *Flight*, issues for September 27, October 4, October 11, October 18, October 25, November 1 and November 8, 1934.

Chapter 16

1. *L'Aerophile* magazine for September 1–15, 1919.
2. *Flight* for Dec. 8, 1921, and *l'Aeronautique* for Oct. 1, 1921; *Flight* for Sept. 28, 1922, and Oct. 5, 1922.
3. Don Berliner, *Model Aviation* magazine for June 1987; *The Aeroplane* for May 17 and May 31, 1933.

Chapter 17

1. Peter Lewis, *British Racing and Record-Breaking Aircraft* (London: Putnam, 1971), pp. 208–320.

Chapter 18

1. Ben O. Howard, *Mister Mulligan, Aviation* magazine, October 1935; official race results.
2. J.H. Meyer, "The 1936 National Air Races," *Popular Aviation*, November 1936; official race results.
3. Cy Caldwell, "Cydelights on the Cleveland Air Races," *Aero Digest*, October 1937; official race results.
4. Cy Caldwell, "Three Days in a Daze at the Air Races," *Aero Digest*, October 1938; official race results.
5. Cy Caldwell, "Review of the National Air Races," *Aero Digest*, October 1939; official race results.

Chapter 19

1. "National Air Races," *Air Trails Pictorial* magazine, December 1946; original notes made by *Cleveland Press* reporters, in author's files; official race results.
2. Alexander McSurely, "Heavy Accident Toll Weighs against National Air Races," *Aviation Week*, Sept. 8, 1947; author's personal recollections; official race results.
3. Robert Hotz, "F-86A Hits Record; Cameras Miss," *Aviation Week*, Sept. 13, 1948; Curtiss Fuller, "Mighty Midgets," *Flying Magazine*, December 1948; official race results; author's personal recollections.
4. Alexander McSurely, "Midget Race Is Close Contest," *Aviation Week*, Sept. 12, 1949; "Cleveland Air Races," *Air Trails* magazine, December 1949; official race results; author's personal recollections.

Chapter 20

1. Author's notes and personal recollections; official race results.

Chapter 21

1. "The Reno Races," *Flying Magazine*, September 1964. Don Dwiggins, "Air Race," *Argosy* magazine, September 1964. Don Berliner, "Air Racing News" *Sport Aviation* magazine, August 1964; Don Berliner, "U.S. Air Races," *Asian & Indian Skyways*, June 1964; Don Berliner, extensive correspondence, reporter's notes and recollections.

Chapter 22

1. Frank Tinker, "Air Racing Revival Meet," *Flying* magazine, February 1966; Don Berliner, "Reno Stakes Claim to National Air Race title," *Air Progress* magazine, January 1966; reporter's notes and personal recollections, plus extensive correspondence; official race results.
2. Don Berliner, "Behind the Scenes at the National Air Races," *Air Progress*, March 1967; extensive correspondence, reporter's notes and personal recollections.
3. Don Berliner, "Forty Thousand Cheer Reno's Fourth 'Annual,'" *Air Progress*, January 1968; reporter's notes, personal recollections; official race results.
4. Don Berliner and James Gilbert, "Racing '68," *Flying*, September 1968; Don Berliner, "Rip-Roaring Racing at Reno," *Air Progress*, February 1969; extensive correspondence, reporter's notes and personal recollections; official race results.
5. Mike Dillon, "Reno Sound, Size and Speed," *Air Progress*, January 1970; Don Berliner, "Reno Race of the Year," *Air Progress*, January 1970; extensive correspondence, reporter's notes and personal recollections; official race results.

Chapter 23

1. Don Berliner, "Showdown at Reno," *Air Progress*, January 1971; reporter's notes, author's personal recollections, correspondence, official results.
2. Reporter's notes, author's personal recollections, correspondence, official race results.
3. Jim Larsen, "The Making of a Champion," *National Aeronautics* magazine, Summer 1973; Don Berliner, "Reno '72," *Air Progress*, January 1973; reporter's notes, author's personal recollections; official race results.
4. Don Berliner, "The Big One," *Air Progress*, January 1974; Jack Leggatt, "Reno Races Smash Many Records," *Sport Flying* magazine, January 1974; official race results.
5. Official race results; correspondence; *Reno Gazette* coverage.
6. Official race results; correspondence; *Reno Gazette* coverage.
7. Official race results; correspondence; *Reno Gazette* coverage.
8. Official race results; correspondence; *Reno Gazette* coverage.
9. Official Race results; correspondence.
10. Official race results; correspondence.

Chapter 24

1. Official race results; correspondence.
2. Official race results; correspondence.
3. Official race results; correspondence.
4. Official race results; correspondence.
5. Official race results; *Reno Gazette-Journal* coverage; correspondence.
6. Official race results; correspondence.
7. John Tegler, "Fast Lane," *Air Progress*, December 1986; John Tegler, "They Came to Race," *Air Progress*, February 1987; Jack Cox, "Reno '86," *Sportsman Pilot*, Fall 1986; official race results; correspondence.
8. John Tegler, "The Unlimiteds Rip Up the Sky at Reno 1987," *Air Progress*, January 1988; Jack Cox, "Reno '87," *Sportsman Pilot*, Fall 1987; correspondence; official race results.
9. Jack Cox, "Reno '88," *Sportsman Pilot*, Fall 1988; official race results.
10. Jack Cox, "Reno '89," *Sportsman Pilot*, Fall 1989; official race results.

Chapter 25

1. Jack Cox, "Reno '90," *Sportsman Pilot*, Fall 1990; *Reno Gazette-Journal* coverage; official race results.
2. Jack Cox, "Reno '91," *Sportsman Pilot*, Fall 1991; *Reno Gazette-Journal* coverage; official race results.
3. Reporter's notes; *Reno Gazette-Journal* coverage; official race results.
4. Jack Cox, "Reno '93," *Sportsman Pilot*, Fall 1993; official race results.
5. Reporter's notes; official race results.
6. Jack Cox, "Reno '94," *Sportsman Pilot*, Fall 1994; *Reno Gazette-Journal* coverage; official race results.
7. Jack Cox, "Reno '95," *Sportsman Pilot*, Fall 1995; *Reno Gazette-Journal* coverage; official race results.
8. Jack Cox, "Reno '96," *Sportsman Pilot*, Fall 1996; correspondence; *Reno Gazette-Journal* coverage; official race results.
9. Official race results; correspondence; *Reno Gazette-Journal* coverage.
10. Jack Cox, "Reno '98," *Sportsman Pilot*, Fall 1998; *Reno Gazette-Journal* coverage; official race results.
11. Official race results; Len Ashburn and Frank Ronco, "Reno 1999," *Professional Air Racing* newsletter, October 1999.

Chapter 26

1. Official race results; *Reno Gazette-Journal* coverage; correspondence.
2. Jack Cox, "Reno '02," *Sportsman Pilot*,

Fall 2002; official race results; Graham White, "Reno from the Pits," *Torque Meter* newsletter, Winter 2003.

3. Jack Cox, "Reno Air Races," *Sportsman Pilot*, Fall 2003; Andy Meisler, "The Fright Stuff," *Los Angeles Times* magazine, Jan. 5, 2003; official race results.

4. Jack Cox, "Reno Air Races," *Sportsman Pilot*, Fall 2004; *Reno Gazette-Journal* coverage; official race results.

5. Jack Cox, "Reno Air Races," *Sportsman Pilot*, Fall 2005; official race results.

6. Jack Cox, "Reno 2006," *Sportsman Pilot*, Fall 2006; official race results.

7. Jack Cox, "Reno 2007," *Sportsman Pilot*, Fall 2007; official race results.

8. Official race results; correspondence.

Chapter 27

1. British aviation magazines, correspondence, author's recollections.

Bibliography

Berliner, Don. *The Complete World Wide Directory of Racing Planes*. Volume I. Destin, Florida: Aviation Publishing, 1997.

_____. *Unlimited Air Racers*. Osceola, Wisconsin: Motorbooks International, 1992.

Forden, Lesley. *Glory Gamblers: The Story of the Dole Race*. Alameda, California: Nottingham Press, 1986.

Foxworth, Thomas G. *The Speed Seekers*. New York: Doubleday, 1975.

Hawks, Ellison. *British Seaplanes Triumph in the International Schneider Trophy Contests*. Southport, England: Real Photographs, 1945.

Kinert, Reed. *Racing Planes and Air Races*. Fallbrook, California: Aero Publishers, 1969.

Lieberg, Owen S. *The First Air Race*. New York: Doubleday, 1974.

Ogilvy, David. *DH88: The Story of de Havilland's Racing Comets*. Eagan, Minnesota: Flying Books, 1984.

Scheppler, Robert H. *Pacific Air Race*. Washington, D.C.: Smithsonian Institution Press, 1988.

Schmid, W.H., and Weaver, Truman. *The Golden Age of Air Racing*. Volumes I and II. Oshkosh, Wisconsin: The Experimental Aircraft Association, 1983.

Index

Numbers in **bold italics** indicate pages with photographs.

ABC-TV Wide World of Sports 154
Aberle, Tom 200, 202, 203, 215, 217, 218, 222, 224- 226, 228
Abrams, Bob 163
Acosta, Bert 55, 59
Adams, Paul 99
Adams, Wayne 158
Aerial Derby 31, 63
Aero Club of France 43, 120
Aero Club of Illinois 38
AeroClassic 235
Aerol Trophy 99
The Aeroplane 18, 36
Agello, Francisco 90
Air Foundation 146
Airspeed Viceroy 110
AirVenture Fly-In 82
Albert A.140 116
Alcock, John 3
Alexander Eaglerock Bullet 80
Alford, Joan 176
All-American Air Maneuvers 147
All Ohio Day 77
All-Ohio Derby 78
Allen, Earl 207, 211, 212
Allison V-1710 engine 62, 214
Amateur-Built Biplane Class (see Sport Biplane Class) 157
American Defender 38
American Legion Day 80
American Motorsports Hall of Fame 15
American Power Boat Association 156
American Team 47
Amerigo, M. 21
Amsoil-Rutan Racer 193
Anders, David 215, 217
Anderson, Neil 195–198
A.N.E.C. Missel Thrush 66
Ansaldo A-1 Ballila 59
Ansaldo biplane 57
Ansalso SVA-9 59
Ansaldo V-12 52
Anspach, Bob 191
Antoinette: monoplane 12, 233; V-8 engine 12, 17
Anzani 11, 12

Aquarius 185
Armstrong Siddeley Genet 82
Armstrong Whitworth Siskin 64; Siskin IV 64; Siskin V 64
Army Balloon Factory 16
Arnold, Gen. Henry "Hap" 121
Arnoux, Maurice 116, 118–121
Around the Island race 31
Around-the World Race 25
Arquilla, Ollie 151
Arrachart, Ludovic 116
Arrow 74
Aslett, Tom 197, 198
Ast, Vince 144
AT-6 Class 236
Atcherly, Richard "Batchy" 66, 90
Atkinson, H.L. 84
Atlantic Derby, Class A 97
Atlantic Derby, Class B 97
Aviatik Arrow 45
Avro 500 31
Avro 539 Schneider 52
Avro Lancaster 62

B-24 Liberator 133
Bach Air Yacht 82
Bacula, Adriano 88, 89
Baker, Marion 185
Balz, Gunther 178, 180
Bardahl Special 163
Barksdale, Eugene 60
Barnard, Frank 63–65
Barnwell, R.H. 31
Barra, M. 21
Barrows, W.J. 80
Batten, E.C. 75
Battle of Britain 88
Bayles, Lowell 103
Beck, Don 181, 182, 184, 186. 187, 189, 192, 197, 198
Beck, Xavier 232
Becker, Dick 139, 141, 144
Beech, Walter 84
Beechcraft 17 Staggerwing 128; Bonanza 235
Behel, Lee 214, 217, 221, 223
Belcher, Lt. 81

Bell P-39 Airacobra 62, 133, 160; *Cobra II* 135, 139, 142, **145**, 163
Bell P-63 Kingcobra 78, 133–135, 142, 160
Bellanca CH300 80
Bellanca trimotor 131
Belle of Bethany 151
Belmont Park 33
Bendix Transcontinental Derby/Trophy Race 81, 97, 99, 106, 154, 170; Jet Division 144
Benjamin, Delmar 105
Bennett, James Gordon, Trophy Race 13, 15, 23, 31, 32, 39, 40, 42, 47, 57, 239
"Benny Howard National Air Races" 127
Bernard HV-220 90
Bernardi, Mario de 88, 89
Berry, Roy 178
Berteaux, French Minister of War 18
Bettis, Cyrus 61, 73
Beville, Steve 137
Biard, Henry 54, 56
Bingham, Sen. Hiram 99
Bishop, Charlie 151
Bissell, Clayton 60
Blackburn, Harold 11, 30
Blackburn Bluebird 124
Blackburn Mercury 30
Blackburn Pellet 56
Blackburn V-twin 64
Blanchard-Bleriot monoplane 56
Bleriot, Louis 3, 14, 15, 18, 23; Type XI 11, 12, 63, 233; Type XII 11
Bleriot Cup 90
Blevins, Beeler 102
Blum, John 96
Bodine, Doug 228
Boeing FB-3 74
Boeing 247 109, 110
Bohannon, Bruce 211
Bohn, Eddie 74
Boland, Bill 166, 170, 172–175, 178–180, 196, 200, 215, 218
Boland *Momgster* 172
Bologna, Luigi 52
BooRay #81 179, 184, 189
Boothman, John 91
Bournemouth, England 5
Bowman, Martie 100
Bowyer, C.D. 84, 85
Boyd *Blue Streak* 203, 211
Boyden, Lt. 81
Breene, R.G. 83, 85
Breese "Aloha" 70, **70**
Breese "Pabco Pacific Flyer" 69, **69**
Brennand, Bill 137, 138, 142, 145
Brickert, Rick 195, 196, 198–202, 205
de Briganti, Giovanni 53, 88
Bristol Badminton 65
Bristol Boxkite 28
Bristol Centaurus engine 168, 195
Bristol Cherub engine 96
Bristol Jupiter engine 52, 64

Bristol Lucifer engine 67
Bristol Type 101 66
British Army Aeroplane No. 1 16
Broad, Hubert 64, 65, 88
Brock, Walter 25, 30, 31
Brock, William 82
Brookins, Walter 34, 35
Brookley, Wendell 61
Brow, Harold 60
Brown, Charles "Chuck" 141, 142, 163
Brown, Ens. F.E. 141
Brown, Henry J. 81
Brown, Michael "Mike" 218, 220, 224, 226, 227
Brown, Stephen 217
Brown B-2 *Miss Los Angeles* 107
Brunner-Winkle Bird 80
Brusse, Lee 100
Bryant Angel of Los Angeles 67
Bryce, Lt. 81
Bucarelli, Ron 24
Buehler, Andy 224
Bugatti racer 122, 123
Buhl Air Sedan "Miss Doran" 70, 71
Buhl Cabin Monoplane 80
Bumford, Jim 203, 204, 207
Bummer's *Bullet* 203, 207
Burgess, W. Sterling 38
Burke Lakefront Airport 170, 188
Burnstine, Ken 183, 184, 186
Burri, M. 45, 46
Bussi, Arthur 131
Butler, Alan 64
Butterfield, Don 168, 169, 171, 172

C-1 (Grumman) 160
California National Air Races 168, 186
Calloway, Steven 60, 61
Camp, Tom 220
Campbell-Black, Tom 109, 110, 112
C.A.M.S 36 54
C.A.M.S 36bis 56
C.A.M.S 38 56
Canadian Air Force 185
Canton-Unné Breguet 30
Cantwell, Robert 75
Carberry, Lord 25
Carney, Linton 141
Carroll, Mike 168, 170, 176
Casale, Jean 52
Cassinelli, Guglielmo 90
Cassutt, Tom 148–150
Cassutt Racer 156, 161, 174, 179, 181, 229; *Aero Magic* #43 194; #22 *Bananas* 231; #63 *Chico Puro* 209; #22 *Dancing Queen* 225; #71 *The Empire Strikes Back* 195; #69 *Flexi Flyer* 195; #18 *Gnat* 189; #95 *Mariah* 214, 217, 218, 223; Martinez #46 **230**; #12 *Outrageous* 217, 222; #59 *Scarlet Screamer* 220, 228; #92 *Yellow Peril* 228
Cassutt Special: I 148; II 150

Index

Cathcart-Jones, Owen 109
Caudron biplane 30
Caudron-Regnier 118
Caudron Type 360 117
Caudron Type 362 115, 116
Caudron Type 366 115
Caudron Type 430 120
Caudron Type 450 117
Caudron Type 460 117, *119*, 128, 129
Caudron Type 461 120
Caudron Type 462 121
Caudron Type 560 119
Caudron Type 561 121
Caudron Type 714R 123
Caudron Type 760 121
Cessa, Eldon 100
Cessna, Clyde 74, 84
Cessna AC 84
Cessna BW 103
Cessna CM-1 *74*
Cessna GC-2 95, 98
Chamberlin, Clarence 67
Chambers, Charlie 184
Charles E. Thompson Cup 83
Chaumont Bearn 450 hp 123
Chester, Arthur "Art" 77, 80, 107, 127, 131–133, 136, 141, 142
Chester *Goon* 130, 199
Chester *Jeep* *97*, 106, 107, 127
Chester *Swee' Pea* 136–138
Chester *Swee' Pea II* 141
Chevalier, M. 36, 37
Chevrolet Brothers 83
Chicago Air Race Corp. 93
Chicago Tribune 93
Christian, Dallas 172, 174, 175, 178, 180
Christie, Jan 151
Christie, Walter 35
Church Midwing *72*
Circuit of Britain Race: (1912) 24; (1913) 25; (1914) 26, 32, 63
Circuit of Europe Air Race 18
Cirrus engine 95
Civilian Unlimited Free-for-All Trophy 75
Clark, C.E. 83
Clark, J.J. 84, 85
Clearing, Illinois 37
Cleland, Cook 3, 138, 141, 142, 143, 144, 146, 168, 173, 193
Cleveland Chamber of Commerce 99
Cleveland Chamber of Commerce Band 77
Cleveland City Band 77
Cleveland Hopkins Municipal Airport 75, 133
Cleveland National Air Races 7, 146, 154–156
Cleveland Pneumatic Tool Co. 107
Cleveland-to-Buffalo Efficiency Race 82
Clouston, Alex 113
Cobham, Alan 64
Cobra #22 192
Cochran, Jackie 130, 133, 134

Cody, Samuel F. 11, 16, 25
Cody Biplane 25
Collardeau, M. 30
Comet engine 84
Comper, Nicholas 115, 117, 118
Comper Kite 124
Comper Streak 117
Comper Swift *115*, 116, 124
Compte de Lambert 14
Conneau, Lt. deVaisseau "Beaumont" de 21–25
Connell, Byron 67
Continental C-85 engine 136
Continental Motors Corp. 147
Continental O-200 engine 172
Continental Trophy Race 147
Coomb, Clarence 59
Cooper, Sherman 176, 178
Corgnolino, Piero 53, 54
Corkille, Johnny 61
Cosmic Wind 136; #5 *Ballerina* **138**, 145, 229; *Ballerina Mk.II* 231; *Little Toni* 138, 144, 168 231; *Minnow* 138, 141, 142
Cote, Ray 3, 168, 169, 172, 174, 177, 179, 181, 182, 184–186, 188, 190–193, 197, 198, 202, 203, 214, 217, 218, 225
Courtney, Frank 64
Covell, George 67
Cowes, England 54
Cox, Ron 209
C.P.R.A. 123
Crandlemire, Scotty 217, 222
Crawford Aviation and Auto Museum 95
Crocker, John 186, 190, 191, 193, 196
Crombez, M. 40
Cross-Country Handicap 29
Crossley, Mick 231
Crosson, Marvel 78
Croydon Aerodrome 63
Cuddihy, George 74, 88
Culbertson, W.D. 58
Cummins, Dr. Cliff 173, 176, 182–185, 187, 188
Curran, James 59
Curtiss, Glenn: 3, 13–15, 33, 34
Curtiss A.1 Triad 45
Curtiss engines: C-12 47; Conqueror V-12 84, 128; D-12 55, 62, 98
Curtiss-Cox "Cactus Kitten" 47, **59**
Curtiss-Cox "Texas Wildcat" 47, 48, 59
Curtiss CR-1 56, 60
Curtiss CR-2 56, 60
Curtiss CR-3 **55**, **56**, 87
Curtiss Falcon 84
Curtiss F6C-3 83, **84**, 98
Curtiss-Kirkham 18-T-1 58
Curtiss O-11 78
Curtiss Oriole 73
Curtiss P-1 Hawk 61, 74
Curtiss P-3A **83**
Curtiss P-36 Hawk 121

252 INDEX

Curtiss P-40 62
Curtiss PW-8B 61, 73
Curtiss R2C-2 56
Curtiss R3C-1 61, **62**
Curtiss R3C-2 88, 92
Curtiss R-6 60
Curtiss-Reed propeller 55
Curtiss-Reynolds Airport 93
Curtiss XF6C-6 98, 99
Curtiss XP-6A 75

Dacey, Mike 228
Daily Express Gold Medal 30
Daily Mail 16, 17, 24
Daimler-Benz 600 62
Dal Molin, Tomaso 90
Damm Field 57
Dansville, NY 148
Dari, Steve 226
David, Gary 228
Davis, Doug 82, 84, 85, 94, 101, 107
Dawson, Leo 62
Dayton-Wright RB-1 47, 49, **50**
DC-7 (Douglas) 160
DeBona, Joe 143
Deerfly #39 **139**, 144, 145, 165
deHavilland dh.4 57, 63
deHavilland dh.37 64
deHavilland dh.50 64
deHavilland dh.60 Gypsy Moth 64–66, 78
deHavilland dh.71 Tiger Moth Racer 65
deHavilland dh.88 Comet 109; #34 *Grosvenor House* 109, 110; *II*; #63 *Black Magic* 109, 110
deHavilland dh.98 Mosquito 62, 140, 143
deHavilland Gypsy Four 95
deHavilland Gypsy Major 116
deHaviland Technical School: TK-1 124; TK-2 124, 126; TK-4 126
Delage V-12 116
Delagrange, Leon 12
de la Muerthe, Henri Deutsch 18
Delgado *Maid* 128
Delmotte, Raymond 116, 118, 120, 121
DeLuca, Vince 182, 184, 185, 187
Deming, Jay 139
Dempsey, Brian 233
Deperdussin, Armand 40
Deperdussin floatplane 45
Deperdussin monoplane 3, 20, 30, 39, 40, **40**
dePischoff airplane 19
Desborough, Lord, Challenge Bowl 32
Deschamps, Paul 179, 180
Desoutter, Marcel 30
Destefani, Bill "Tiger" 4, 196, 199, 200, 203, 204, 207–209, 211–215, 218, 226, 227
Detmer, Eugene 75
Détré, Georges 115, 117
Detroyat, Michel 119, 128, 129, 206
Devereaux, E.J. "Red" 80
Dewey, Mike 165
Dewoitine D.412 90

Dilley, John 201
Dixie Derby, Class B 96
Dole Race 67, 75
Dollar Special 170
Doolittle, Jimmy 3, 88, 92, 101, 102, 105, 128, 133, 239
Doran, Miss Mildred 70
Douglas A-1 Skyraider 163
Douglas A-26 134
Douglas DC-2 109–111, 129
Douglas DC-7 173
Douglas DC-7B 176
Douglas O-2H 78
Dowd, John "Dusty" 191, 194
Downey, Bob 139, 156, 163–165, 168–172, 181, 182, 189, 193
Downey-Miller *Ole Tiger* 164
Drew, Bob 199
Driggs Skylark 80
Dulles International Airport 181
Dwelle, Tom 216
Dyott, George 38

EAA Biplane 157, 166
Eaglerock Bullet 79
Eaker, Ira 102, 103
Eastchurch, Kent 36
Eckner, Hugo 86
Ecole des Beaux-Arts 12
Edmondson, "Woody" 135
Edwards Air Force Base 164
Eldridge, Kevin 209, 224, 226, 227
Eliot, Lt. 74
Ellehammer, Jacob 11
Entriken, Birch 220
E.N.V. 11
Espanet, Gabriel 43, 44, 46
Etampes 47
Etheridge, Dot 174
Etrich "Swallow" 38
Eucker, Bob 141
Evansville, Indiana 183
Experimental Aircraft Association (EAA) 82; *Sport Aviation* 152
Experimental Aircraft Association AirVenture Fly-In 149
Experimental Aircraft Association Museum 97, 122

F2G Super Corsair 3, **143**
Fabre, Henri 42
Fahey, Claire 78
Fairbanks, Don 192, 194, 196–198, 200
Fairchild 71 80
Fairey III 51, 64
Falck, Bill ("Willie") 3, 145, 148–151, 163, 164, 165, 168–172, 174, 176, 177, 179, 181, 182, 184, 187, 191, 208
Falck *Rivets* 145, 165, **180**
Farman, Henry (or Henri) 12, 14; biplane 17, 21, 30

Farman, Maurice biplane 31
Farman monoplane 115
Farman V-12 engine 115
Faulkner, Charles 84
F.B.A. flying boat 45
Federal Aviation Administration (FAA) 155
Felixstowe 64
Ferguson, Cris 226
Ferrarin, Arturo 88
Fiat A.14 53
Fiat A.S.5 90
Fiat A.S.6 90
Fiat V-12 89
Fischer, Clem 171
Fisher, E.B.V. 28
Fisk CF-10 Spirit of Los Angeles 67
Flanders F.3 28
Flagg, Claude 96
Flagg *Phantom I* 96
Fleet 2 79
Floyd Bennet Field 106
Fogg, Phil 194
Fokker F10 82
Folkerts, Clayton 93, 129
Folkerts *Toots* 128
Folkerts SK-3 Jupiter *Pride of Lemont* 129
Folz, Edith 79
Forbes, Dave 175, 182
Ford, Henry, Museum 49
Ford, Maj. Vernon 144
Formula Air Racing Association 230
Formula One (190 Cu. In. Class) 161, 172, 239
Formula V 235
Formula World Championships 179
Ft. Wayne, Indiana 149
Foss Special 165
Fowlie, Danny 96
Franco, Charles 120
French Grand Prix 230
Frey, Andrey 38
Friburg Special 199
Frost, John 69
Fuller, Frank 129–131, 134
Fulton, Dale 134

Garden City, Long Island, N.Y. 57
Gardner, Marvin "Lefty" 186
Gardner Trophy Race 74
Garland Pack's *Grey Ghost* 164
Garros, Roland 18, 21, 23–25, 43, 46
GeeBee 3; D Sportster 102; R-1 Super Sportster **101**, 104, 119; Y Sportster 102, 103; Z Super Sportster 102, 103
Gehlbach, Lee 105
George, King V 63
Gibert, Louis 21, 23, 24
Giboney 228
Gidovlenko, Howrd 141
Giffen, James 67
Gilbert, Dan 213

Gilbert, Eugene 39, 40, 114
Gilbert *Shadow* 213
Gill, John 78
Glasair 162, 214, 215
Glenn Curtiss Trophy Race 74
Glenview Naval Air Station 93
Gloster IVB 89
Gloster Grebe 66
Gloster III 88
Gnome rotary engine 38–40
Goddard, Norman 69
Goddard Sport "El Encanto" 69
Goebel, Art 70, 75, 97, 102
Golden Age of Air Racing 152, 239
Goodyear F2G Super Corsair 138, **143**, 146, 160, 193, 198, 208, 209, **221**
Goodyear Tire & Rubber Co. 136
Goodyear Trophy Race 138, 140, 187
Grahame-White, Claude 17, 34, 35, 38
Grahame-White Bi-Rudder Bus 32
Grahame-White Boxkite 31
Grahame-White Cup #3 29
Grand Speed Handicap 30
Granville Brothers 103, 104
Granville-Miller-DeLackner R-6 *Q.E.D.* 106, **110**, 128
Gray, Kathy 211
Gray, Col. Leon 137, 140
Great Miami Air Race 182
Great Week of the Champagne 10, 15, 239
Greenamyer, Darryl 3, 157, 163, 170, 171, 173, 178, 180, 184, 187, 188, 218, 221, 222, 224, 225, 227
Greer, Charlie 218, 220, 223, 225
Greve Trophy Race 107
Greig, D'Arcy 90
Grey, C.G. 36
Griffen, Bennett 69
Von Grote, Rod 225
Grove *Madder Maxx GR-7* 213, 217
Grumman F4F Wildcat #2 *Bisquit* 220
Grumman F7F Tigercat #1 *Big Bossman* 220
Grumman F8F-2 Bearcat 154, **158**, 160, **163**, **167**, 180, 186, 208, 216, 222; *Rare Bear* **192**, 193, 195, 201, 202, 206, 207, 211, 220, 224, 227
Guazetti, Frederico 89
Guthrie, Giles 113

Haizlip, Jimmy 94, 99, 105
Haizlip, Mary 98, 100, 103
Haldeman, George 75, 82
Halfpenny Green 230
Hall, Charles (Chuck) 170, 171, 173, 183
Hall, James 102, 179, 181
Hall, Robert 102, 103
Hall-Scott engine 47
Halle Department Store Trophy 137
Hamel, Gustave 31, 36–38
Hamilton, Charles 35

Hamiltonian 34
Hamersley, H.A. 52
Hamilton, Lloyd 199
Handley Page HP.5 E. 31
Hannah, Bob 213
Hannah, Kirk 198
Hanriot monoplane *38*, 39
Hansen Trophy 189
Harold's Club Transcontinental Trophy Dash 157
Harris, Grace 141, 145
Hartney, Harold 57, 60
Haviland, William 58
Hawker, Harry 25, 51
Hawker Sea Fury 160, 168, 170, 176, 179, **185**, 195, 207, 216; Blind *Man's Bluff/Critical Mass* 200, 216; *Dreadnaught* 195, 199, 200–202, 207, 210, 213, 223, 225, 226; #232 *September Fury* 218, 223, 224; #105 *Spirit of Texas* 223
Hawks, Frank 94, 99
Hayden-Baillie, Ormond 185
Heath, Eddie 79, 80, 82, 96, 97
Heath, Lady Mary 79
Heath *Baby Bullet* 80, 82, 96, 97
Heath *Cannonball* 96, 102
Heath Parasol 97
Heath Super Parasol 79
Helen, Emmanuel 114
Henderson, Clifford 76, 81
Henderson, Phil 76
Hendon Aerodrome 17, 63
Hendon 8-lap Handicap 31
Hendon Empire Day Meeting 30
Hendon 4-lap Cross-country Handicap 31
Hendon International Air Contest 31
Hendon Trophy 31
Henshaw, Alex 124
Hertz, John 93
Hevle, Ron 193–196
Hines, Logan "Pat" 187, 192–194, 196, 218
Hinton, Steve 188–190, 193, 196, 198, 200–202
Hispano (-Suiza) Type 42 48, 52, 53; W-18 90
Hobbs, Basil 52
Holm, Skip 193, 196, 198, 199, 204, 206, 216–218, 220, 222
Holman, Charles "Speed" 74, 79, 82, 94, 99
Holste, Max, 20 123
Honolulu, Hawaii 3
Hoover, Bob 157, 178, 181
Hoover, David 223, 224, 226, 228
Hoover #11 *Endeavor* 216, 223, 228
Hope, Wally 66
Howard, Ben O. 93, 95, 97, 99, 102, 103, 127, 128
Howard DGA-3 "Pete" 95, **95**, 97, 99, 103
Howard DGA-4 *Mike* 127
Howard DGA-6 *Mr. Mulligan* 106, 127, 128
Howell, Randy 213

Hubler, Gary 217, 218, 220, 222–226
Hucks, Bentheld C. 829
Hunter, Walter 100, 102
Hurel, Maurice 56
Hurlburt, Margaret 134

Indianapolis 500 153
Ingalls, Laura 128
Inland Sport 98, 100
Instone Air Line 63
International Aeroclassic 165
International Aeronautics Federation (FAI) 93, 136
International Air Races 162, 189
International Experimental Limited (IXL) Class 188, 190–192
International Formula Midgets (IFM) 193
Irvine, Rutledge 56
Irving, Livingston 69
Irwin, William 70
Isle of Man 64, 176, 229
Isle of Sheppey 36
Isle of Wight 51, 54
Isotta-Fraschini V-6 54; W-18 90
Israel, Gordon 95
Italian Air Force Museum 91

Jackson, Dale 103
Jackson, Matt 226
Jacobson, Joe 128
Janazzo, Tony 139
Janello, Guido 52
Jensen, Martin 70
Jet Class 241
Johnson, Anson 141, 142
Johnson, Fonda 60
Johnson, Harold 101, 102
Johnson, Ruth 137
Johnson-Nelson, Patti 207, 209–213
Johnston, Alvin "Tex" 3, 135
Jonathan Livingston Seagull #76 179
Jones, "Casey" 73
Jones, Howell C. "Nick" 168, 169, 174, 184, 186
Jones, H.W.G. 64, 65
Jones, John Paul 165, 182, 184
Jury, Bud 164

Kansas City, Missouri 3
Kansas City Rotary Club Trophy Race 74
Keefe, Howie 178, 179
Keith-Miller, Jessie 79
Keith Rider B-1 96
Keith Rider R-1 *San Francisco* 107
Keith Rider R-2 102
Keith Rider R-3 Marcoux-Bromberg 106, 129
Keith Rider R-4 *Schoenfeldt Firecracker* 129, 130, **131**,
Kellner-Bechereau **116**
Kendall Trophy Race 137, 141
Kennedy, John F. International Airport 33

Index

Kentucky Derby 153
Killips, A.W. 97
Kimmerling 22, 23
King's Cup Race 63
Kinkead, S.M. 89
Kirsch, Georges 47–49, 114
Kistler Special 164
Klabo, Waldo "Klay" 187
Kling, Rudy 129, 130
Klingensmith, Florence 103
Knight, Ken 137
Knight Twister 157, 158, 166; #5 *White Knight* 192
Kramer, Al 192, 193
Kunz, Opal 98, 103

Lacey, Michael 218
Lacombe, Yves 117, 119, 121
Lacy, Clay 171
Lacy, Clay's P-51 **166**, 170
Ladies Stock Plane Class 234
Laidley, Richard 180
Laird Commercial biplane 75
Laird LC-DW-500 103
Laird LC-LW-300 103
Laird LCR-300 84, 103
Laird *Solution* 96, 99, 103
Laird *Super Solution* 101, 102
Laird-Turner LTR-14 *Meteor* 129, 130
Lambert, Merle 102
Lambert Field 60, 72
Lancair 162, 214, 216; IV 217, 218; Legacy 221, **227**
Landon, M. 19
Landry, Katherine "Kaddy" 141, 145
Lasne, Frenand 114
Las Vegas (Nevada) National Air Races 163
Latham, Hubert 12, 14
Latham L.1 56
Leblanc, Alfred 34, 35
Lecointe, Sadi 47–49, 52, 53
Lee-on-Solent 64
Leeward, Jimmy 151, 201, 224
Lefebvre, Eugene 13, 14
Lemartin, M. 19
Lemoine, Gustave 115, 116
Lemon, Dot 141
Levasseur, Pierre 45, 46
Leverton, Irene 158
LeVier, Tony 130–132, 134, 135, 137, 144
Levitz, Gary 183, 186, 212, 213
Lignel Mistral 30 123
Lignel 20 121, 122
Lignel 30 122
Lillywhite, R.J. 32
Lindbergh, Charles 67
Livingston, John 76, 96, 97, 102
Lo, Jeffrey 224, 226
Lobet, William 231
Lockheed Air Express 81, 97
Lockheed Altair 100, 102, 103
Lockheed Orion 100, 101, 102, 128, 134
Lockheed P-38 Lightning 62, 133–135, **141**, 160, **183**, 205, 207
Lockheed P-80 Shooting Star 137, 140
Lockheed Speed Vega 84
Lockheed Vega 5 75, 81, 97, 100, 102
Lockheed Vega 5B 97
Lockheed Vega "Golden Eagle" 69
Lockwood, Bruce 213–215
Loening, Mike 178
Loening R-4 60
London Aerodrome Silver Trophy: #12 30; #16 30
London Aviation Meeting 30
London-Paris-London Race 25, 133
London-to-Melbourne Race 108; Handicap Division 112; Speed Division 112
Long, Dave 142
Lorraine Radium V-12 90
Los Angeles International Airport 75, 105
Love, Bob 158, 181, 182
Love, Philip 78
Lowers, Jack 186
Lucky Lager Championship Race 178
Lufberry Field 57
Lund, Bettie 103
Lund, Freddie 79
Lund, Hal 168
Lundberg, Ted 80
Lunken, Eddie 141
Lycoming O-290 177
Lyford, Chuck 155, 157, 163, 167, 170, 173
Lyford's *Challenger* 167
Lympne Lightplane Races 79

Macchi-Castoldi MC.72 90
Macchi M.7 52
Macchi M.7bis 53, 54
Macchi M.17bis 54
Macchi M.19 53
Macchi M.33 87
Macchi M.39 88, 89
Macchi M.52 89
Macchi M.52R 90
Macchi M.67 **89**, 90
Macchi Naval M.7 53
Macmillan, Norman 64
MacReady, John 60, 96
Mahoney, Lee 179
Mahoney *Sorceress* 179, 181, 182, 192
Maitland, Lester 60
Mallard, Henri 52
Mantz, Paul 134, 136, 140, 141, 143
Marquis of Anglesey Cup 31
Marsden, Kit 151
Marsh, Fred 229, 231
Martin, Dan 227
Martin, L. 38
Martin B-26 Marauder 143
Martinet-Regnier 119
Martinsyde A.D.C.1 65

Martinsyde Semiquaver 48, 49
Marty, Philippe 31
Maryland National Air Races 172
Masotte, Raymond 118, 120
Matheson, Eric 228
Matthews, T.K. 73
Maughan, Russell 60
Maxwell, Sam 203
Mayson, Thomas 136
McArthur, J.H.G. 145
McBride, Helen 145
McClain, Roy "Mac" 183, 185, 186, 190, 191, 193
McConnaughey, I.M. 83, 85
McCormick, Mrs. R., Trophy Race 94, 98
McCormick, Robert R. "Bertie" 93
McCowen, Ian 231
McDonough, W.J. 66
McGrath, Margrete 138
McIntyre, Bruce 170, 171
McKillen, Ben 145, 146, 221
McMillan, Jack 79
Melbourne, Australia 3
Menasco C4 96
Mendell, Loren 80
Men's Non-Stop Derby 97
Mercury Air *Shoestring* 139, 148, 150, 161, 165, 184, 193; *Pole Cat* 191; Wagner *Judy* 197, 199, 202, 204, 228
Messerschmitt Bf.109 62
Messerschmitt Bf.110 62
Messerschmitt Me.109V 173
Mexicali, Mexico 189
Meyer, Lou 217
Meyers, C.W. 75
Miami, Florida 3
Midget Monocoupe 174
Midget Mustang 142, 161, 182
Midget Racer Design Competition 229
Midway Airport 38
Miles, Lee 107, 127, 128
Miles & Atwood Special 106, 107
Miles M.2L Hawk Speed Six **125**
Miles M.5A Sparrowhawk 124, **125**
Miller, Howell 104
Miller, Jim 148, 151, 165, 183, 197, 198, 200, 202–204, 206, 207, 209, 212
Miller, Walter 61
Miller *Little Gem* 148, 165
Miller *Pushy Cat* **197**
Miller *Pushy Galore* 211
Miller *Texas Gem* 184
Mills, Harry 73
Milton 82
Mines Field 75, 105, 128
Minor, Roy 106, 107
Mirley, John 231
Miss DARA 151
Miss Foxy Lady 186
Mr. Zip 151
Mitchell, John, Trophy Race 61, 73, 74, 81

Mitchell, Reginald J. 88
Mitchell Field, Long Island, NY 57, 61, 73
Model Farms Field 73
Moeller, Col. Bob 179, 182, 184–186, 188, 189
Moisant, John 36
Mojave Desert 3, 179, 183
Moll 110
Mollison, Amy 109
Mollison, Jim 109
Monaco 43
Mone, Clifford "Kip" 144, 145
Mong Sport 157, 161, 166, 171, 172, 175, 196, 197, 200, 202, 205–207, 213; #88 *Glass Slipper* 214; *Phantom* **219**, 221, 224
Monnett Sonerai *Miss Annapolis* 233
Monocoupe 102
Monte, French Premier 18
Monti, Giovanni 89
Monville, Albert 118, 119
Moore, A.L. 81
Moore, Ray 102
Morane monoplane 21, 22
Morane-Saulnier 31
Morss, Dave 200, 202, 214, 215, 217, 220
Mortensen, Danny 193, 196, 197, 205, 206
Moseley, Corliss 57, 58, 60
de la Muerthe, Henri Deutsch 114, 119
Mulcahy, Francis 60
Musée de l'Air 35, 41, 49
Musso, Paul: *Real Sporty* 191; #76 *Spirit of '76* 186
Mustang Mountain 154
Myers, H.G. 100
Myhres, H.S. 82, 85

Napier Lion engine 51, 54, 56, 88
Naples, Italy 54
NASCAR 7
National Advisory Committee on Aeronautics (NACA) 133
National Aeronautic Association (NAA) 93, 99, 136, 154
National Championship Air Races 7, 153, 160, 233, 239
Naval Aircraft Factory TR-3A 55
Nazi German 130
Neumann, Harold 93, 127, 128
Neville, John T. 77
New Englnd Air Museum 96
New York-Spokane Derby 74
Newhall, Wilson 78, 142, 145
Niagara Falls, New York 148
Nicholas Beazley Barling NB-3 80, 82
Nicholl, Vincent 51
Nielsen, Prof. Klaus 153, 154
Nieuport & General Goshawk 48
Nieuport biplane: 29V 47, 48, **49**, 52, 114
Nieuport-Delage 29 53
Nieuport-Delage 450 90
Nieuport-Delage sesquiplane 114
Nieuport monoplane **34**, **44**; type IIN 36

Index

90 Cubic Inch Class 235
Noel, Louis 31
Non-Stop New York-to-Spokane Race 74
North American AT-6/SNJ 134, 157, 161
North American B-25 197
North American P-51 Mustang 3, 62, 134, 135, *140*, 155, 160, 207; *Bardahl Special 159*; *Beguine 144*; *Dago Red* #4 193, 195, 198, 209, 211, 217, 220, 224, 227; *Galloping Ghost* 141, 142, 173; *Jeannie* #69 187, 188, 190, 191, 193, 201; *Miss America* 178, 210; *Oogahonk Special* 181; *Precious Metal* 186–188, 195, 202, *208*; RB-51 #5 *Red Baron* 184, *186*–189, *189*; *Strega* #7 195, 200, 224; #84 *Stiletto* 196; *Vendetta* 201; *Voodoo* 213
North American T-28 216, 236
Northrop Gamma 128
Noyes, Blanche 128

Oakland-to-Cleveland Derby 80
Odegaard, Bob 221
Odom, William 144–146
O'Donnell, Gladys 79, 96–98, 102, 103
O'Driscoll, Frank 60
Oftsie, Ralph 88
Ogilvie, Alex 35, 37
Ohm, Dick 148, 150, 151
Ohm & Stoppelbein Special 150
Omaha, Nebraska 58
Omlie, Phoebe 79, 96, 97, 100, 102, 103
190 Cubic Inch Class ("Goodyear Midgets") 136, 153, 154, 158; *see also* Formula One
Ong, Bill 95, 103, 134
Ormond Beach 13
Ortman, Earl 129, 130
Oshkosh, Wisconsin 149
Otfinovsky, George 117
Owl, George 162, 174
Owl Racer 161, *162*, 174, 194, 198; #4 *Alley Cat* 203, 214, 217, 218, 222, 226; *Fang 177*, 184

P-51R *Miss Ashley II* 212–214
Pacific Derby, Class A 96
Pacific Derby, Class B 96
Packard Motor Car Co. 62
Packard 1A-2025 47; V-12 57
Page, Capt. Arthur 99
Page, Jane 134
Panama Pacific International Exposition 26
Pangborn, Clyde 109, 113
Paris Air Show 165, 181
Paris-to-Madrid Race 18
Parker, John 188, 190, 192, 218, 220, 222–225
Parmentier 110
Parsons, Clyde 158, 166
Passaleva, Alexandro 54
Paulhan, Louis 17
Payen, Roland 119
Payen Flechair 123
Payen PA-100 119

Pearson, Alex 61
Penkith, Mike 203
Penney, John 209, 211, 212, 220, 222, 223, 226, 228
Penrose, Paul 137, 138
Percival Mew Gull 124, *126*
Percival Vega Gull 113
Petit, Lt. Col. 140
Pheasant H10 biplane 77
Philadelphia-to-Cleveland Derby 80
Phoenix, Arizona 209
Pickles, Sidney 31
Piper Cherokee 180 157
Pitcairn PA-4 84
Pitcairn Sesqui-wing 75
Pitts, Curtiss 142
Pitts Special 48, 161, 170, 174, 202, 20, 205–207, *210*, 211; *Class Action* 215; *Magic 213*; *Miss Gianna* 224
Pitts *Pellet* 142
Pixton, Howard 31, 45, 46
Pizet, C.P. 28
Plains of Betheny 9, 14
PN-9 67
Pobjoy Niagara 96
Pomeroy, George 129
Pond, Robert 205, 208
Pond Racer 160, 205
Porter, Bob 148, 156, 158, 162, 165
Porter, Hep 204, 207, 218, 220
Portland-to-Cleveland Derby 79
Post, Wiley 97
Potez R-9B engine 115
Potez Type 53 115, 116, *118*
Potez Type 53-2 117, 118
Potez Type 53-3 117
Powder Puff Derby 157
Pratt & Whitney R-985 Wasp Jr. 84, 105
Pratt & Whitney R-4360 Wasp Major 138, 193, 195
Pratt & Whitney Twin Wasp 129
Pratt & Whitney Wasp 105
Preston, Alan 199, 200, 202, 210
Prevost, Maurice 39, 40, 43, 46
Price, David 209–212
Princetau, Lieutenant 19
Prix de la Vitesse 1
Prix de Tour de Piste 14
Professional Race Pilots Association 1, 136, 148, 153, 154, 174, 235
Proud Bird 187, 190
Puckett, Ron 138, 145, 146
Pulitzer Trophy Race 73
Putnam, John 190

Quarton, Jerry 156, 169
Quarton Cassutt Racer *156*
Questair *Venture* 214, 217; #25 *Eggstra Special* 215; #71 *Fool's Gold* 218
Quinby, Ray "Spud" 80

258   INDEX

Rache, Thea 78
Racing Biplane Class 194, 196, 202, 218, 221
Rae, Roger Don 107, 129
Raikes Trophy 28
Ranger V-12 engine 137
Rankin, "Tex" 79
Rawdon, Herb 85
Ray, James 74 75
Raymond, Bruce 141, 142
Raynham, Frederick 31, 49
Reaver, Stanley 143
Rechenmacher, Fred 166
Red Bull air races 240
Regnier 180 hp 119
Regnier 220 hp 115
Reichers, Lou 102
Reims (or Rheims) 3, 9, 11, 39
Reims-Champagne Aeroport 11
Renault Bengali engine 115
Renaux, Eugene 25
Reno, Nevada 3, 7
Reno Air Racing Association (RARA) 236
R.E.P. monoplane 21
Republic AT-12 143
Republic F-84 Thunderjet 144
Republic P-47 Thunderbolt 129
Rheinschild, Bill 204, 213
Rheinschild, Erin 204
Ricard, Paul, auto racing circuit 230
Rice, Jim 151
Richardson, L.G. 66
Richet, E. 30
Rider, Keith 93
Riffard, Maercel 117
Rinehart, Howard 48, 49
Rittenhouse, David 55
Roberts, Verne 80
Robertson, Sir MacPherson 108
Robinson, Billie 144, 145
Rocket Racing League 240
Rodgers, Arthur 67
Rodgers, John 67
Roe, A.V. 11
Rogers, K.E. 81
Rollason Aircraft Ltd. 229
Rollason Beta 229; #74 *Blue Chip* 230; #56 *Forerunner* 230, **232**
Rolls Royce Lion engine 52; Griffon 90, 184, 189, 212; Merlin 62; R engine 90
deRomanet, Bernard 47, 48
Rose, David 215, 218, 221, 222, 226
Rossi, Alberto 209
Rowe, Basil 74
Rowe, John 186
Rowland, Earl 75
Royal Air Force Museum 17
Royal Aircraft Factory SE.5 57, 66
Royal Automobile Club 16
Royal Dutch Airlines (KLM) 109
Rutan, Burt 205

Sadi-Lecointe 114
Saint Louis Flying Field, Missouri 60
St. Petersburg, Florida 155
St. Petersburg International Airport 162
Salel, M. 116
Salmon, Herman "Fish" 138, 141–143, 158
Salomons, Sir David 16
Sanders, Brian 207, 208, 209, 210, 212, 215, 223
Sanders, Dennis 213
Sanders, Frank 178, 179
Sanderson, Lawson "Sandy" 60, 61
Santos-Dumont, Alberto 9, 114
Savoia Marchetti SM.79 113
Savoia S.12bis 52
Savoia S.13 **53**
Savoia S.51 54
Scapinelli, Pietro 90
Schiller, Duke 74
Schilt, Christian 88, 89
Schlessinger Race 113
Schneider, Jacques 39, 42
Schneider Cup Race 31, 42, 85, 114, 239
Schoenhair, Lee 75, 81, 97
Scholefield, E.R.C. 65, 66
Scholl, Art 164, 168
Schroeder, R.W. "Shorty" 49, 93
Schulze, Lester 60
Science Museum (London) 56, 92
Scott, Charles W.A. 109, 110, 112, 113
Scoville, John 148
Scoville *Stardust* 148
Seattle Chamber of Commerce Trophy 75
Seattle Spokesman-Review Trophy 75
Selfridge Field, Michigan 60
Seversky SEV-S2 129, **131**
Seversky SEV-3M 127
Shankle, Joan 103
Sharp, Jon 194, 197–200, 202, 204, 206–208, 210–213, 215, 222, 224–228
Sharp Nemesis 162, 204, **205**, 206, 213; Gilbert *Miss B Haven* 218
Sharp Nemesis NXT 222, **223**, 224
Shealey, George 80
Shell Oil Co. 94
Shell Speed Dash 99, 105, 107
Shell Trophy 30
Shelton, Lyle 168, 173, 178, 180–186, 191, 193, 195, 201–204, 206, 207, 209, 211–213
Sherman, Denny 151
Siddeley Puma 52
Simplex Racer 82, 83
Skeel, Burt 61, 73
Skelton, Betty 174, 235
Skliar, Bill 189
Sky Ranch 154, 155, 165
Slack, R obert 31
Slayton, Donald "Deke" 194
Slovak, Mira 158
Smith, J. Wesley 80, 82, 97
Smith, Jim 207, 212, 215

Smith Miniplane 157, 166, 175
Smoot, Sherman 226
Snyder, Jimmy "the Greek" 163, 165
Sohio Trophy Race 137, 141, 145
Somes, Jason 222, 226
Somethin' Else 186
Sopwith, T.O.M. 28, 63
Sopwith Camel 63
Sopwith Tabloid 31; Rainbow 48; Schneider 45, 107
Sorenson, Keith 144, 145
S.P.A.D. 40; 20bis5 47, 48; S.20 52
Speed Handicap 30
Speer, Bill 209
Speer, H.A. 80, 82
Spooner, Miss Winifred 66
Sport Biplane Class 161, 188, 219, 221, 233, 236; rules 177
Sport Class 162
Springfield *Bulldog* 105
Springfield, Illinois 148
Stainforth, George 92
Stanton, Stan 95
Stead, Bill 154, 156–160, 165, 168, 198, 233, 234
Stead Air Force Base 167, 191
Stearman, Lloyd 85
Steinhauer, Earl 135
Stevenson, Jim 184
Stewart, Jimmy 143
Stinson, Eddie 74
Stinson monoplane 74
Stoffler, Ernst 45
Stolp Starduster 157
Stoner, Rex 61
Storey, Tom 229, 231
Street, St. Clair 60
Sturgis, Kentucky 186, 235
Sullivan, Bill 231
Sundancer #1 182, 184, 187, 192, 193
Super Gold Race 209
Super Sport Class 227
Supermarine S.4 88
Supermarine S.5 89
Supermarine S.6A 90
Supermarine S.6B 91, *91*
Supermarine Sea Lion I 52
Supermarine Sea Lion II 54
Supermarine Sea Lion III 56
Supermarine Spitfire 62, 88, 145
Swallow "Dallas Spirit" 70
Swearingen SX300 162, 214

T-28 Class 236
Tabuteau, Maurice 22
Tait, Maude 102
Teeside 230
Tegler, John 172
Telling, Fred 217
Texaco Oil Co. 94
Thaden, Louise 78, 128

Thaw, William 45
Thomas, Tommy 181
Thomas *Miss Q* 181
Thomas-Morse MB-3 57, 73
Thomas-Morse MB.6 59
Thomas-Morse MB.7 59
Thomas-Morse R-5 60
Thomas-Morse Scout 74
Thompson, Steve 195, 196
Thompson Cup Race 94, 107
Thompson Trophy Race 80, 94, 99, 138, 154, 157, 206; Jet Division 137, 140
Thomson, John 151
Thousand-Mile Race 176, 178
350 Cubic Inch Class 5
Thunder Mustang 217, 218, 224; #75 *Rapid Travel* 228
Tiger Club 229
Tinnerman Trophy Race 137, 145
Tissandier, Paul 13, 14
Tollerton 230
Tomlinson, William 88
Top Turkey #93 188
Town & Country Club Trophy Race 73, 74
Train, Louis-Eile 18
Transcontinental Free-for-All Speed Dash 100
Transcontinental Handicap Air Derby 100
Transpo 72 181
TravelAir 75, 103
TravelAir D-4000 79, 82
TravelAir 5000 "Oklahoma" 69
TravelAir Mystery Racer 3, 82–84, 94, 99, 101, 105
TravelAir Speedwing 83, 99
TravelAir 2000 80, 98
Tremaine Hummingbird 67
Triptane fuel 142
Trygg, Anders 225
Tsunami 160, *194*, 199, 201, 202, 204, 206, 208
Tucker, Charles "Chuck" 135
Turner, Lewis 30
Turner, Roscoe 3, 81, 84, 85, 93, 97, 104–107, 109, 113, 127, 129, 130, 132–135, 239
Turner Meteor/Pesco Special 3, *132*
Tuttle, Glen 186
200 Cubic Inch Class 5
Tygert, Don 150

Ueno, Takehisa "Ken" 206
U.S. Army Air Service's Engineering Division 57
U.S. National Aerobatics Championships 154
University of Nevada 153
Unlimited Class 142, 157
Unlimited Hydroplane Hall of Fame 154
Unlimited Transcontinental Race 158
Unwin, Miss 25
Uwins, Cyril 66

INDEX

Valentine, Jimmy 20
Vance Flying Wing 103
Vandam, Rick 221
Vedrines, Emile 25, 40
Vedrines, Jules 21–24, 39
Venice, Italy 52
Venture (Questair) 162
Vernhol, Capt. 116
Verrept, M. 21
Verrier, Pierre 30, 31
Verville-Packard VCP-R 47, 57, **58**
Verville R-1 60
Verville-Sperry R-3 60, 61, 73
Verville VCP-1 57
Vickers Vixen 65
Vidart, Rene 21, 23, 24
Vivinius 12
Vliet, Jim 235
Voisin brothers 12; biplane 12; Gabriel 12
Vought F4U Corsair 133–135, 160, 170
Vought VE-7 57

Waco ATO 98
Waco CTO 102, 103
Waco F 100
Waco Taperwing 79
Waco 10 biplane 75, 79
Wade, Leigh 57
Waghorn, Henry 90
Wagner, Judy 179, 187, 193, 234
Walgreen, C.R. 93
Walker, Bill 231
Waller, Ken 109, 113
Walling, Charles 141
Warner radial engine 95
Warren, D.C. 100
Warwick, Bill 178
Warwick, Guy 66
Warwick *Hot Canary* 177
Washington National Airport 94
Waterman, Waldo 82
Way, Norman 206, 213, 218, 221, 224, 228
Webster, Sidney 89
Wedell, Jimmy 93, 94, 103, 105
Wedell Williams #17 95
Wedell-Williams #44 103, 107
Wedell-Williams #57 **104**, 107, 127, 129
Wedell Williams #92 95
Weiner, Ed 170
Welch, George 135
Wells, Theodore "Ted" 79, 82
Wendel, Fritz 173
Wentworth, Chuck 195, 197
Western Flying Trophy 75
Westland Widgeon 66
Weymann, Charles 21, 23, 36, 37, 43–45
White, Sid 170, 171, 184–187
Whitehead, Ennis 60

Whitehouse, E. Ronald 31
Whittington, Don 186–189, 191, 193, 195
Wickliffe, Dr. Clark 170
Wijnmalen 22
Wilbur Wright Field 61, 73
Will, Rittner 214
Williams, Al 60, 62, 73
Williams, Art 144
Williams, Errett 80, 99
Williams, Jim "Yogi" 150
Williams *Estrellita* 144
Williams *Falcon* 189
Williams "Mic" 196
Williams *Stinger* 194
Winkle, William 80
Wise, Ralph 194
Withers Cup 30
Wittman, Sylvester Joseph "Steve" 77, 93, 127, 129, 141, 142, 145, 148, 150, 151, 156, 157, 165, 168–170, 177, 198, 235
Wittman *Bonzo* 141, **149**
Wittman *Buster* 136, 137, 148
Wittman *Chief Oshkosh* 129
Wittman V-12 *Bonzo* 106, 127
Wofford, Fred 187, 190
Women's Air Derby 78, 79
Women's AT-6 Race 137
Women's Stock Plane Race 158
Women's Trophy Race 145
Wood, Eric 84
Wood, John 81
World Seaplane Speed Record 90
World Speed Record 92, 190
World War II 130
Worsley, Oswald 89
Worthen, J.A. 107
Wright Brothers 11
Wright-built Hispano V-8 59
Wright F2W-1 61
Wright 1903 Flyer 4; Baby Wright Racer 35, 40; Wright Racer 33; Wright Roadster 35
Wright NW-2 55
Wright R-3350 Cyclone 18 engine 173
Wright T-2 engines 55; E-4A V-8 55; J6 Whirlwind 83; T-3 V-12 61
Wurtsmith, P.B. 81
Wynmalen, Jan 38

Yakovlev Yak-3 160
Yakovlev Yak-9 160, 214
Yakovlev Yak-11 201, 208; *Czechmate* 226; *Perestroika* 203, 206, 207
Yancey, Bob 203, 206–208
Young, "Smokey" 228
Yout, Pierre 232

Zanetti, Arturo 53, 54

www.ingramcontent.com/pod-product-compliance
Ingram Content Group UK Ltd.
Pitfield, Milton Keynes, MK11 3LW, UK
UKHW041933140426
5217IPUK00014B/461